Fat Is a Family Affair

Fat Is a Family Affair

How Food Obsessions Affect Relationships

SECOND EDITION

Judi Hollis, Ph.D.

Hazelden
Publishing

Hazelden Publishing
Center City, Minnesota 55012-0176
hazelden.org/bookstore

Library of Congress Cataloging-in-Publication Data
Hollis, Judi.
  Fat is a family affair : how food obsessions affect relationships /
  Judi Hollis.—2nd ed.
    p. cm.
  Previously published: Center City, MN : Hazelden, 1985.
  ISBN 978-1-56838-980-6
    1. Compulsive eating. 2. Compulsive eaters—Family
  relationships. 3. Codependency. 4. Obesity—Psychological
  aspects. I. Title.

RC552.C65 H653 2003
616.85'26—dc21   2002038898

19 18 17   6 7 8 9

Editor's note

The personal histories presented in this book are composites of stories from many different patients and do not present the literal details of any individual's life. Recommendations are offered in a general way, not as prescriptions for treatment. Readers are advised to consult a helping professional to adapt these concepts to the specifics of their personal history and situation.

Cover design by Theresa Gedig
Interior design and typesetting by Kinne Design

To Hope

Beyond a wholesome discipline,
be gentle with yourself.

– "DESIDERATA"

Contents

THE WEIGH IN

THE WEIGH OUT

PREFACE

Fat Is a Family Affair was my Ph.D. dissertation in 1983. At that time, the nation's first self-help–oriented eating disorders unit—which I had opened—was well into its eighth year. Many imitators were springing up, and I, characteristically, was done with pioneering and wanted to move on. I decided to turn my dissertation into a book for a popular audience so that I could say what I had to say and then get out of the treatment field. I was disillusioned with how the insurance industry was corrupting the family treatment model. I thought the book was my swan song. Instead, *Fat Is a Family Affair* became a national best-seller, and I was slam-dunked into the field. I appeared on TV throughout the nation. I was on many of Oprah Winfrey's early shows, had a regular spot on *Hour Magazine,* and lectured around the country training counselors in how to manage family therapy and the special denial and resistance needs of over- and undereaters.

Now, close to twenty years after that first launch, I welcome the opportunity to update some of that initial material and to share further experience treating addicted families. In my later books, I refuted some of what I'd said in the first edition of *Fat Is a Family Affair.* In this second edition, I have noted those changes, as well as other developments in the treatment and recovery of over- and undereaters. For the most part, however, the main message remains intact: To maintain a weight loss, you must surrender to the idea that you can't do it alone and that it is an inside job involving a spiritual/psychological transformation that will affect everyone you know.

I can summarize the focus of this book best with a brief

conversation I had with my main mentor. The idea of needing a mentor, of following direction from another fellow sufferer on the path, is key to making this treatment approach work. For me—intelligent, successful, cunning, and driven—eating was the one area of my life I could *not* control. No force of will, firm resolve, or teeth-gritting, fist-clenching declaration could endure for more than three or four days. The weight piled on. Food knocked me to my knees. It forced me to ask a fellow human being for direction, to acknowledge I didn't have the answers. That first acknowledgment opened the door to the significant difference between this treatment program and all others.

Instead of advocating goals and resolve and pushing, the approach to healing that I've outlined in this book has to do with surrender.

Early on I tried to impress my mentor with all I knew about my own psychodynamics. I was a therapist after all, shortly out of graduate school, just licensed as a marriage and family counselor. I had learned a lot about my own "process."

I explained to her, "I think I keep this weight on because I am afraid to get thin."

She replied, "Why don't you get thin and then we'll talk about it."

Whew! Trimmed my sails and stopped me dead in my tracks. This approach was about doing and seeing what you felt when you'd arrived. It wasn't about conjecture and mind games.

Then I decided to criticize the treatment methods.

"I like everything about this program except the spiritual part," I cajoled.

"There is no spiritual *part* to this program," she answered emphatically. "It *is* a spiritual program. It's all spiritual and nothing but spiritual."

Finding our way between the spiritual and psychological and developing a personal treatment plan that can include both is the crux of this book. So this book differs from all the others out there in those two distinctive ways:

1. You can't do it alone.
2. You need spiritual direction.

Your family must also accept these premises and adapt accordingly. If not, you will all remain obsessed with food and weight.

In this second edition I have also addressed the concept of obsession more than the concept of addiction. I found over the years that some people focused so much on the addiction aspect that they made food an enemy, called themselves "food addicts," and became just as obsessed with not eating as they once were with eating. Others would examine checklists or medical journals and find the loophole to make the situation not applicable to them. They decided they didn't need to take drastic measures because they felt they didn't fit the proper diagnostic categories for having an eating disorder. For that reason, I am not writing solely about eating disorders.

Eating disorders have become too popularized as a concept. Medical practice is looking for quick fixes, with most centers prescribing drugs. Many want to find some childhood incident that "caused" the food obsessions. These ways of thinking don't apply to those of us facing lifelong, chronic obsessions. After a few months of media attention, food obsessions are still virtually ignored, helping us to fail at addressing our national epidemic and obsession. America's drug of choice is *food!* I am addressing persons who *know* that they are obsessed with thinking about food and their relationship to it.

These people are not necessarily diagnosable as E-Ds (eating disorder sufferers) as I'd named them in the first edition. We will now call them F-Os, meaning anyone who is food obsessed.

Similarly, I have changed the name for their family members. In the first edition, I was one of the originators of the term "codependents," as we'd been using that in our family treatment program for years. Many have written extensively from that base, often quoting the first edition as their guide. The term has now become so overused that I want to move away from it so that we can really focus on the pain suffered by these loved ones. I tried to get to the core of the relationship the family member has to the F-O and decided to use the name C-P for confluent personality. C-Ps have lost perspective of their own ego boundaries and have melded into concern for their loved ones. This confluence is what has to change in order for them to grow into full-fledged separated beings and to allow their loved ones to do the same. I regret that at this writing, O-Anon, the self-help group created for family members of F-Os, seems to be defunct. I strongly recommend that family members find other help.

Those who are food obsessed and their family members face roadblocks to recovery because the ideas about sugar addiction have remained controversial. At a time when most nutritionists and medical personnel were recommending carbohydrate loading and exercise, my experience and that of my patients was that we had an intolerance to sugar and carbohydrates. It set up cravings, which forced us to eat more fats to soothe ourselves. People who had that experience bought this book. Now, many years later, the research is proving that eating "fat-free" has made us all fatter, and it is now conjectured that yes, maybe sugar is somewhat the culprit. There are many volumes out there explaining this in great detail. This book is not one of them. It is not a diet book and is not about food. It's about you and your relationship to food. I continue to ask you to trust your own experience. You know.

ACKNOWLEDGMENTS

Yves Luc Bolomet was my editor, companion, best friend, and seer through the first publication of this book. He helped birth this project when many others had abandoned the task. He also managed our treatment centers and encouraged me to continue on the spiritual path that is now producing yet another book. He died on his Triumph motorcycle just before his sixtieth birthday. I'm sure that's the way he would have wanted to go. His kindness and encouragement live on in these pages. As professional mentors, William Ofman, Ph.D., taught me the "good faith" of honest relating, while Walter Kemplar, M.D., showed me how to move whole families along the journey to intimacy.

Thanks to my dad, Gilbert Stockman, who expected me to be a full and honest person, and my mother, Rebecca Stockman, who showed me the strength I'd need. Thank God for my brother, David Stockman, whose counsel in the midst of our family was such a comfort and reassurance that I saw the situation clearly.

My deepest appreciation and joy go to the thousands of patients and counselors who have shared the hope of their recoveries. It is a humbling privilege that they allow me into their lives. Special thanks to Elaine Paxson and Muriel Zink, who listened to my inner voice until I could hear it myself. Thank God for the Twelve Steps.

We're As Fat As We Are Dishonest

Fat is a family affair. If you are obsessed with food and dieting, you and your loved ones have been living with a dishonest person who seeks to survive by living a lie. Not only that, but your loved ones have helped you live the lie as they have lived out their own. As food-obsessed individuals, to win love and admiration, we acquire an "as if" personality, becoming what others need, gaining excess weight, and losing a sense of a true inner self. When that true person cries out to be heard, we drown it out with food. Recovery from food obsessions requires a precious journey to find the real Self. Most of us are unable to find the way on our own because we wear blinders when forks loom up in the path. It is easier to trudge the well-beaten, painful path than to risk the unknown.

As long as we keep eating, we can ignore internal messages that say, *Something is wrong here. I'm living the wrong life. I don't belong in this body or these roles.* In my case, I was a very successful therapist weighing in at 222 pounds, on a small 5'4" frame. I had no idea that anything about my lifestyle was at all related to the poundage I'd amassed. I was counseling heroin addicts and alcoholics and getting praise at how well I understood the addictive personality. I actually thought I was a nearly perfect human being— my only minor flaw was the fat. If I'd lose weight, I'd be perfect and so would my life. I'd lost thousands of pounds before, as a college freshman on pills, then each of the nine times at Weight Watchers, as well as countless other failed attempts. Each time, despite a gorgeous body, nothing had changed in my personality. Despite pushing out a false bravado, I felt very inadequate underneath. I still never felt deserving of the good life and couldn't endure the stress of success. Slowly the weight crept back.

These past three decades have been different. I've not only kept the weight off, but I've also lost my childish demands to be rescued. Instead, I found the very wise, sensitive, and real adult I'd been smothering with excess food. You might say, "Well, surely someone should grow up in thirty years." But if I'd continued with my food obsession, I wouldn't have learned any of the lessons in this test of life. You've certainly known people who have aged chronologically but still act like demanding children. That would have been me. I would still be waiting to grow up. Instead, a whole new life was created within this very lifetime. I did not continue in the direction I was headed. I had to be reborn and become a baby first. Then I could grow up without excess food. As a result, I had to renegotiate every relationship in my life and establish a new identity for success.

To recover from food obsessions, we have to give birth to our true self, find a way for it to be heard, and then carry it with us into a new life. Through suggestions in this book, you, too, can find a new way to relate to recover.

Relate to Recover

Eating is a substitute for true intimacy and risk. If we want to change our bodies, we have to change our relationships. Then we won't need the excess. Whether bingeing, vomiting, or starving, our disordered behaviors around food symbolize how we relate in our world. Overeaters, anorexics, and purgers all have this in common. Whether fifty pounds underweight, three hundred pounds overweight, or struggling with the same fifteen pounds daily for years on end, each of us must examine the same issues of control and vulnerability.

Problems arise when we try to get nurturance without being vulnerable. The only way to do that is with food. Food is that single, solitary, lonely substance that is ever-ready and never fails. Food never expects anything of us. We don't have to entertain it with small talk, and we don't even have to take a shower for it to love us. People aren't quite that predictable or dependable. People sometimes expect too much. Refusing to risk the pain of separateness from others, we choose the controlled security of food. Eventually the food itself becomes uncontrollable. Then we must give up food and return to others. We have to give up an obsessional relationship with food for a riskier intimacy with other human beings. This affects everyone in our lives. This book is for you and all of them.

Renegotiating relationships is much harder than fasting or gulping down at water coolers or endlessly talking about diets. Eating less and drinking more water won't heal a thing. You might be turned off to this approach, thinking of it as too hard. But you already know the "quickie" books don't work. They're tossed in your bedroom corner with the Snickers wrappers. For you, the question must be "Do I want to have another quickie just this once, or do I really want to get on with it, once and for all, whatever it takes?" It's a clear and personal choice. If you're not ready, go ahead and toss this book onto the pile. You might eventually walk over, stoop down, and pick it up again. Don't worry. It's good exercise. You don't even have to take care of it in *this* lifetime. I'm not pushing you. Whatever growth you are avoiding will still be waiting for you the next time around. However, consider this: denying your true self left you irresponsible. You avoided living your own true life. A fat buffoon threatens no one. If you keep failing, no one will expect too much. Neither will you. This book is about taking yourself seriously and gaining respect from yourself and others. Your life is at stake.

You have nothing to lose but your fat.

When I sent this book proposal to a number of publishers, I was overwhelmingly rejected with "The approach is too serious." Here is some of what I was told:

> A very thorough proposal and an excellent book idea. The trouble is, I think, that most people want a quick, new diet program that works for them. So, while a book for behavior modification for the whole family and/or friends makes some sense, I don't think it can compete with those other books.
>
> My experience with books having to do with eating disorders is that the more serious they are the less well they sell and that books that don't provide diets don't sell at all.
>
> Unfortunately, as we all know, the diet books that work are the "magic" books, and while they may not be healthy, they offer people what they want.
>
> *Fat Is a Family Affair* is not only *not* a diet book, but one which requires a great deal of time and effort on the part of the person who suffers from the problem and from the family members as well. In other words, I think it's just too much work.

Another rejection letter said the following:

> *Fat Is a Family Affair* could be the hottest diet book since sliced pineapple and papaya and still I'd think it was chopped liver!

Despite such rejections, this book eventually found a home and went on to be a national best-seller. It has been required reading in treatment centers around the world. I take pride and compliment in the words of my detractors. I wish I could tell you that the world has changed since first publication, but it hasn't really. Although this book continues to touch a tender spot in the hearts of over- and undereaters who want to get honest with themselves, the general trend is toward diet books and get-well-quick schemes that focus on food instead of self. Looking at changing ourselves still seems like too damn much work.

If those are the reasons for rejecting this manuscript, I offer all these "reasons" to you, the current reader, as a tribute to your dedication to finally take on the difficult task. As we joked in high school when asked to try something new, "May as well, can't dance. . . ."

· THE WEIGH IN ·

CHAPTER 1

Relate to Recover

I was never truly thin until I grew up and became an adult. I can't say I've as yet fully accomplished the task, but most days I choose more adult behaviors than I used to. While waiting to grow up, I was still looking for a "big daddy" out there to "fix" me. That was years after I had lost and gained thousands of pounds, but emotionally, I did not know how to be independent and responsible for myself. I had a mistaken sense of responsibility. I tried to prove my worth by helping others. I didn't have a clue how to heal me. So I ate.

I became a therapist hoping that by delving into *why* I ate, I would one day be able to stop eating compulsively. Life would begin when I got thin. I also hoped that helping others would heal me by osmosis. Regrettably or fortunately, that plan backfired. Helping others drained me, and intense therapy only left me lonely and depressed. So I did what any compulsive overeater would do—I ate. It was a roller coaster: gaining, losing, bingeing, abstaining, examining, ignoring, and, ultimately, eating.

Even though eating became a larger and larger part of my life, I did manage to develop a career. Professional success helped hide my bingeing. I was certain hiding it would make it vanish. However, I became fatter and fatter and my "secret" became more and more obvious.

I was a gifted teacher and trainer in the addiction counseling field. I lectured internationally about the problems of addiction for heroin abusers and alcoholics. Just before stepping on stage, I agonized about my posture and appearance. I contorted like a twisted pretzel to keep the bulges from showing. Sometimes I would actually binge before a lecture to gain enough confidence to speak. In those days, food was still working for me. In 1972, at the Dusit Thani Hotel in Bangkok, Thailand, I burped at the podium for the International Congress on Alcohol and Drug Dependence. This ended my speech and punctuated my behavior at the buffet an hour before. These are the kinds of **P**ainful **a**nd **I**ncomprehensible **D**emoralizations referred to in *Alcoholics Anonymous*, affectionately known as the Big Book. Food obsession sufferers share a common experience that more-normal individuals can't understand. We've **PAID** our dues.

My bulges weren't the only thing to hide. While I was lecturing, I also kept secret the fact that I was married to a practicing alcoholic who beat me periodically. He beat me the night before my first appearance on TV. Extra makeup covered the bruises as neither of us knew how to weather the stress of my new success. Life was offering new opportunities, and we were still caught up in continuing past suffering. Excess weight kept us married to the past. Despite all my best efforts, I could not fix him either. I had helped so many other families, but my own life was in shambles. The stronger the facade I projected, the more I kept falling apart. Only one thing kept me strong enough to keep up the front—food.

It was very easy to counsel and help alcoholic families but impossible to see myself in the same situation. Colleagues marveled at how well I worked with the addictive personality. They felt I had a natural gift for understanding alcoholic patients. Not one of them ever made the connection that I was just as sick and pained as the people I helped. I know now that my true illness was the denial of my own neediness, masked in the service of helping others. We all denied the severity of my illness. After all, although alcoholism certainly seemed severe and deadly, we all assumed my problem was merely a struggle of willpower, and as soon as I mustered enough of old Will's power, I would pull myself up and do something. I always assumed that I would do it on a Monday. (I always binged on the weekends.) I showed a strong facade as a therapist, while I denied my own painful obesity. "Knowing it all" for my clients certainly didn't help me.

One September afternoon I walked past a store window and saw a horribly fat reflection in the glass. She wore a dress exactly like mine. It stopped me cold—the wind was knocked out of me. I stared fixedly into the glass and, somewhere deep within, a small voice whispered, *That lady in the window is* you. I could not speak or move—I was transfixed as I realized that my self-destructive journey was every bit as deadly and uncontrollable as that of any alcoholic I'd ever treated. With all my best efforts, I weighed 222 pounds! I had *dieted* myself up to that weight. I had not done it by willy-nilly eating. My life consisted of brief periods of controlled eating followed by excessive bingeing. Dieting always began with firm resolve, clenched teeth, and white-knuckle abstinence. When the pain of living became unbearable, I was soon back with my tried-and-true comforter.

I saw alcoholics who kept alcohol at bay by finding nurturance among people. I had been counseling them and their families into Alcoholics Anonymous (AA) and Al-Anon for years. It suddenly seemed axiomatic that the cure for compulsive eating must follow a similar course. It might be harder for overeaters; we have to control the substance daily. However, the fact that it is difficult doesn't make it impossible. That "impossible" feat, abstaining from compulsive eating, has been accomplished by myself and thousands of others with the plans described in this book.

Recovering from food obsessions involves turning away from self-administered comfort and turning instead to nurturance from people. The hardest part is acknowledging how hard this is and accepting help. If you could have recovered on your own, you would have. The crucial step is admitting your own personal vulnerability. Once you can allow yourself to ask for help, you are well on the road to recovery. Overeaters Anonymous (OA) works very well and offers help to large numbers of people. This book will show you how to accept help and make Overeaters Anonymous work for you. You will see that as your personality changes and you become more vulnerable, the people in your life will be adjusting to the changes. They will need help as well. Family members will learn how to get help from others and remove their false expectations to cure you.

You may say, "But this will take too long. I might be forty before I'm thin." Well if all goes well, you're going to be forty anyway. And you may stay thin for more than a half-hour flight over Chicago. These long-lasting results will keep you from returning to compulsive eating. You'll feel better with abstinence than you ever felt bingeing. There's nothing so bad that a binge won't make worse.

Your dishonest relationships with loved ones helped you deny and kept you fat. You were able to isolate yourself from others as long as your best friend, food, filled your needs. When you give up food (and by this I mean your old attitudes and behaviors toward it), you will give up defiance, and you will need to get nurturance from others. When you learn how to get your needs met by other people, the craving for food diminishes. In other words, instead of looking at food, glorious food, as the problem to address, we will instead look at *you* and your relationships. Your new neediness will affect every person you know. This is what makes fat a family affair.

For recovery to be lasting, your relationship with food changes, and then all relationships change, from near and distant relatives, to co-workers, friends, and new people you haven't even met yet. *You* will change, not just your food plan, but *you*.

CAUTION: Reading this *will* mess up your relationship with food. You won't be able to eat in the same old way. You will be too conscious of what you are doing. If surrender and support are the focal points of this recovery program, *consciousness* is at the heart of it. You can't afford to be unconscious about what and how you are eating, and you can't be unconscious in your actions with other human beings. You have to pay attention to the choices you make and accept responsibility for many of the situations you create in your life. This consciousness begins at every meal, with every bite you put in your mouth. I have developed a video, *The Divine Dine*™, which shows viewers how to develop conscious eating techniques. This consciousness is what families learn in treatment programs and you will learn as you read on.

Food As Love

Loving food is safer than loving people. This certainly sounds like a crazy idea. What does one thing have to do with the other? Food and people are our most intimate comforters. Actually, *eating is the most intimate experience any of us knows*. Think about it. When you take food into your body, you are bringing a foreign substance across your own personal boundaries and incorporating it into your very being. When you eat, the "outside" enters your own personal temple, juices from your own body mix with it and use it to make new cells. *The food changes form and becomes new parts of you*. Not even sexual intercourse or pregnancy involves such an intimate merging. This is total union. Seeking that total union and intimacy, we turn to food because people don't usually work as well.

Baby Wants a Bottle

While in the womb, you felt secure. You couldn't really separate where you began and Mommy ended. Life was safe and required little effort. You never had to ask for a thing. The world anticipated your needs before you even knew what they were. You were full and safe without even knowing the possibility of feeling differently.

When the nurturing, effortless environment was disturbed by birth, you had to get out there and live. Suddenly, you became an infant. As an infant, you experienced the differentness between *you* and *the world*. Much of your early development involved reaching for new and strange objects in the new environment and discovering the difference between inside you and outside you. Even your own toes proved fascinating. You learned the difference between touching *your own* toes and touching *someone else's* wooden crib. There *was* a difference. You also learned that sometimes you felt different inside. Sometimes you felt full, and sometimes you felt empty. When you felt the emptiness, you didn't like it, so you cried and *someone else* fixed it. Satisfying your feeling of emptiness may have taken a few minutes, but sooner or later Mom came with bottle or nipple poised, ready to fill your needs. *What took you so long?* you wondered. *There was a gap between the time when I knew I needed something and you fixed it. Why did I even have to cry? Why didn't you know what I needed? Isn't the rest of the world inside my skin? I don't like these delays. I definitely don't like the effort it takes to live out here; it's a hell of a lot of work.*

"Thanks a Lot, I'd Rather Do It Myself"

Because you learned early that life required effort and might even sometimes be difficult, you decided to find another way to get your needs met. Other people are usually disappointing. Consider the following for a minute. Other people can't help being "wrong" for you. They are going to have their own bad days. They have their own needs they're trying to meet. And, most important, they are not inside your skin; they can't anticipate your needs and save you from the effort required to know and ask for what you want.

Your decision to turn to food instead was actually somewhat wise. That choice saved you from the painful realizations and disappointments that accompany the difference between you and other people—the reality that *they* may not be there for you. Because you felt you could not weather those disappointments, you decided to nurture yourself without *them*. That's what bingeing does. You are totally secure and safe while bingeing. Your need for nurturance is being met at a steady pace, and you are totally in control of food. You buy it, prepare it, and devour it. That makes you totally self-sufficient. You don't need anyone else. In fact, when you are alone with food, you don't think of anything else. You feel at one with the universe; the separation is gone. There is a continuous motion between your elbow's bend and your jaw's chewing, and the precision of the act is perfection. The world is yours. Ashley Montagu quipped in his book *Touching* that we are all looking for "a womb with a view."

The anorexic, while refusing to binge, carries the self-nurturance even further. With anorexia, you are saying, "Not only don't I need *you*, I don't even need *food.* I am so self-sufficient, invincible, invulnerable, and self-contained that I can live on air. I have overcome any 'human' (said with a sneer) neediness and am completely in charge of my life. *I'm not needy!*"

Each behavior around food is a way to feel in control and protected from the need for human nurturance. To avoid disappointment, you transfer all your neediness to an unnatural love affair with food. There's really nothing inherently destructive or problematic about this decision until carried to extremes. Although your case may not yet be extreme, it is your unnatural relationship with food and the use of it to avoid human nurturance that can lead to painful obsessions. You are using food to avoid the risk of life. In this book you will learn how to risk life to give up food obsession.

You will learn ways to risk showing the world exactly who you are and of turning to other people to help you. You will learn how to express your needs and feel grounded. Too often you ate to amass body size so you could feel solid. When you discover adult interdependence, you won't need all that flesh to prove you exist. The only freedom from your obsession with food is a new, healthier dependency on other people instead. People with broken legs use crutches, and people with food obsessions can turn to other people.

Giving Up Means Growing Up

Whether you are emaciated or obese, your decision to deny your own neediness and seek solace in food is a way to stay in control, albeit while suffering. Staying focused on food has been a way to avoid growing up and accepting the reality that *they* can't fix it. Maybe they should, but they can't. They can aid, but they can't fix. As a demanding, disappointed child, you have proclaimed, *they* should be different. *They* should be there for me. *They* are trying to hurt me. Because *they* (Mommy, Daddy, spouse, friend, employer) failed, you turn to a substance to keep filled and safe with the fantasy that instant gratification and a fix will always be there. Rather than face the disappointment that you might not be cared for well enough, you decided to do it yourself.

This is a survival mechanism. Perhaps your childhood was spent being your own parent, or parent to your parent. This is often true if you were born into an addicted family.

Your addicted parent certainly could not be there for you, so you learned to do it yourself. Whatever the causes, the choice to binge or starve came quite honestly. If anorexic, you probably started out with a weight problem (food to excess) and now seek to control the problem. Starving is your "solution" to food and other life problems. The obsession with food once worked, but now it's turned on you, and the way out is to face the disappointment. First, food has failed you: you can't control it. Second, people have failed you: they don't anticipate or meet your needs fast enough.

Facing such disappointments is a way to grow up. How can you still turn to others knowing they might sometimes fail you? "Sometimes" is the key word here. If you spread your neediness and shop around, you are bound to find someone who can offer help when you need it. You might later be in a position to return the favor. If you don't learn this crucial timing issue, you'll eat. It's that simple. In recovery you will grow up strong enough to know that others can care about you but can't fix you. They also can't be up for you all the time.

I will never forget calling my mentor in a snit about something someone had said that offended me. She politely and quietly responded with, "I'm sorry, dear, but I am eating lunch right now. Can I call you back in twenty minutes?" I was initially quite offended and further incensed. I wanted to scream at her about how difficult it was for me to even make the call in the first place, how I didn't like feeling so humbled, how she should know how hard it all was for me. Instead, I waited quietly. She called back. We all lived. I wanted recovery more than I wanted my righteous indignation.

You will learn that recovery is an inside job for which you use others as allies and aids, but it is a job that you must take on for yourself. You will learn to weather those crucial, painful moments from when your obsession starts to when it finally passes—and it will pass. You will see that you can survive the length of time when needs aren't met. Most compulsions last about fifteen minutes. You can seek the aid of others to help you pass on a binge.

You will learn what a C-P, or confluent personality, is and how most over- and undereaters are also C-Ps. As a C-P, you want to rescue those you love from the painful reality of growing up and facing disappointment. In zealously rescuing them, you have contributed to their problem and certainly not helped yourself. The best way for family members to help is to start helping themselves. Living and facing life honestly is the road to recovery. Sometimes you may be honestly fed up with rescuing. Then it's time to express your discontent and stop jumping in to "save the day."

One relationship that often involves confluence is the parent-child relationship. Parents and children need to separate with love. The relationship of parent and child has to be severed and then slowly soothed and healed into something new. As long as parents feel overly responsible for their child, the child will not grow up and face life on his or her own. This separation is not just a matter of age or geography; it is a deep emotional commitment and tie that must be broken for survival to occur. Sometimes the dependence is transferred to a mate. You marry into a situation where you still believe someone else will fix you. As long as you both believe and perpetuate the myth, the obsession with food will continue.

However, to grow up, the first and most crucial relationship change you have to make is with your best friend, food. As your most significant love object, food serves as both nurturer and punisher. It works when all else fails. It helps mask all your neediness and helps you avoid your own life. Most important, it helps you weather the stress of change. It plants you firmly in concrete so you won't ebb and flow with the tide of life. Without the binding security of food, you will acquire the flexibility to flow with changes in your life.

Food As Avoidance

You have used an obsession with food to *avoid*. With food you avoid

- the risk of knowing how much you need other people
- the possibility that you won't have the world as you'd like it
- taking responsibility for your own life
- the probability that if you really want to, you could be ecstatically happy most of the time
- the reality that even if life is great, there will also be bad days
- the reality that *they* are not in your skin
- sensual, sexual pleasures
- the responsibility of success
- the difficulty of avoiding others' expectations

You must learn to change an unnatural relationship with food into a new relationship with others. Food will become cardboard. It is only a substance to stoke your engine for a twenty-four-hour period. It is not love, God, sex, or rock and roll—it is just food.

And you are just you. You may not be all the things you thought you'd become or others planned you'd be, but you certainly are someone to yourself. This is your life. Your responsibility is to live it. Food keeps you away from the fullness of your life. You can denigrate with "You're full of it!" Or you can celebrate with "You're full. Love it!"

You may be drowning in esoteric discussions of self-worth and personal image. What does it all have to do with anything? What is self-worth? Does a chair have worth? A table? Its worth is in how you use it. Do you have use for a table? If you don't need a table, what's it worth? Do you have use for your life? It's here for you to enjoy. With the food obsession out of the picture, you'll be able to see what you've got and put it to full use.

Food As Punishment

Maybe you can't enjoy life because you think you should be punished. You may be confused about nurturance and punishment. Mothers, in addition to being our chief nurturers in early life, are also our chief socializers. Mom teaches us how to adapt to our culture and fit in with the environment. Noted psychiatrist, R. D. Laing, wrote that "the Stone Age baby is born to the twentieth-century mother and that's where the process of violation begins."

At birth you possess the same genetic programming and the same potentials bred into the savage Stone Age baby. However, you were born into a society where Stone Age behavior is not appropriate. Your mother's job was to teach you to survive in this culture. Some of your savage behavior had to be corrected and modified. You were told no, and you felt deprived; there was conflict between your wants and society's dictates. You received punishment and nurturance from the same source, so you were confused about which is which.

This confusion above all else distinguishes F-Os, or those who are *food obsessed,* from "normies." Others don't use food in a punishing way as we do. Food became your punisher as well as your solace. By the time you have picked up this book, it is difficult to sort out what is what. You may think you eat to get soothed, whereas you actually binge to punish yourself.

We Are *How* We Eat

Food has been your major coping mechanism. To know who you are, just watch how you eat. Do you see yourself as a lady or gentleman sitting down to a genteel leisurely meal in a serene state of mind with classical music and place mats, or do you drive while eating in a garbage-strewn car with straws and wrappers and crumbs stuck in the cushions?

Eating with a driven frenzy, whether it is the pizza you obsessed about all day or the spontaneous decision to guzzle at the kitchen sink, is compulsive eating. Eating compulsively is a measure of your anxiety and inability to handle the frustration and stress of your life. Food takes the shaking away. It seems to relieve the stress and help you cope. "Stressed" spelled backward is "desserts." Some people who fancy themselves as secure, independent, extremely competent individuals may reject the idea that eating frenzies have anything to do with stress. They have lives fashioned around showing how well they can manage things.

That was certainly true in my case. At my top weight I was needed by and helpful to a lot of people. How could I believe that I was also needy? The food kept me from having to admit that fact. The only way you will find out how truly needy you are is to stop eating compulsively. Until you stop the behavior, all your ideas about why you eat will be philosophical conjecture with no basis in life experience. I surely thought seeking the why of my behavior would be the way out. I studied and became a therapist in order to figure out why I ate. I found many reasons. Some were quite depressing, and *I ate over them.*

What else could I do?

To find out *why* you eat . . . DON'T.

The only way to learn the reasons for your behavior is to stop the behavior and observe what develops. If you want to find out why you eat compulsively, don't eat compulsively. With little effort on your part, when the eating stops, your true life will emerge. Without the excessive feeding and the obsessional frenzies around food, whatever you have been submerging about yourself and your life will automatically bubble up.

In my case, I found I was scared to death to appear on TV shows so I had binged my way through. As I continued to curtail my eating behavior, I stopped running around Hollywood impressing TV studios with how brilliantly I could host a new show. I was a workaholic, and food helped me succeed and achieve. However, the more I made abstinence the number-one priority in my life, the more clearly I saw that my life had to change. I just couldn't run around selling myself, convincing network executives that I could deliver them a hit show. I believed in my work and myself, but I didn't want to be selling. It didn't seem to fit with the new-found ways I was learning in recovery programs. I knew I had to reprioritize my activities. Let the chips fall where they might. Not bingeing had gradual but dramatic effects on the total personality I was to become without excess and over-load at its core.

One morning I chatted with my brother while I boiled two eggs and sliced a grapefruit for breakfast. He said, "You might regret not having your own TV show."

I answered, "Yes, but maybe I'll be thin."

I wanted to lose the weight more than I wanted fame or fortune. I realized that if my number-one priority was to stay healthy, then I would have to stop running. I would have to just stop. I stopped running and impressing and selling and manip-ulating. I waited for my Self to show up. Interesting events began to occur. I was asked to be on countless shows as a guest. I watched what a host actually did on a show and the pressure each lived under. I knew it wasn't a job I'd enjoy. I found out that I liked being a guest, showing up to say my piece and then leaving. I was asked to explain things I was passionately involved with. I did it well and walked away.

I've never regretted that major personality change. I've never regretted waiting to find out what my inner being really wants. I do get impatient and want my answers more quickly, but I've learned that it takes whatever time it takes.

Whoever you think you are is who you have become with

food obsession. You really don't have any idea yet who you might be without obsessions around food. That new person will gradually emerge. You'll see. So will your family and friends.

Eat to Live or Live to Eat

If you eat only when hungry, you certainly don't have any need to examine your life as a way to change your relationship with food. You are obviously only using food to stoke your engine for a twenty-four-hour period. You are not obsessing about food or overindulging to relieve stress. This is true for my little dog, Samson. He lies around most of the day. He feels secure about his life. He has very few performance expectations for himself or from others. He's content. He can let a bowl of food sit all day. He often leaves half his bowl and returns later to finish. I've even known humans like this. I might invite them to eat, and they'll refuse seconds, saying something like, "No thanks, I'm full."

I always wonder, *What does hunger have to do with it? Don't they see what good stuff is here? Why do they push away a half-eaten plate?* They eat like my dog. Their eating is a natural life function, like breathing. Their attitude toward food is "I'll take it when I have to, but I really don't care much about it either way." Can you imagine? They don't need this book. They eat to live.

And then there are those of us who live to eat. If you fall into this category, you spend a large part of your time thinking about and taking in food. You have adapted your life to make sure regular feedings fit into your schedule. You might obsess about it a lot or just graze and don't even know when you are eating. Filling yourself and feeling sedated have become integral parts of your life. They help you handle feelings and needs that you might have judged as too excessive. Let's look at some of those needs. Recovery from obsessive eating will involve finding a way to get those needs met without food.

APPRECIATION. Comedian Rodney Dangerfield laments, "I don't get no respect." He's also fat. What about Jackie Gleason as Ralph Kramden on the *Honeymooners* TV show, who struggled to make his wife Alice listen to him? Also fat. Would the character be more appreciated if he were slender? Is he made to look more ludicrous because he is fat? Often the fat person has colluded with those who don't respect him by making a joke of himself before anyone else can. Even so, eating is a way to assuage the disappointment at not being appreciated. Many women start to gain weight soon after marriage. After the romance and excitement of the wedding settle down, the bride stops getting all those pats on the back and appreciative best wishes. Hubby doesn't profess his love and devotion as often as he used to. Similarly, if the strokes from work aren't forthcoming, both men and women sometimes handle the disappointment by turning to food.

The weight gains women experience after childbirth have been explained mostly as metabolic. It has taken extreme headliner cases such as Andrea Yates to alert us to the vast numbers of mothers with postpartum depression (PPD). You might remember that Andrea Yates is the mother in Texas who drowned all five of her children in June of 2001. PPD is an extreme incidence of lack of appreciation. Even though there are hormonal changes that affect the new mother's mood, she is also depressed because of the unrealistic expectations of what childbirth would deliver. She is supposed to be so joyous that there is no allowance for her to voice her disappointment and aloneness.

This disappointment after childbirth is a great truth that dare not speak its name. It is hardest for these mothers to admit to themselves that maybe motherhood is not the big deal it was cracked up to be. It is difficult to speak openly about this. All the relatives and friends are fluttering around oohing and aahing. How could you possibly complain when everyone is telling you how happy you are? All kinds of presents and well wishes come from near and far for the new infant. Yes, Mom gets flowers and then is supposed to get enough joy and enough of a present just by holding the new baby. Where is there a place for her to say, "Oh, my God! What have I done to my next twenty years? Where do I get mine?" The easiest answer is through food on the plate.

When the mother does accept the birth of the child with joy, she then dedicates herself to raising it well. After twenty-odd years, if she's done a good job, the child leaves the nest. Again, "Where's mine?" With much discussion of the empty-nest syndrome and women's needs for fulfillment, little specific attention has been paid to the mother's need for appreciation. In treating menopause, hormones are prescribed when a few pats on the back might do wonders. It is no accident that most women enter alcoholism treatment in their forties. They are finally facing issues around lack of appreciation. Many women who don't cover up their needs in a bottle do it by overeating.

In recovery you will learn how to identify your desire for appreciation and turn to people who can congratulate and applaud you as needed. They may not be family members, as family members may feel too jealous and are angry at being jealous. By the time your covering up with food has progressed to its excessive stages, you may need appreciative pats on the back, not just from one or two people, but from crowds of people, a whole group. You need to be cautioned not to "take your bucket to empty wells." You may tend to insist and demand that you get those strokes of appreciation from the very person who can't give them. This is self-defeating. For example, the mother whose nest is being abandoned may demand that the adult daughter who is struggling to break away be the one to show her appreciation. This is a no-win situation. In order to make the break, the daughter may have to rebel and reject before she can later be ready to appreciate. The mother may instead need to turn to other mothers to get appreciation. Similarly, the daughter can't get support from the mother she is leaving. She will need to turn to other daughters for appreciation of her struggle.

Since I haven't had children and have channeled my birthing instincts into developing eating disorders units, I experienced this struggle for appreciation in my professional work. I worked with a well-known media psychiatrist who served as an early mentor, almost like a father figure. We met when I was assigned to him as an intern while still in graduate school and still fat. Throughout our ten-year association, I changed tremendously. After losing weight and then founding innovative treatment programs, I wanted appreciation and respect from him at the very time I needed to grow up professionally and move out from under his protective wing. He also needed appreciation for all he had taught me. We were both needy as well as strong. He couldn't see my individual growth. We parted badly with him screaming, "I made Judi Hollis!" He once even yelled the codependent's hidden cry, "I liked you better fat!" Unable to receive appreciation from one another, we each had to turn to others for support in weathering the separation. In my case, I had to seek out appreciation or return to the comfort of the plate.

APPROACHING THE NEW. Newness and change can be terrifying. Instead of acknowledging and weathering the discomfort of new situations, many simply assume false bravado and plunge in with both hands and a knife and fork. Without food, you may have to feel the threat and challenge of new situations. At a party, you may have to feel the awkward shyness you have on first meetings instead of staking out your ground at the buffet table and cracking a thousand jokes. On the job, you may have to sit back and learn more instead of showing off your brilliance and then running to the cafeteria. In other words, slow down and wait. You are right to be cautious and a little apprehensive in new situations. Let yourself feel the fear of change. Let the threat of the new come to the surface, and then it can pass. Denying the threat of the new will keep you locked in the old. This is especially true if the change is for something better and more positive than what you knew before. It's the good life that is hard to take.

RELAXATION. Eating is often seen as a way to relax and soothe tensions. At most jobs, a coffee break is acceptable and allowed, whereas twenty minutes of quiet meditation seems self-indulgent. Instead, if you can't relax by taking quiet time, you binge at your desk. Eating, anxiety, and work are tied together. You may often judge your wish to be alone and quiet as being too withdrawn and isolating, when, in fact, you need the separation in order to regroup and listen to your own inner voice. When that voice isn't heard, it wants to eat.

HABIT. Some eating is simply habitual, a tried-and-true response to various life situations. You expect to eat when the clock strikes noon whether you are hungry or not. Certain events evoke nostalgic feelings about certain foods. Rarely do you give yourself a chance to decide whether you really wanted to eat turkey on Thanksgiving or not. What about eggs for breakfast? Is that really what you wanted to eat, or is it habit?

Sometimes certain friends awaken cravings for certain foods. My friend Jennifer and I used to telephone each other with "Wanna go 'porkin'?" This meant we would hit both Baskin-Robbins and See's Candy and ride around eating in the car until we were nauseated. For many years after I gave up these forays, it was difficult for me to get together with Jennifer without craving a return to our habitual relationship. We had to learn new activities or else give up the friendship.

SEXUALITY. Have you ever described a hot fudge sundae as orgasmic? Much sexual energy is sublimated into licking ice cream cones and slurping puddings. Since the first publication of *Fat Is a Family Affair*, I have written an entire book about the extremely important topic of eating due to sublimated sexuality titled *Hot & Heavy* (Health Communications, Inc., 1998). The healthiest approach to both eating and loving are the same: mindfulness and consciousness. These days, women feel at liberty to speak freely about their sexuality. Many women complain that they feel much more sexual and horny than their macho male partners. They also seek more conscious and connected sexuality. This outspokenness can be threatening in a culture previously based on male dominance and women's coy submissiveness. Guilty over such sexual feelings, many women have decided to become fat rather than sexually demanding. The partner may then use the fat as the reason for his lack of interest. During the woman's recovery, these men feel threatened when the weight comes off and the excuse is removed. The relationship has to be renegotiated. When the option to eat the sundae is removed, you may experience tremendous sexual urges. Try not to be afraid of these, but accept them as what you have been pushing down with the food.

COMPETITION. It's natural and healthy to put angry energy into achieving something positive. Trying to accomplish much more than humanly possible, however, creates more anger and resentment, so you relax with a Snickers bar or a bag of Fritos. These munchy, crunchy foods are another way to express rage. You give your mouth a chance to gnaw on your perfectionistic standards for yourself and others. You must find ways to express your anger that are not self-defeating.

COPING. Your major coping mechanism has been on your plate. When all your coping tools are funneled onto your plate, you have not learned the other tools necessary for survival. Your tools have been inadequate responses to life situations, a way to fill your need to please and manipulate others. You are also covering up your feelings of inadequacy and low self-worth. In recovery you will find a form of self-acceptance that makes you feel that whatever you can accomplish will have to be enough. Do the best you can and aim for progress, not perfection. You might then be able to survive others' expectations as well as your own.

Using Food to Cope Is Disordered Eating

If you cope with life by eating to excess, you are probably suffering what has been labeled an eating disorder. Using food as a Band-Aid to make it through a day is disordered eating. Since the first publication of this book, there have been countless treatises on eating disorders, including many popular tabloids' exposés of suffering movie stars. You can find the definitions for the various eating disorders in any basic text. We have become inured to the concept, making the maladies commonplace. Many use the checklists and diagnostic criteria as a way to tell themselves, "I'm not that bad yet. I don't fit the diagnosis."

For these reasons, I have changed the focus in this second edition to look at all these behaviors as *food obsessions,* something with which many more people identify. Rather than adhering so clinically to definitions for someone with an eating disorder, an E-D, we will instead look at the clearer indication—*food obsession*—and refer to all sufferers as F-Os. In the next chapter you will learn more specifically about your condition.

CHAPTER 2

Who's the F-O?

Are you an F-O? Does it sound like I'm calling you a name? By picking up this book, you've shown some interest in food obsessions, fat, health, dieting, and so on. Many people, to live as full-blooded, card-carrying Americans, need to use some kind of substance in order to cope. We consume excesses of heroin, cocaine, marijuana, and alcohol. Sixty to eighty million Americans are fat, 30 percent of all college women binge and vomit, and one in ten high school girls are anorexic. As many as 60 percent of children under age ten qualify as obese. So, it seems America's "drug" of choice is food. If you use food to cope with life rather than to stoke your engines, you are an F-O. This applies whether your unnatural relationship is one of bingeing on excessive quantities or swearing off food to the brink of starvation. These are merely opposite sides of the same coin. F-Os eat or starve to cope and compete.

It's Hard As Hell!

The suffering you have as an F-O is woven into every cell of your being and cannot be exorcised with a quickie diet or brief stint in psychotherapy. It's bigger than all of that. If these simple solutions would have worked, I'd never have had the struggles I did, nor would I have written this book, nor would I have brought thousands into treatment programs.

You've already tried to get away with the simple quickies. It is time to focus on the hard-core issues that are rooted in character and personal responsibility.

Bringing attention to the seriousness and difficulty of your problem is not meant to depress you; it is meant to comfort and encourage. You have spent much of your life hearing how *easy* controlling your food should be. That made you feel much worse. Let's face it. No other addiction is treated more off-handedly. For some reason, probably because no one wants to face the seriousness of the issue, we keep acting like weight loss is a simple matter. Every women's magazine carries articles about easy weight loss. The editor of *Family Circle* even reported that the magazine's covers must include a picture of a scrumptious dessert, with a promised recipe inside and an announcement about a diet. The picture attracts us, promising indulgence, and then the diet article takes care of things by promising how easily we will rid ourselves of the effects. This type of presentation minimizes and even trivializes the task at hand.

Because I have been in the treatment field for thirty years, I can't stand cocktail-party discussions of weight loss. For this reason, I am careful not to tell anyone seated next to me at a dinner or on an airplane about the work I do. However, someone invariably starts a discussion about all the simple, new ideas he or she knows. Most people offer me theories as well as excuses. As I was finishing up work on this second edition, I retreated to Palm Springs, where I have only a cell phone available. For some reason, the phone gave out, and I raced to my local service center. All three of the lovely people who worked with me on the phone were clearly obese.

One employee looked up my company's name on the computer, HOL SEM, which stands for *Hollis Seminars*. She asked what kind of seminars I present, and when I told her that they are motivational talks about weight loss and changing your relationship with food, all three initially showed keen interest. I told them how I had maintained a large weight loss for many years and emphasized that I knew how difficult the task was. Each immediately offered me their evaluations about why they'd been unsuccessful. One said she needed to exercise more. The man said he was just lazy. The other woman speculated that her two pregnancies caused the problem.

Each of them was clearly recounting ideas and excuses they'd repeated thousands of times to themselves and to others. We all have been programmed to think we know what it takes to lose weight and why we haven't done it. That very way of talking tends to help us minimize the problem. It's really more than all of those ideas put together. Instead of facing the enormity of it, everyone in this country can tell you his or her own personal theory on weight loss, as if it is such an easily solved problem. I wanted to ask, but remained silent, "Then why does the nation keep getting fatter?"

This conversation reminded me of the first time I appeared on *The Oprah Winfrey Show*. This was the early 1980s, and Oprah had just gone national. I had been asked to appear as a guest expert on a show titled "Diet Failures." The producer prepped me well, explaining that Oprah (still quite large at that time, before her first weight loss using a protein drink) would be surrounded by an audience full of obese women who would be discussing all their failed attempts at weight loss. I would then come on and give them my answer about the attitude change needed, telling them what works.

I was a bit full of myself, imagining the glorious and appreciative response I would get. As they shared all the approaches that had not been working, I waited in the green room for my chance to emphasize the disease concept and a plan I knew worked, not for the short run, but for the long haul. I was very hyped up and couldn't wait to get into the discussion. I was on my stool squirming, thinking *Let me at 'em, coach!* Finally my segment came, and I was announced to come on. Oprah asked, "Okay, Judi, tells us what works."

I responded so importantly, "Well you see, Oprah, it's a disease and . . ."

Oprah quickly interrupted, "It's not a disease."

Then she turned to the audience, egging members on to disagree with what I'd just said. People started blaming and talking about cop-outs and excuses and generally putting down the whole idea.

I was in shock. This was my first appearance on national TV, and based on what the producer had told me, I never expected this response. My sphincter tightened and my throat closed. I stared wildly straight ahead, and when I could get a word in, I smiled politely and tried to make some points. At last the show ended. I made dutiful and relieved thank-yous to Oprah and her staff, vowing to myself that I'd never do this again.

Within a week the producer called me, as they'd received tons of mail and numerous phone calls from people asking them to have me back. The general feeling from viewers was "Why didn't you let her speak?"

I did go back on the show two more times. But as Oprah lost weight using a protein drink and then with a trainer and personal chef, the idea that weight loss is difficult and needs deeper work had basically been discarded by the media.

The media is abundant with promotions and advertising for easy solutions to this complex problem. But we don't see TV ads promising easy treatments for alcoholism or cocaine addiction or heroin abuse—and those are substances you can live without. Once you give them up, you never have to go back to them again. Overweight people, however, are ridiculed and criticized and seen as weak and lazy. It's the last acceptable prejudice in our society.

Racial epithets and slander are definitely discouraged in our culture, but fat bashing is commonplace. Profiling individuals due to race is strongly criticized in our liberal establishments. A child would be strongly reprimanded for using the "N" word, but schoolyards resound with children calling each other "you big fat . . ."

Living in a society that minimizes the difficulty of your weight-loss efforts makes you feel even more like a failure. After all, you failed at such an "easy" task. Instead, this book emphasizes that recovery will be *the hardest thing you've ever done*. Everything else was accomplished with your best friend, food. You'll take on this project without that comfort.

It seems so much more honest and humane to warn you in advance and let you know that I know how hard it is. Letting you face what you're up against is much more effective than all that stiff-upper-lip minimizing. This way you can face what's in store for you and mobilize your own resources for the journey.

I wanted that clarity when I underwent a minor surgery. The doctor told me I would feel pain for "a few minutes." I decided that "a few" meant three minutes. For me, "a couple" meant two minutes and "a few" meant three. As it turned out, I remained in pain for twenty minutes until the anesthetic took effect. Later I told the doctor I was concerned that maybe I had complications because I hurt for so long. He quickly brushed aside my concerns, assuring me that most people hurt "for about twenty minutes."

In his vocabulary, "a few" meant twenty minutes. I told him that I might have been less fearful and agitated if I had known exactly how long I would hurt. As it was, I became afraid because I expected the pain to end much sooner. I would have preferred some clearer advance warning. In other words, if I knew what was to come, I might have been more willing to flow with the pain and cooperate with my body. The doctor cautioned me that if he told people to expect pain, they might manufacture more than necessary.

Despite what my doctor said, I have found it is better to let F-Os know in advance how painful recovery will be. Too much time and money has been spent on minimizing, pretending, and hoping for easier ways. If it were easy, you certainly would have done it already. You will now look at the seriousness as a way to face the problem. After you acknowledge that recovery will be hard, you will be shown a way out.

Let's first see whether you are an F-O. You may be fat or emaciated. You are not being evaluated at the scale or at the clothing rack. This is not a matter of physical presence, but of psychological and spiritual energy. Are you obsessed with food and dieting? No matter what your size, has food assumed unnatural importance in your life and come to dominate you, both psychologically and, ultimately, physically?

F-O Questionnaire

Please answer the following questions to determine
the actual level of food obsession in your life.

	YES	NO
Do you feel guilty about eating?	☐	☐
Do you consume large quantities of junk food?	☐	☐
Do you hide food or hide from others while eating?	☐	☐
Do you eat to the point of nausea and vomiting?	☐	☐
Are you sometimes repulsed by food?	☐	☐
Do you relish preparing foods even if you don't eat them?	☐	☐
Have you ever forced yourself to vomit?	☐	☐
Do you take laxatives to control your weight?	☐	☐
Do you weigh yourself on a scale more than once a week?	☐	☐
Have you found yourself unable to stop eating?	☐	☐
Have you fasted to control your weight?	☐	☐

	YES	NO
Is your eating pattern abnormal and embarrassing?	☐	☐
Do you eat until your stomach hurts?	☐	☐
Does eating cause you to fall asleep?	☐	☐
Do certain occasions require certain foods?	☐	☐
In your lifetime, have you ever lost more than fifty pounds?	☐	☐
Does a "good" restaurant serve large portions?	☐	☐
Do you eat snacks before going out to eat with others?	☐	☐
Do you eat standing up?	☐	☐
Do you "inhale" your food?	☐	☐
Do you become irritated when eating is postponed?	☐	☐
Have you heard others call food "too rich" and felt confused?	☐	☐
Do you awake from sleep to eat?	☐	☐
Does your wardrobe fluctuate among three or more sizes?	☐	☐
Does eating sometimes make you hungrier than not eating?	☐	☐
Do you feel like an object as others describe your body?	☐	☐
Do you usually clean your plate whether hungry or not?	☐	☐
Is your eating rather continuous?	☐	☐
At a party, do you spend most of your time at the snack table, or do you consciously avoid the food area?	☐	☐
Have you tried more than one fad diet?	☐	☐
Do you make fun of yourself before others can?	☐	☐
Do you feel exhilarated when you control food?	☐	☐
Are you afraid to be "normal"?	☐	☐
When you know certain foods are in the cupboard, do they "call" to you?	☐	☐
Do you buy clothes either too big or too small?	☐	☐
When your friends eat like you do, are they embarrassed?	☐	☐
Do you postpone joys with "wait till I control my weight"?	☐	☐
Do others see your body shape differently than you do?	☐	☐

———————◼———————

Cultural Link

In addition to your own psychological tendencies, there is a strong link between culture and food obsessions. Eating disorders only occur in western, industrialized societies. People from other countries who come to the United States and adopt the American diet and attitudes often end up becoming obese.

Moving from Sin to Sickness

How many times have you said, "I was really 'bad' during the holidays, but I'm going to be 'good' for the new year"? You have been using food as a way to evaluate "good" and "bad." In actuality, your eating behavior has nothing at all to do with whether you are a sinner or a saint. You have an illness. You have tried your best to control your compulsive relationship with food but to no avail.

Finally, medical science is catching up to this reality. There are now clinical diagnoses for people who suffer from eating disorders. You are not a bad person but a sick person. It was not until 1957 that the American Medical Association declared alcoholism a disease. For centuries before that, alcoholics died from their compulsion to drink. Similarly, schizophrenics were jailed and tortured before investigation revealed their underlying chemical and psychological malady.

You can help yourself by taking a more medicinal attitude toward your eating behavior. My major motivation for creating hospital treatment units was to allow the patient to move from the sin to the sickness model. I had seen such an approach do wonders for alcoholics. Receiving treatment in a hospital setting, where a doctor acknowledged the seriousness of the illness and the patient got respect rather than punishment, helped the patient become willing to get well. Those suffering with food obsessions need the same respect and attention to their serious, lifelong, chronic illness. The minimizing, punitive solutions don't work.

If you have chosen food as your drug of choice, you clinically fall into one of two major categories of eating disorders: bulimia or anorexia. (See the "Bulimia" and "Anorexia" sections later in this chapter for an understanding of how these terms are used in this book.) I don't want to give too much importance to these diagnoses, as their definitions change each time psychologists revise their diagnostic manual. Over my many years in the field, I have watched the diagnoses undergo changes that are motivated by the political and personal concerns of the writers. I would rather you look at the obsessional nature of your relationship with food than the criteria listed in such checklists. In my experience, anorexia and bulimia are really the same illness. I see them as opposite sides of the same coin or opposite points on the same spectrum. One of you is fat, the other thin. Though you look different physically, you both exhibit the same personality profiles. To divide you into categories, fat or thin, is unnecessary. You both have the same personality structures, struggle with the same control issues, and, therefore, need the same treatment to recover. In fact, a person whose weight changes frequently and who never maintains a stable body configuration may have both disorders. Quite possibly, you weighed 90 pounds last year and ate only lettuce, but this year you weigh 180 pounds and eat nonstop. Your body changes as frequently as the weather.

More than likely, you have been both fat and thin. Some people with childhood onset obesity have experienced special metabolic, genetic, and cultural influences. But even these people have also had periods of slimness, along with periods of excessive starvation diets, whether they stayed fat or lost weight. There are many very obese people who meet many of the diagnostic criteria for anorexia. In nearly all cases, anorexics started out with overweight problems, began dieting, got high from not eating, and now are emaciated and obsessed with avoiding food. They found their solution to the eating problem. They don't eat. Still, food remains their number-one topic of discussion and obsession.

Whether fat or thin, you contain the characteristics of your opposite side. You might want to deny that side, but she exists. If thin, you are sometimes repulsed by the fat lady and don't want her anywhere around. And fat ladies say, "What do I have in common with a skinny little bitch like that? She flaunts her body." In either case, your recovery will depend on making friends with that opposite side of yourself you'd rather avoid. Your biggest project right now will be removing poundage as your evaluation criteria. You will have to see that *your disorder lies in your relationship with food, not your poundage.* Recovery will involve renegotiating your relationship with food, not obsessing about the numbers on your scale. Those who are thin but talk incessantly about food and dieting are still food obsessed and not in the kind of healthy recovery I am advocating.

Forsake the Scale God

If you have bought what I have proposed thus far, you can surely see how absurd it is to go to your health spa and brag, "I just lost three pounds." That's the same three, or thirty, pounds you lost last year and the year before. Poundage is not the issue. You must be ready to have a totally new relationship with food. Bowing down to a scale every morning is all part of the obsession. That very behavior must stop.

You have made the scale your god. Each morning you bow down to ask, "Who am I, God?" You are really trying to find a way to beat the system and eat. You are really asking this god, "Did I get away with it?" You want to know whether there were any consequences to the eating you already feel guilty about. If you ate and didn't gain, you sigh, "Phew, I got away with it." Maybe you check in with the scale god because you are dieting and want quick reinforcement for your deprivation.

You bow down to ask the god, "Do I get a quick payoff for my suffering?" In either case, you are looking to an external, spring-driven contraption to verify who you are. Whether the scale god shows a loss or a gain, it is usually an excuse to binge. If you've lost weight, you say, "Well, I'm doing pretty well, no need to rush it, I think I'll eat a little." If you haven't lost weight, you complain, "This isn't fair, I may as well eat." In either case, weighing leads to eating. Weigh yourself right now, as you begin this book, and then don't weigh again for one month. You may find that it is harder to give up the scale than to give up the food. Try it and see what happens.

As you give up the focus on poundage, you become more ready to accept your illness as a medical reality instead of a moral affliction. Let's take a look at how the diagnostic categories have been presented.

Bulimia

"Bulimia" is derived from the Greek word "buli," which means "to eat like an animal, or animal hunger." It does not mean "to vomit," even though that interpretation has evolved in popular usage. Instead of referring you to diagnostic checklists and manuals, I would like to encourage you to honestly face the disordered nature of your attitudes toward food. You don't need other people's questions and charts as much as you need rigorous self-honesty. The illness is the unnatural manner of "shoveling in" food. *Bulimia refers to the manner in which you take in food, not how it gets out.* You may keep the food in, as fat, or you may vomit it out, or exercise or diet it off. The main ingredient of bulimia is bingeing.

Commonly used in TV newscasts and recent magazine exposés, the term "bulimarexia" has come into our vocabulary to designate people who binge and then vomit. This term is not in professional writings but is used by the public. If you binge and then vomit, you can rest assured that you've got just simple bulimia.

Anorexia

Now, what if you are just as obsessed with food but to the opposite extreme? You are driven and obsessed *not* to eat. A major problem in trying to diagnose yourself is your own denial. You may not see the situation clearly. If you are anorexic, other people in your life may point this out long before you recognize the problem. With anorexia as well as bulimia, it is not your weight that is of utmost importance. The essential factor is your *attitude* toward food and dieting. If anorexic, you have an unnatural fear of food. You may be repulsed by your own body, especially if it is normal-sized.

Trying to find the seriousness of your problem will be difficult in a society in which everyone is made to feel guilty about eating. Someone who was once considered normal and shapely, say Marilyn Monroe, is by today's standards considered plump. Size ten was once normal, but now women try for size two. Unrealistic social pressures coupled with personal distorted body images keep us denying our problem. Fat people see themselves as thinner than they really are, and skinny people think they're fat. You can see, therefore, how these disorders come from internal messages and have nothing to do with weight. They have more to do with accepting reality and yourself. Ultimately, your recovery program must include finding a way to love yourself and get more love from others. That is why "fat is a family affair."

Beyond Labels

While it's important that your disorder be considered a disease, be careful to not get stuck on the label and not move any further. Until very recently, medical practice has been bent on naming things but not on fixing them. Do you hang out in the self-help section of your bookstore seeking a new name for what ails you? Would you like this book to offer even more checklists of symptoms to which you could say yea or nay?

Wouldn't that make things a little easier? Wouldn't it be easier if we could just treat this disease called life?

Don't blame yourself for wanting your problem a bit more tightly wrapped and packaged for shipping. You came by it honestly. Most of us look for labels to help us continue to deny the fact that physically and spiritually *we create* our own lives. This prospect seems too much to bear. Once you recognize this bottom-line basic fact, you may sink into deep regret about wasted time. That can get very depressing.

Despite the comfort we may briefly feel from esoteric diagnoses, having a name for what's wrong with us is *exactly* what is wrong with us. Our inner being knows there's much more to it than the medical label. She also knows that if we buy too much into the labeling mentality, we'll stop listening for internal signals altogether. We might even work harder to shut her up. After all, most of our upbringing, our "civilizing," has been in the service of devaluing our inner yearnings.

Medicine has been part of that murder of the spirit by too readily naming legitimate human drives and needs as sickness. At the beginning of your journey to recovery, you can use these labels to help remove blame and get off your own back so you can seek help and support. Later you will be able to throw away the labels and find your own personalized healing.

Recovery means looking beneath the labels for who we really are. It means being more respectful of our elusive inner selves. But our culture teaches the opposite. For example, I was working on pre-interviews with the producer of a nationally syndicated talk show presenting "Women Who Hate Their Bodies." I'd been appearing on TV for more than a decade and was nauseated at the gradual degeneration of media reporting and the tactics they used to increase their audiences. Although I was somewhat embarrassed to continue appearing,

I was convinced that any way I could carry the message could be worthwhile for someone.

Our conversation got quite heated as the producer shouted that he needed four specific categories of guests: "I need an exercise freak, a vomiter, a plastic-surgery makeover, and a starver. Maybe we could throw in a laxative abuser as well. Main thing is, they have to be average middle America types. Not too serious; no one saying they have a 'disease.' We used that angle last month."

This producer didn't realize that with his categories he was actually bordering on a heady debate I'd seen brewing at professional conferences for two decades. Psychiatrists spent hours debating new diagnostic categories to decide whether patients should be labeled anorexic or bulimic, or given the new label of binge eating disorder (BED). These fine-line demarcations always left me cold. The debate usually centered around consumption or elimination behaviors. "If she vomits only three times a day, we'll still call her anorexic, but if more often, she might qualify as bulimic."

Then there were those endless discussions of what purging meant. Could excessive exercise be purging? Was laxative abuse considered bulimic if done by a fat man? Recent studies had shown that even grotesquely obese women suffer from anorexia for long stretches at a time.

Considering all of these anomalies made categorization virtually impossible. Whose needs did these categories serve? How could medicine explain a three-hundred-pound woman who vomited six times a day?

I found diagnostic discussions not only boring but also a useless attempt to avoid deeper issues about treatment. Not knowing how to help these patients, doctors wasted everyone's time debating labels. They seemed more concerned with accountability and making sure that they understood each other's nomenclature than with actual healing.

You Are an Addict

Although recovery from eating disorders is psychological and emotional, we cannot underestimate the physical component to these illnesses. I have grave concerns about the direction of medical science when its practitioners diagnose these illnesses as purely psychological. This is exactly what was done with alcoholics years ago when they were put into mental hospitals rather than alcoholism treatment centers. Professionals denied that some of the abnormal behavior was *caused by the drinking*. With F-Os, some of the abnormality is *caused by the eating*. After alcoholism treatment units showed patients with successful recoveries, it was found that only 2 percent had a serious psychological illness that required treatment. That was the same proportion as the general population.

Since this book first came out, we've witnessed another very dangerous result of looking only at the psychological aspects of eating disorders. Many Americans are on Prozac and other drugs of that same family. These are known as selective serotonin reuptake inhibitors, or SSRIs. It was as if these drugs received Federal Drug Administration approval and then manufacturers immediately took doctors on junkets and luncheons to teach them about the benefits of prescribing them.

The female population suddenly developed an epidemic of Prozac deficiency. This was coupled with managed-care clerks insisting that medical teams prescribe these drugs. Also, the patient population became educated and learned that the drugs supposedly had an appetite suppressant. What they didn't realize was that the actual claim said that these drugs did not cause as much weight *gain* as other antidepressants. All this new data merged, and countless food-obsessed individuals begged their general practitioners for Prozac. It didn't even need psychiatric monitoring. Years later, I admitted to inpatient units patients who were on

Prozac and still bingeing and vomiting and also gaining weight. The appetite suppressant aspect only worked on anorexics. Bingers ate right through the Prozac.

There was also more difficulty getting off these drugs than medical personnel had predicted. They assured people with addictive personalities that the drugs weren't addictive. They forgot to consider the person involved. You can't just look at the drug without looking at the drug taker. Medical people have contemplated this process since the dawn of modern medicine. Louis Pasteur was father of the germ theory and thus fathered modern medicine. Before his work, we didn't really know that germs cause disease. After Pasteur, we created more antiseptic environments for people to heal, we "pasteurized" our milk, and we promoted scientific approaches to healing while abandoning some other more psychologically and spiritually oriented methods. However, during his lifetime, Dr. Pasteur kept asking, "If germs cause disease, why is it that some people get sick and others don't?" He figured that there must be some reciprocal relationship between the germs and their host organism, that they colluded in creating the sickness. Without going as far as many New Agers today who say we cause our own cancer, Pasteur did keep a careful watch on what kind of host environment might welcome illness. On his deathbed, he declared, "Forget the germ theory. The host is everything."

While we want to avail ourselves of all medical knowledge, in addictions, we have to pay careful attention to our experience as "hosts." Alexander came to my group after he had been on SSRIs for eight years. He reported that he just saw a psychiatrist on the east side of Manhattan who charged him $225 for a half-hour session to tell him he must move to yet another SSRI. The doctor, after outlining all the side effects of each, told him, "You pick one." Alexander brought this to group totally confused and angry.

For much less money, we advised him to consult the doctor about taking him off *all* drugs he was on. He complained fearfully that he didn't want to get worse. He forgot to look at how bad his life was anyway. He was sleeping most days until noon, at risk of losing his sales job, deep in debt, bingeing, having flare-ups of violence, seeing a psychologist and a psychiatrist, attending group, and still depressed most of the time. I suggested that he might want to give *life* a chance. It was hard to tell at this point how much of his life was him and how much was the drugs and all their infinite side effects. I asked him to give it a try as a present to his newborn daughter. He knew the drugs weren't working. It was just hard to face that his life would be up to him.

When you accept that even if sick, you are still in charge of creating and developing your own life, you have a new attitude for the future. Sickness is no excuse. You are still accountable to yourself.

An important aspect in creating your new life is seeking treatment. But remember that treatment for addictive disorders follows a different approach than treatment for psychiatric disorders. If the psychiatric approach would have worked, I surely would not have been a successful 222-pound therapist. I spent much time in intensive insight therapy laboring to find out *why* I ate. I presumed that when I figured out why, I would miraculously stop eating. Unfortunately, therapy helped me deny there was a physical component to my illness. In addition, if I did not stop overeating first, I would not be awake enough to honestly examine why. In other words, food is a drug. In my seminars I give out a stick of chocolate packaged as a Band-Aid. I emphasize that we are dealing with the use of food for medicinal purposes. Excess food dulls the senses and relieves pain. It takes the edge off. It works.

What once solved the problem has now become the

problem. You might have gotten warnings from countless medical professionals holding up your thick, heavy medical record admonishing you for continuing the behavior and asking, "Don't you see what this is doing *to* you?" A fellow sufferer will look at you compassionately and not *ask* but *tell*, "I know what it does *for* you." Therein lies all the difference. We have to admit and face what it does for us. This admission is embarrassing and perhaps disconcerting. It is not glamorous to acknowledge that a piece of chocolate cake has got the better of you. I often wished I were an alcoholic instead of food obsessed. Alcoholics include famous jazz musicians, senators, comic and serious movie stars, even space heroes. Who of note ever admitted to needing to eat, no matter what price, and to having an unnatural, destructive response to a pastry?

More recently, we have seen many celebrities who had food-obsession problems along with other addictions. They include John Belushi, John Candy, Chris Farley, and Jackie Gleason. We know that Mama Cass choked to death on a sandwich, and Totie Fields overate to the point of developing diabetes and having a leg amputated. Some young starlets have recently acknowledged their bouts with anorexia and bulimia. Even established personalities are becoming more visible in the throes of this obsession and are admitting how hard it is. Liz Taylor, Oprah Winfrey, Liza Minnelli, and others have let us watch their struggles.

What Makes You an Addict?

A simple but workable definition of addiction is "When you don't have it, you feel bad; when you have it, you don't feel good." Does this define your relationship with food? Despite the way it seems to smooth out the rough edges, it doesn't help you really soar into your life. You don't wake up joyous and happy to be alive. In fact, in the later stages of addiction, you may wake up slightly hung over from the binge of the night before. You will overeat because you have to, not because you want to. By the time you recognize that this substance has the best of you, you are well into full-blown addiction. Medical science has characterized three distinct aspects of addiction.

1. Initial *high tolerance* for the substance.

    You can put away much larger quantities than others and then experience minimal, if any, discomfort. This is apparent when you find yourself eating everyone out of house and home. You may also find others commenting that some foods are "too rich." You are puzzled by what "rich" means. As they push away these "rich" plates, you finish them up while clearing the table. Your tolerance for the substance is quite different from their tolerance.

2. *Withdrawals* when the substance is removed.

    If you have found yourself sluggish and irritable when trying to diet, you are experiencing light withdrawal symptoms. Some F-Os may experience violent tremors, inappropriate mood swings, crying, shaking, and sometimes even convulsions. Medical science has not adequately monitored these withdrawal symptoms.

    In the early days of alcoholism treatment, sufferers complained of withdrawal symptoms and medical personnel tended to minimize these reports. Even medical personnel don't want to acknowledge the dire consequences when drinking is carried to excess— perhaps because of their own drinking patterns. After all, "everyone likes to have a drink once in a while." However, we are quite willing to acknowledge the monstrous effects of heroin withdrawal. But a little-known fact is that people do die in the throes of alcohol withdrawal but rarely die during heroin withdrawal. Alcohol, like food, bathes every single body cell and, therefore, affects every single organ system. If we've minimized alcohol's addictive qualities because we all want to drink, imagine what kind of minimizing and denial goes on with food.

3. *Cravings* after withdrawal.

Even after you have given up the offending substance, you will still experience psychological cravings long after the physical hunger pangs have ended. These cravings are what take every sufferer back to the offending substance. That is what makes the treatments proposed in this book so necessary. You need help long after you have stopped the bingeing and the obsession. The illness is cunning, baffling, powerful, and patient. It *will* come back. You *will* miss what that old standby did for your feelings. When the feelings become too much to handle, when life intrudes on diet plans, it seems simpler to return to the substance than to change your life. With the plan outlined in this book, you will find a way to diminish the cravings because you are going to change your life.

Upon its first publication, this book was a groundbreaking treatise comparing the alcoholic's relationship with liquor to an overeater's compulsion to binge. After its initial success, this book was and continues to be used in treatment centers teaching the addictions model. Sometimes that use had deleterious effects. Some people have come out of those treatment centers convinced they are addicts and that food is their enemy. I have seen their fear, and I have watched some of them go to extremes. They control their food and become anorexic, sometimes falling off the wagon, only to binge again and regain hundreds of pounds. In my second book, *Fat & Furious*, I went to great pains to refute some of what I'd initially set into motion.

Food is not our enemy. We all have to eat. Food must be handled and thought of cautiously, but it can't be forsworn. Our work is to change the relationship we have with food, our dangerous substance. We just can't use it the same old way. It can't be our Band-Aid for emotional pain. Though alcoholics and drug addicts can give up their substances, we have to make friends with our caged animal, take it out of the cage at least three times a day, walk it, use it moderately, pet it, and then get it back in the cage. In my Divine Dine™ workshops and videos, I teach conscious, mindful eating techniques so that you can make friends with food and take it in spiritually rather than ravenously.

Addicted to What?

If you were raised on a typical American diet, that is, off our supermarket shelves, more than likely you are a "junk food junkie." Your addiction is to simple sugars and refined carbohydrates. You eat quickly assembled, easily digested junk food that provides little nurturance but sets up immediate cravings. The sugar high lasts in the system for about eighteen minutes. Then you plummet into withdrawals. Eating too much of anything will put excess sugar into your system.

Numerous nutrition treatises will explain sugar addiction in greater detail. In recent years, we've seen popular best-selling books such as *The Zone, Sugar Busters!,* and *Protein Power.* Please refer to these sources for more specifics about the addictive nature of your relationship with sugars and an outline of which foods cause the most problems. To keep this treatise relatively simple, I simply suggest that, to decrease your sugar consumption, just avoid cellophane. What do I mean by that? I mean that if you can eat whole foods, which are the most natural, rather than ripping open cellophane bags to munch on something refined, then you will be avoiding most of the hidden sugars that have made America fat.

Since the early 1970s, Dr. Atkins has been leading a diet revolution that expounds the evils of carbohydrates and the values of fats and proteins. That kind of plan doesn't work for those of us who eat compulsively and obsessively. Even if it curbs our unnatural physical relationship with sugars, we still have the psychological obsession to overeat.

Any type of excessively restrictive diet feeds into our obsessional thinking. Many have criticized such diets, telling themselves that they didn't want to feel *deprived*. Well, any time I can't have what I want when I want it, even if *I'm* the one saying I can't have it, I am *deprived*. If I eat less than I want, which is most of the time, I am *deprived*. In a Buddhist sense, we have to lean into that emptiness. The danger in these diets is not the deprivation itself but the continued promotion of obsessive thinking. They all make food important and the individual merely a secondary piece of machinery.

As this second edition went to press, Gary Taubes wrote an article for the *New York Times Magazine* and created a frenzy in the media. He wrote about the national fear of fat and how it has contributed to our epidemic of national obesity. He noted that even though consumption of fast foods took a leap in the 1970s and 1980s, it was not nearly as great as the rise in the number of obese Americans, from 13 percent in the 1960s to 25 percent in the 1990s. His main point was that our national fat-free mentality has created phobic dieting, making us hungrier and heavier. Eating fat-free foods loaded with sugar makes us binge. He reinforced what I'd offered in this book's first publication—that sugar was the addictive and problem substance. It's not the fat; it's the sugar.

For those who fall into the category of being addicted to sugar, here are some telltale symptoms of withdrawal:

fatigue	crying spells
dizziness	poor memory
irritability	mood swings
depression	temper outbursts
fainting spells	blurred vision
insomnia	indigestion
night sweats	asthma
suicidal tendencies	impotence
shaking	headaches

After treating so many food-obsessed individuals for so many decades, I can assure you that the worst withdrawals occur in the fourth through sixth days. If you can let yourself sit and shake and cry and do whatever you have to do, the discomfort will pass. Unfortunately, rarely has anyone addressed how hard withdrawals will be. When you experienced them before, you just self-medicated with more food. If you have trouble accepting this addiction idea, just consider how many times you've given up your diet on Thursdays (the fourth day). You always start on a Monday, and when Thursday's withdrawals start, you decide instead to binge for the weekend and start fresh next week. I know this occurrence so well that I am writing an entire book titled *The Four-Day Diet*.

Though you didn't ask to be an addict, it seems you've ended up here. When I worked with heroin addicts on the streets of New York, their evolution to addiction differed greatly from the gradual and insidious addictions of alcoholics and F-Os. Heroin abusers knew they were injecting an illegal substance, and they knew it was addictive. This is not the case for alcoholics or F-Os who are just trying to socialize and be like everyone else at the party.

Since 1967, I have heard stories from all kinds of persons— street junkies to addicted doctors and nurses—all using quite a few different drugs, and they all knew they were taking an addictive substance. Some were addicted house-wives whose physicians had gotten them into drug use. A few were patients who weren't weaned from painkillers after surgery. But the majority of drug addicts *knew* what they were doing and *chose* to step off the beaten path. Their drug use was not so normalized into daily life that they uncon-sciously strayed down the road of addiction.

If you suffer a food obsession, however, you are unfor-tunately finding yourself addicted without asking for it. You are not superior to other addicts but instead more to be pitied, as you were in essence tricked into a full-fledged self-destructive obsession that started as an innocent search for nurturance.

Some explanation comes from Manuel E. Cheraskin, nutritionist, dentist, and researcher at Louisiana State University. In his book *Psychodietetics,* Dr. Cheraskin told of feeding a group of mice delicious pellets full of nutrients and fiber and low in salt, sugar, and fat. He gave these mice a choice of drinking water or alcohol. They were all repulsed by the alcohol and chose water. Later he separated the mice and kept half of the group on mouse pellets while the other half were fed junk foods from Cheetos and Fritos to salami and chocolate cake. The second group of mice, those fed the junk food, chose alcohol instead of water. These junk food mice were experiencing withdrawals from the sugars. Alcohol soothed their raw edges. (Alcohol is sugar in liquid form.) The mice, like humans, needed soothing when com-ing off junk foods. Are we feeding our children to be future alcoholics as well as obese?

William Dufty pondered these questions in *Sugar Blues,* where he makes a case for sugar addiction. American con-sumption of sugar has grown to 158 pounds per person per year. Hidden sugar is found in nearly every packaged prod-uct on the grocer's shelf, even salt. Baby food is loaded with sugar too—not for the baby, but because the baby's feeder prefers the taste. Long before the poor baby can decide, it is addicted and withdrawing. Even cigarette tobacco is laced with sugar in the curing process. It is interesting to note how many people who give up smoking cigarettes turn to eating sugar compulsively. Alcoholics crave sugar when giving up booze. Without making a personality change, we may all simply transfer addictions and stay in the cycle.

To make matters worse, diet-food manufacturers have learned how to capitalize on our food obsessions and sugar addiction. Do you use large amounts of Equal to sweeten your food and drinks? Next time, read the label. You will find a warning to diabetics not to use it without a doctor's consent. Then look at the first two ingredients: dextrose and maltodextrin, both forms of sugar. When I confronted representatives from NutraSweet about this, I was told that the amounts are negligible, even though they are the first two ingredients, meaning they are most prevalent. Then they assured me that a person would have to use large quantities before having any negative effects. Who do they think uses Equal? People who eat and drink moderately? Finally, after my continual complaints, they admitted that the malto-dextrin is used to provide bulk to the powdered Equal so it won't blow away when poured. I asked why they don't use sawdust as some cereal companies do. The truth is, sugar is cheaper than sawdust.

As a crazed dieter, have you learned that fat has twice as many calories as sugar, so you should seek out fat-free foods? If you look at the ingredient labels of fat-free products, you will find that sugar is high on the list. You have to get taste from something. They've traded fat for sugar, and though it has fewer calories, it sends those of us who get withdrawals from excess sugar out for another box of cookies or another vat of salad dressing. There is always a trade-off between sugar and fat to make the product taste good. If it has no fat, it usually has more sugar. If it is labeled sugar free, it probably has more fat. There is truly no free lunch. You might initially lose weight by cutting down on fat, but you will suffer and eventually binge on more sugar.

Says Who?

Are you aggravated? I don't blame you. After all, who wants to think of him- or herself as an addict? You want to believe you have control of this situation. You have bought all those magazines with easy diets inside, and you know you can take care of the problem yourself. "I can handle this whenever I want to" is the woeful refrain of every addict. "I just don't want to yet." When you sit down honestly and alone with this book, you must ultimately acknowledge what you have always known to be true. It does have the best of you, maybe not forever, but at least for today. When you finally face this truth, there's no going back. We don't know exactly when a cucumber soaked in brine becomes a pickle. We just know that once pickled, it can never be a cucumber again. Who wants to face how obsessed they really are? I saw myself clearly one day when I realized I had two shoeboxes full of recipes I'd clipped from magazines, knowing I would try them one day. I was hoarding these brown crumpled harbingers of future comfort as tightly as a baby holds a favorite stuffed toy.

While you may exhibit similar addictive symptoms, the idea of sugar as an addiction remains quite controversial. Physicians who read this book will probably write angry letters about the use of an addictive model for a simple food we all "need." I once gave a presentation to a group of prominent doctors. Among them was a man who angrily denounced what I was saying. He claimed the sugar addiction idea is a fallacy. "There is no scientific evidence to prove what you are purporting here!" he shouted. "I have been an endocrinologist for many years and have found no scientific evidence to corroborate these ideas." I offer you the same answer I offered him. Even though this idea may not yet be proved, it helps people by removing the blame from themselves and gets them out of a punitive, self-loathing cycle. They can then see themselves as sick people seeking a cure rather than morally bankrupt transgressors wanting pity. The addictive model takes morality out of food obsessions. Maybe medical science hasn't yet caught up with what you already know about your eating behavior. You know it's an addiction. Your recovery should be similar to what works for other addicts.

But I'm Anorexic and Don't Eat at All

Even if your refusal of food keeps you suffering, the addiction model still applies. As an anorexic, you are addicted to the high, clean, superhuman feeling you have when you don't eat. There is a physical high that comes from not eating. Hindu mystics have encouraged fasting for centuries as a way to seek enlightenment, spiritual fulfillment, and light-headed ecstasy. You may crave that clean feeling and feel sluggish, repulsive withdrawals when you try to eat.

Early in 1983, the *New England Journal of Medicine* published a highly controversial study that compared feelings and lifestyles of anorexic teenage girls and forty-year-old male runners. The study revealed some startling similarities between the two groups. They both felt exhilarated by the feeling of pushing their bodies past the normal limits of human endurance. Runners call this "hitting the wall." Anorexics often delight in testing their endurance the same way. They serve elaborate meals to others and eat nothing themselves. They experience the same type of high. In addition, many anorexics have a drugged look; they stare blankly as if not involved in what is going on around them. Runners report the same "alone" trancelike state when they exhaust themselves. Their "runner's high" is just as addicting as the anorexic's starvation.

Gimme Fuzzies

In the early 1970s, doctors began studying a mechanism within the nervous system that produces a morphinelike effect, helping to alleviate pain and subdue trauma and shock. These morphinelike substances are called endorphins, and they are secreted to soothe pain, take the edge off, and promote general well-being. Some research indicates that overeaters and alcoholics produce fewer of these endorphins than normal people. Medical science is also researching evidence that some people's metabolism breaks down sugar differently than others. Sugar works to soothe the savage beast. Since you produce fewer endorphins, you often feel on a raw edge. Eating sugar increases endorphin production, so when you eat, the rawness vanishes.

Some of the justification for prescribing so much Prozac was that the Prozac aided serotonin uptake, which produced the endorphin-like effect, and thus helped the brain to soothe itself. These drugs have been so randomly and irresponsibly overprescribed that the *individuals* taking them are largely forgotten. Because they don't eliminate excess sugar before taking the drugs, they still haven't had a chance to find out what they could accomplish on their own without medication.

Some people have availed themselves of other non-chemical, self-soothing techniques. Some of us have learned how to eat mindfully and live consciously and thus soothe ourselves. If you are not aware of getting this sedation effect from sugar, you may not need this book. You might have some sugar and then take it or leave it. You may already soothe yourself with endorphins you produce naturally.

If anorexic, you get the same kind of soothing from the "high" of not eating. That exuberant feeling comes from the endurance high of pushing yourself beyond your limits, much like the "runner's high" mentioned earlier. These sedating feelings are hard to give up. But don't despair, there is an alternative method to increase endorphin production, and it doesn't involve bingeing or deprivation. It involves hugging. That's right, hugging. When you turn to a fellow human being and you put your arms around one another, endorphins start flowing and the raw edges are removed by the warmth of a loving friend.

Just look to the animal kingdom to confirm this theory. Animals in nature huddle and cuddle whenever they want to. Similarly, your dog is no dummy when he jumps up for a rub on the chest or pat on the head. He's getting his endorphins up and keeping himself mellow. There aren't any obesity treatment programs for animals. These animals get their hugs and don't need to binge. The only overweight animals are those force-fed by humans or domestic pets of people who, fat themselves, overfeed to show love.

The effectiveness of this theory is also evident in other cultures. The Chinese are high on hugs and low on obesity. In China, mothers carry babies on their backs or slung at their sides for many years. The baby is rarely far from the warmth of the mother's body and, when hungry, is brought immediately to the breast. They also deal with discipline differently than in the United States. Babies are not disciplined until age five, when they are considered at the age of reason and thus able to distinguish right from wrong. Despite a few exceptions (those who gain weight to show wealth), the Chinese do not have obesity problems. To give up food, you need to take in love. If you find this idea embarrassing, do it for health reasons. Hug medicinally. You have to get hugs to keep from eating. It's all part of your recovery.

Hugs are not always physical. I am personally not a hugger type. Sometimes it feels like being hugged when I have an honest and touching conversation with a friend or a powerful session with a therapy client. Sometimes being alone and serene with nature feels like a hug. Sometimes letting yourself be quiet while listening to others at a party can feel like a hug. It is a feeling of connection and intimacy that is achieved without food. As you spend less time obsessing about food, you will develop more abilities to let yourself be vulnerable and let the world come at you. Being hugged is a metaphor for letting yourself receive and for being vulnerable and penetrable.

"Will Power" Died of Obesity

Other people who don't suffer as you do will sometimes try to tell you it's all in your mind. This is a variation on the "use a little willpower" approach. But it's more than a matter of simple willpower.

You experience *cravings*. You continue to have cravings even after you're "off the sauce." Those people who encourage you just to try a little of this or that have no idea what a setup that can be for you. Your addiction has to do with your attitude when you take in food—your relationship with food. A normal person seeks food to alleviate hunger or provide sustenance. He or she does not worry about being "bad." Guilt is the most predominant detrimental attitude toward eating suffered by the obese as well as the anorexic. When eating is accompanied by guilt, you're in trouble. Normal people don't eat with guilt. If they are going to be guilty, they simply refrain. F-Os project the guilt, wallow in it, beat themselves for it, and then eat anyway.

When someone decides that they definitely do want to eat compulsively and perhaps ravenously and want to eat things that aren't on their usual and customary food plan, I encourage them to eat it with relish and savor and enjoy it. Then, when they return to a more disciplined plan, I ask them to smack their hands as if to say "that's done" and to immediately get on with things with no guilt or remorse. Wallowing in guilt is actually counterproductive and a form of further indulgence. Go for it and then finish with it. If you eat, then *eat,* and when done, be *done.* I attribute no greater asset to my long-term recovery than the ability to get back on the horse and ride it in the direction it's going.

We need to take the guilt out of our eating. In my Divine Dine™ seminars, I encourage participants to savor and suck and enjoy their food. I know that if eaten well, a little dab'll do ya. Similar ideas are encouraged by William Clower in his book entitled *The Fat Fallacy,* where he notes that French people savor high-calorie, fatty, but tasty food in small quantities and have a low incidence of food obsession.

When the American Medical Association initially declared alcoholism a disease, a key factor in diagnosing the illness was "a person who has *tried* to quit." If the person has tried to stop the behavior and still kept it up, it was an indication that he or she is addicted. You see, normal people don't *try* to quit. If they see a problem with certain behavior, they just stop it. If they don't see a problem, they feel no need to even think about quitting. An addict *tries* to quit. Over and over and over again, he or she tries to control an obsessive relationship with food and, despite brief periods of control, returns to obsessive eating. Our natural state is bingeing.

You've tried to quit and couldn't. You judged yourself harshly instead of accepting that you suffer from an illness and can't help it. More than likely, you eat compulsively with an inordinate amount of both guilt and despair. It's all in the attitude.

Let's look at attitude as it relates to alcoholism and see whether you can draw any parallels to your own addiction. When drinking is done with guilt, the incidence of alcoholism is much greater. This is clear in Mormon and Muslim populations. Both groups look upon drinking alcohol as sinful. When persons from either of these groups drink even a slight amount of alcohol, guilt and remorse immediately set in.

They often drink to cover the guilt, and they end up drunk nearly every time. I find clients from both of these groups the hardest to treat. They find great difficulty in moving from the sin to the sickness model.

To recover, you must accept that you are ill. When you stop giving food the power to make you feel "good" or "bad," you will stop turning to willpower and ask instead for help from other people.

Your Illness Is a Disease

You have a "disease" when you are not "at ease." Something is wrong. Alcoholism is a disease and so is disordered eating. When we think of disease, we look at a *physical addiction* coupled with a *psychological obsession.*

Nearly all your efforts at controlling the disease have centered around physical approaches, not on the addictive quality of eating behaviors. Some people have even had half their intestines cut out to gain control of the eating. A few surgeons have then referred these patients to me to teach them mindful eating techniques. The surgeries are a useful tool to force them to practice the techniques I teach. But even after drastic surgeries, many regained lost weight.

Without treatment of the psychological aspects, a person will not change. You must acknowledge the physical aspects but also look at the psychological obsession. You can't minimize either part of the disease. Now, let's take a look at the gradual and insidious progression of the psychological aspects of this obsession.

Eat to Celebrate and Eat to Mourn

As a full-fledged F-O, you eat in any heightened awareness state. You eat to level out emotions, good or bad. You eat to achieve numbness. You eat when your team wins, and you eat when it loses. It is pointless to ponder the reasons for eating. Such investigations may prove interesting to you after you have stopped the eating, but for now, they accomplish little. As long as eating sedates you and soothes the rough edges, you won't really uncover true and clear information to help you. Therapy for someone who is still eating compulsively is like counseling someone who is drunk.

Insight does not change eating behavior. Changing eating behavior, however, can change insight. Or, simply said, you can't think your way into right action, but you can act your way into right thinking. You have probably taken a long time flowing into your food obsessions. You got this far, slowly and insidiously, over a long period of time. It is practically impossible to be aware of this gradual progression while you are in it.

Early Stages

If you were born to two fat parents, you have an 80 percent chance of being fat yourself. If born to two alcoholic parents, you are 50 percent likely to be alcoholic. As evidenced by the statistics, both illnesses, alcoholism and food obsession, are largely genetically predetermined. That doesn't mean you are doomed. It just means it is going to be a difficult and lifelong journey. That has been true for me and will probably be true for you as well. You have a genetic tendency to accumulate more fat cells. From the starting gate, you already have a few strikes against you.

Now, do you think fat parents taught you to eat normally? Most likely not. You were trained early to overeat. You learned that what others might call humongous portions, your family saw as meager. You developed an overeating style. Both heredity and environment played a part in determining your future as a food obsessive. Most important, however, was your training to use food to relieve stress. In a stressful environment, you were programmed to take that rough edge off through the use of a simple, time-honored, immediate ritual—putting something in your mouth. You didn't know any other way to reduce stress. You didn't consider that changing your life could help reduce stress. Food was immediate and easy. You developed a style of expecting immediate relief or immediate gratification. You did not practice deferring gratification. ("I want what I want when I want it.") You learned this attitude long before the "age of reason," and it will be hard to give up even after the "dawn of insight."

Because you didn't practice deferring, you now have a very low tolerance for stress. You don't know how to weather it; you only know how to smother it. So, as you grow and your life becomes even more complicated, you have more stresses and more need for food. The needs increase outside your awareness.

Obsessional Stage

Because you have fashioned a lifestyle with food abuse at its base, you feel the need to carefully guard both your supplies and your consumption. You may start to feel a creeping sense of embarrassment about the amounts you eat and how you "shovel" them in, so you may start to take more meals and snacks alone. Sometimes this means stolen moments away from a crowd, when you have to gulp your food quickly so no one will find out. Thus, you develop a pattern of eating even when you don't feel like it. You eat out of fear—the fear that you may end up hungry. You don't want to be out socially and appear hungry. You don't want people to think you overeat. So, to forestall any problem, you eat at home to "get a buzz on" before the party to help you endure the difficulty of making small talk. You don't enjoy or savor your eating, but instead eat just in case. You become preoccupied with food and shopping and ensuring that you will get enough. By this time, however, enough is never enough.

Secret Life

You know you are out of control. Brief moments of clarity arise, but you quickly eat to avoid them. Food makes you feel better and takes away the guilt momentarily. Guilty about your eating behavior, you eat to make that feeling go away. You develop a denial system to convince yourself that it's not that bad. Your eating becomes a secret, not only to others, but also to yourself. You eat while shopping or standing over a sink. You deny all weight gains. You see no relationship between the food in your mouth and the fat on your body. At the time you are eating, you completely block out the possibility of consequences. You have been learning how to fast and then binge, so in the moment of eating, you tell yourself, *It doesn't count. I'll fast tomorrow.* This develops the catch-up-ball phenomenon. Binge today, fast tomorrow. The pendulum swings from excess and numbness to guilt and swearing off. Eventually you learn how to turn off even this denial mechanism. You resent thin or normal people and avoid discussions of food or dieting. *If I ignore it,* you hope, *it will go away.*

Full-Fledged Compulsion

Instead of going away, your compulsion gets worse. You continue eating until nauseated, even though food no longer works. You feel unable to cope emotionally, and to complicate things, you start having physical withdrawals periodically as you make futile attempts at testing your willpower. Even though food does not work, you have no other tools for coping, so you keep on the same merry-go-round, returning to food again and again. Sometimes you even experience periods of memory loss as you become excessively preoccupied with food and weight. Nothing else matters. *When I get thin, it will all matter again,* you think. With no memory, you can conveniently forget the quantities you are eating. When moments of clarity do arise, you resort to elaborate alibis and justifications for your eating. Since you can't truly believe you are out of control, you project reasons for this weird behavior on outside persons and situations. It is hard to believe that your best friend, food, has turned on you. Despite what you eat, you still feel moody, depressed, and grouchy. *It must be them,* you think. *Who wouldn't eat with a life like mine? My stressful job* (or boss or wife or kids or friends or parents or siblings) *forces me to binge.*

Getting Ready

At some point, the alibi system will break down, and you become ready to change your life and give up the obsession. Dishonesty about your food intake has spread to dishonesty in your whole life. You deny that this is your life. Instead, you see life as a dress rehearsal. You tell yourself, *Life will begin when I get thin.* You lose self-esteem by continually breaking promises to yourself. You begin grandiose, perfectionistic behavior as a cover-up. You may resort to a PIP (Privileged Invalid Position) complaining that you can't help it. As badly as you feel, you keep drawing attention to yourself. Your entire identity revolves around being a person with a weight problem. You are trying to get out of the problem but don't know how. You return yet again to food. However, what used to solve problems now becomes a problem in itself. With any luck, you come to see that you have to stop the yo-yo cycle with food. Only then can you see what your life is really about. You can only be ready when you are ready. At this ready stage you are not only fed up with food and its effects, but you are *sick and tired of being sick and tired.*

In the next chapter, we'll watch how your loved ones have traveled a similar progression.

---■---

Progression toward Psychological Obsession

Use the following checklist to note some of your own demarcations on the path to psychological obsession.

Warning Signals

- ☐ Have a hereditary propensity for overeating
- ☐ Have a low tolerance for negative feelings (anger, sadness, fear, etc.)
- ☐ Have a high stress level, that is, are easily stressed out
- ☐ Resent thin or normal people and often compete with them

Abuse

- ☐ Use food to escape worries
- ☐ Use food to hide from other issues (sexual, employment, etc.)
- ☐ Spend too much time thinking about food (shopping, cooking, dining out)
- ☐ Avoid discussions about food and weight
- ☐ Constantly discuss food and weight
- ☐ Diet constantly (fasting, bingeing)
- ☐ Secretly eat while shopping or driving
- ☐ Anticipate shortages and overeat to avoid "hunger"
- ☐ Feel compelled to eat again and again within short periods of time
- ☐ Feel compelled to eat soon after a meal
- ☐ Keep eating after physical fullness

Addiction

- ☐ Eat to the point of bloating or nausea
- ☐ Eat to relieve negative feelings (guilt, shame, remorse)
- ☐ Deny weight gain, seeing no relationship between food eaten and weight gained
- ☐ Deny physical complications caused by eating (back, knee, and skin problems, headaches, etc.)

- ☐ Deny powerlessness by making promises to limit or control eating and then breaking them
- ☐ Have periods of memory loss (blackouts) or go into a trancelike state while eating
- ☐ Don't know what normal-sized portions are
- ☐ Feel trapped (food is salvation as well as destruction)
- ☐ Make desperate attempts to control eating and weight through fad diets, pills, excessive exercising, etc.
- ☐ Frequently feel shame, guilt, or remorse after diet failures and eat for relief
- ☐ Lie about eating or other behaviors; steal food or money
- ☐ Feel scared or different, that is, alienated from other people
- ☐ Find your eating interferes with normal activities or relationships (job, family, community)
- ☐ Feel hopeless, anxious, depressed, or suicidal

CHAPTER 3

———————■———————

Who's the C-P?

As a family therapist, I feel it verges on malpractice to treat only one part of a family system without at least warning the others involved about the possible effects on them. If you have been watching someone commit slow suicide, you have been affected. You are also affected when this person turns around, stops being self-destructive, and starts taking personal responsibility—and when he or she sets limits on bad behaviors from others, thus demanding better treatment for him- or herself.

The analogy to slow suicide can also apply to the loved one who stands by and watches. In fact, in my thirty years as a therapist, I have had only one client ever commit suicide. He was not a drug addict, an alcoholic, or a food obsessive. He was the husband of an alcoholic, and he shot himself after his wife got sober. When she was drunk, he ministered to all her needs as she sat in front of the TV. He spent a lot of energy joking and trying to cheer her up. None of what he tried worked. Finally, when she went through our hospital treatment and got sober, she went with other women to AA, returning to tell jokes she'd heard from a speaker at the meeting. She started becoming cheerful in her own right. Her husband was jealous, displaced, and depressed. He was addicted to her addiction. He was a confluent personality, finding his worth in ministering to others. When no longer needed, he perished.

The confluent personality (C-P) is someone whose life is intertwined with an addictive or self-loathing person. The dictionary definition of confluence is "a flowing together of two or more streams." A further exposition talks about merging and running together and the making of one out of two. But if carried to an extreme, it is noted in the definition that this merging can become something negative, such as a mass of sores or a rash. What may initially be a positive adaptive trait can fester into an illness. With food obsessions, confluent persons have personal missions to blend with and cure the food abuse. They forget their own lives to help another.

In the first edition of this book, I used the term "codependent" instead of C-P but changed it here. The term "codependent" has become so misused and generic that people use it to describe any helpful behavior. (For excellent explanations of the term "codependent," consult Melody Beattie's *Codependent No More,* in which she quotes much from the earlier edition of this book.)

I wish to stress that the C-P suffers too, sometimes even more than the food obsessed. In my earliest units we had multiple family groups where the C-Ps had their own counselor and own chance at rehabilitation. As of late, C-Ps have been virtually ignored in many treatment circles.

Although food obsessions and dieting crazes get a lot of focus in the media, in medical practice we've taken large strides backward in terms of helping families quell the rising tide of obesity. The obsessions continue to be minimized and ridiculed, and help for families is virtually nonexistent. Most insurance companies will not authorize payment for family therapy. It usually requires creative record keeping for claims to get paid. Even the self-help group O-Anon, which was created to help family members of F-Os, is now defunct due to lack of interest. All that remains for families are private consultations with therapists like me or the short, weeklong treatments offered at some treatment centers. And at these facilities, families are brought in primarily to learn how to support the F-O. Their own pain and suffering is rarely addressed.

This ignoring of treatment for C-Ps is not new. In the early 1960s, when alcoholism treatment programs were beginning to take form, no one paid attention to family members. It was assumed that these people had no specific needs of their own. We just wanted them to get out of the alcoholic's way. We also assumed they would be ecstatic when their alcoholic stopped drinking. We found instead that when a spouse's drinking stopped, depression sometimes emerged in the partner. Some family members actually worked to sabotage the alcoholic's treatment. Many formerly helpful spouses sought divorce. They had stayed during all the bad times, but when change came, they had to leave. Most couples broke up in recovery. Often spouses left to marry another alcoholic.

I once treated a woman who had married seven alcoholics—one of them twice. She adamantly swore off getting involved with another alcoholic with each divorce. But without examining her own needs and wants as a confluent personality, she was doomed to repeat her endless cycle.

An addict who is in recovery from food obsessions presents difficulty and necessary change for the C-P. As a family member, you may have picked up this book thinking it will help you help them. It's always so much easier to focus on the other person. To really get practice, I became a therapist. But the plan here is not to teach you how to help them but, instead, how to help yourself. You might have assumed we'd discuss how to food-proof your kitchen or give you helpful hints for cajoling your loved one to stop being self-destructive. That's not what you need. Instead, this is a chance for you to learn what your own needs are in the situation and to safely step out of the way. In this book, the C-P will find help to survive recovery.

We're all C-Ps. . . . That's right. We are all people whose lives have been affected by someone else's food obsession. Being overweight extends to such a large segment of the American population that we are all affected as a society. We have jumped to a 27 percent obesity rate with 30 percent of grade school children clearly obese. We care. We want to help. After all, we will be paying health care bills later. And, most important, we feel frustrated by not knowing what to do. Each individual has to evaluate clearly what *is* and *is not* his or her job. To get a better understanding of how to act, let's first look at how a confluent personality intertwines with a food obsessive.

Confluence

A confluent personality type refers to people who have no sense of their own ego boundaries. In other words, it is hard for them to know where they stop and another person begins. They have no boundaries. Clinically this is referred to as enmeshment. Everyone seems to ebb and flow into each other: When you have a splinter, my finger hurts. You have a stomachache, so I'll take the antacid.

The quality of being perceptive and aware of the other person, the ability to walk in another's shoes, can be an asset called empathy. When anyone in a family system has genuine empathy with a detached caring, everyone in the system benefits. Empathy makes for many terrific actors and actresses, nurses, doctors, and psychologists. Empathy also helps in dangerous situations because you can deftly sense what is going on in the other person and thus develop a healthy, cautious attitude.

In families, however, empathy can go to an extreme.

When based on fear, empathy becomes confluence, which leads into a tangled web where you lose your own identity in the service of others. In addictive families, members become so enmeshed in each other's needs and identities that it takes extensive work to get untangled. In the mother-daughter individuation struggles that I illustrated in *Fat & Furious,* daughters develop whole identities based on their moms' pain and anger.

However, it is important that each family member learn how to speak for him- or herself and develop separateness. You may think you know what your loved one is thinking long before he or she says it. Often you may be right, but assuming you've got this person figured out is actually disrespectful. You rob him or her of the chance to feel like an exciting, evolving person. You also rob yourself of the chance to be surprised and learn something new about your relationship.

It is safe to say that C-Ps are addicted to another's addiction. They consider curing this person to be their mission in life. They become obsessed with solving their loved ones' problems. Whether their loved one is fat or emaciated, they take on the role of food monitor and diet prescriber. On the one hand, they relish the idea of discussing someone else's problems, but on the other hand, they have great difficulty talking about their own lives. They can talk endlessly about the diets they've put their loved ones on. They can often recite weight fluctuations and actual poundage and which year. They know each new diet and gym membership, often having financed it all. They feel full ownership of this other person and have no sense of how violating it is to talk about this loved person as an object. They continue this discussion to avoid talking about themselves. They can recount very little else about themselves independent of the food obsession.

If you are reading this book because of your emotional involvement with someone who is suffering from a food obsession, more than likely, you're also hurting. You are strongly invested in helping this person. You may even be more involved and interested in that person's life than he or she seems to be. You are the one providing the energy and impetus to the relationship while this person is out to lunch. This chapter is for you.

While many C-Ps are not food obsessed themselves, some fat people develop their own confluence, to keep others around who are even fatter so they can worry about these other people instead of themselves. It could even become a "mutual suicide pact," for example, between an alcoholic and an overeater: "I won't say anything about your drinking if you won't say anything about my eating."

A confluent's involvement in the food problem can extend beyond caring to a dogged insistence on being able to solve the problem. This can be seen with mothers of anorexic girls. The anorexic daughters pick up on their moms' intense need to fix them and learn to control their mothers by alternately demanding and rejecting help. The mother starts to suffer as much or more than the daughter. This is especially true in anorexia, where we see fearful and distraught parents whose daughters shrug and sneer, "No problem." It is important to know, however, that real compassion comes in helping others solve a problem, not feeling it more than they do.

To help better assess your situation, look at the following attitudes, which are signs of impending confluence:

"I feel safest when I am giving."

"I know more clearly what you want than what I want."

"I only feel good about myself when I have your approval."

"I am very concerned with how you look because you are a reflection of me."

"When you are hurting, I often feel it more deeply than you do."

"If you have a bad day, I react."

"If you have problems, I feel I must come up with a solution for you."

"I need to be needed."

"I don't develop many of my own interests but respond to yours."

"Before speaking, I carefully gauge what effect and reaction I want to achieve from you."

"If someone is angry with me, I find that intolerable."

"I diminish my social circle to get overly involved in you."

"I focus on your problems a lot so I won't have to face any of my own."

"I am critical and judgmental, then I feel guilty."

"I think I can convince you to like yourself."

C-Ps need help as much as the food obsessed. They need help to take care of themselves without guilt or excessive feelings of responsibility. Whenever I am scheduled to lecture on the family aspect of overeating, most participants expect three fairly standard discussions. They think I want to talk about

1. the genetic aspects of obesity
2. how families need to adjust to new food plans
3. how family members can best help their loved ones maintain their commitments

I address none of these topics. For help maintaining commitments, I recommend professional nutritionists or others similarly afflicted, like people in Overeaters Anonymous. As to the food plan, that's not the family's business. Regarding genetics, at this point, it doesn't make much difference how we got here. We all need help getting out. The discussion must instead center on C-Ps getting help in order to detach with love.

------■------

Are You a Confluent Personality?

Use this questionnaire to evaluate the extent of your involvement.

	YES	NO
Do you force diets?	☐	☐
Do you threaten to leave because of weight?	☐	☐
Do you check on the diet?	☐	☐
Do you make promises based on pounds lost or gained?	☐	☐
Do you hide food from an overeater?	☐	☐
Do you worry incessantly about an undereater?	☐	☐
Have you "walked on eggshells" so as not to upset the over- or undereater?	☐	☐
Do you throw food away so the overeater won't find it?	☐	☐
Have you excused the erratic, sometimes violent mood swings resulting from sugar binges?	☐	☐
Do you change social activities so the overeater won't be tempted?	☐	☐
Do you manipulate budgets to control spending on food and clothing?	☐	☐
Do you purchase and promote eating the "right" foods?	☐	☐
Do you promote gyms, health spas, and miracle cures?	☐	☐
Do you break into emotional tirades when you catch the overeater bingeing?	☐	☐

	YES	NO
Are you constantly disappointed when you see relapse?	☐	☐
Are you embarrassed by an over- or undereater's appearance?	☐	☐
Do you console the over- or undereater when he or she is embarrassed?	☐	☐
Do you set up tests of willpower to tease the over- or undereater?	☐	☐
Have you lowered your expectations of what you might like?	☐	☐
Does your weight fluctuate with your loved one's (for example, yours up when his is down)?	☐	☐
Have you stopped attending to your own grooming?	☐	☐
Do you have many aches and pains and a preoccupation with health?	☐	☐
Are you drinking heavily or using sleeping pills or tranquilizers?	☐	☐
Do you bribe with food?	☐	☐
Do you talk about the eater's body to him or her or to others?	☐	☐
Do you feel life will be perfect if your loved one shapes up?	☐	☐
Are you grateful you aren't "that bad"?	☐	☐
Do you feel the eating disorder gives you license to run away?	☐	☐
Do you feel the eating disorder gives you an excuse to stay?	☐	☐
Do you leave "helpful" literature around the house for your loved one to find?	☐	☐
Do you read diet books even though you have no weight problem?	☐	☐
Do you think you have the perfect home, except for the F-O?	☐	☐
Have you spent much time in your own therapy talking about the F-O?	☐	☐

If you found the foregoing questions descriptive of your relationship, read on. This book will show you the benefits to be gained by emotionally detaching yourself from your loved ones' problems. You will find a way to keep loving your partners, your children, or whomever you are enmeshed with without having to like their behavior around food. You will learn a way of being more interested but less involved. The keystone is in letting this become more their problem and less yours. As long as you worry about their food behavior, they don't have to. The best way to help is to detach.

Enabling Punishers

Confluent types travel quickly between two extremes—enabling and punishing. One minute you might be overly protective, helpful, and conciliatory and the next minute raging and criticizing and threatening abandonment. You try hard to be helpful because you want to "make a difference," "have an effect," "be worthwhile." When all efforts fail, you become punitive and enraged and demand immediate perfection. All your efforts at helping are a way to prove you are "okay," "a nice person." If the F-O stays sick, you take this personally. You feel that makes you "not nice."

As attempts at controlling the eating continue to fail, you become disappointed and angry at the overeater's broken promises. You alternate between understanding the problem and quietly fuming with rage. You feel like they're doing it *to* you. The truth is they are just doing it—and mostly to themselves, not you. You become a nagger and scolder, obsessed with watching another eat. You make comments about weight and diet to family and friends. This may be your way of excusing the eating and also showing you are actively working to do something about it. In truth, *it's not your job.*

In such relationships, difficulties develop when messages are unclear. Trying to present a helpful, "enabling" image, you may actually be enraged. Smiling icily through clenched teeth, you seethe, "You really don't want to eat that, do you, dear?" Later, you get fed up with enabling and decide to crack down. You declare, "I'm sick and tired of putting up with paying your bills and watching you kill yourself. If this doesn't stop, I'm through!" Despite the speech, the check is written yet another time and threats to leave are idle. So no one believes what anyone else says, and the cycle continues.

Monitors

Steve had spent years trying to help his wife, Melinda, with her problem. They had an agreement that he would monitor her weight. Each morning, Steve stood over Melinda as she weighed in on the bathroom scale. He carried a chart attached to a clipboard and diligently recorded each reading. Melinda gained thirty pounds during the first month of this plan. Steve's involvement promoted guilt and fear in Melinda. She coped with her rising anxiety by eating "at him."

Their case is not uncommon. Husbands often try to help with their wives' weight problems. They are actually the least likely person to be helpful; they are too personally involved and too invested in success. There is also often an unconscious fear about success that can work to sabotage their efforts.

In 1979 researchers at the University of Pennsylvania began to examine some of the investments husbands had in their wives' weight problems. While the wives were enrolled in the university's weight control program, husbands were surveyed to determine their attitudes about the project. They were asked the following questions, with interesting results:

1. Do you want to see your wife lose weight?

Yes	50
No	3
Don't Care	2

73

2. Are you willing to assist your wife in losing weight?

Yes 27

No 17

No Answer 11

3. Is your wife heavier now than when you were married?

Yes 41

No 8

Same 6

Notice how the numbers change in the first two questions. Nearly all the husbands wanted to see their wives lose weight, but when asked to offer help, their interest faltered. The answers to the fourth question are especially significant.

4. In your own words, what changes would weight reduction by your wife mean to you?

Loss of eating as a shared activity 29

Loss of a bargaining position in arguments 27

Loss of wife in *divorce* 21

Worry about *infidelity* 17

Notice how loss and fear permeate the responses. In their own words, these men were worried that they would (1) lose a binge buddy; (2) lose the advantage of saying, "You fat slob, what do you know?" In addition, they didn't anticipate the joy of having an attractive spouse but instead feared that their wives' heightened self-image might destroy the relationship. She might have new options: divorce and infidelity. These men anticipated fear of loss more than joy of success.

As a spouse, you are not the right helper to enlist in the weight-loss game. Despite your best intentions, there may be too much at stake. At the end of Woody Allen's film *Annie Hall,* one man tells another about his weird brother who thinks he's a chicken.

The second man asks, "Why don't you take him for treatment?"

The first man answers matter-of-factly, "We need the eggs."

Don't fall into this same needy trap. Your wife might try to enlist you as helper, but I strongly suggest you decline. Wives who want to eat will set you up as their punitive parent and then beg you to twist their arms to make them give up their food plan "just this once." For you it's a no-win situation. Despite my warnings, countless women try to use their husbands as food monitors. It's always a setup to eat. It also helps you believe you can keep it in the family, and it again denies the seriousness of the problem and the extent to which the C-P has his or her own suffering that needs attention.

Some studies even show that husbands exert a negative rather than positive influence on the wife's project. Couples enrolled in weight-loss programs were observed through video- and audiotapes to determine their behavior patterns around food. Even though wives were trying to take their attention off food, husbands constantly brought up food-related topics. They asked their wives seemingly insignificant questions about dinners and menus for no apparent reason. While eating together, the husbands were the ones most likely to keep offering extra helpings to their spouses. It was almost as if they were working very hard to show how truly lenient and disinterested they were. However, when wives did give in to eating, husbands were quick to blame and ridicule their wives' behavior. They rarely praised abstinent eating behaviors but were quick to point out any slips in the food program.

To sum up, C-Ps want to see weight loss and success as long as they can control it. If they have involvement and can take credit, they will help, but if it is done by and for F-Os themselves, spouses may sabotage. This point will be important to remember throughout this book as sometimes family members feel they have more to lose than to gain and thus will try to pull an F-O away from recovery programs. Often family members get angry at me, the therapist, declaring, "How come she listens to you and she won't listen to me when I say the same thing?"

Remember the displaced husband whose wife laughed at the AA speaker's jokes and not at his? You are bound to feel displaced. To be helpful, a spouse can develop a style of interested disinterest. You must show care and support but clearly give the message that what the F-Os do, they are doing for themselves only. Keep your eyes on your own plate. More succinctly, mind your own business.

Viva la Company

Employers may also become the well-meaning monitors, using established poundage standards to control eating. Such techniques have never worked as a long-range solution. I treated hundreds of flight attendants from major airlines who endured weight checks for continued employment. The airlines were unrealistic, demanding that a forty-year-old flight attendant have the same weight as when she hired into the company at age twenty-two. (One major airline reneged a little by instituting a flexible schedule that allowed employees to gain three pounds each decade.) The idea that a scale determines competence is part of the problem.

The weighing-in procedure tended to promote sick-leave abuse. The overweight flight attendant simply called in sick during the weigh-in week and then used amphetamines to control her appetite and laxatives to eliminate any effects. When she reached her weight limit, she reported in to record her poundage. As long as her weight was okay for that week, she was safe. Never mind the next month when she regained twenty pounds. Some attendants were so over the weight limit that they were out months on sick leave with other "complaints," all the while abusing their bodies trying to comply with weight standards. I once treated a stately flight attendant who resorted to weekly hydrocolonic enemas to keep her weight down.

The airlines' insurance carriers would pay for flight attendants to get alcohol or drug treatment and would pay for all the consequences of the dieting, purging, and weight gains (rapid weight gains and losses are potentially dangerous to the heart), but they would not pay for treatment for the psychological obsessions the airlines helped to create.

Airlines have since discontinued weight checks for a couple of reasons. First, there was the case of a male flight attendant who was also a weight lifter. He had a low-fat mass, was nearly all muscle, but weighed in on the heavy side for his height (muscle weighs more than fat). He was fired because of it. His appeal went all the way to the U.S. Supreme Court but was still denied. Even though the airlines won the case, they didn't look good with such a policy. Second, with all the recent dissolutions and consolidations of airlines, seniority places older and older employees as flight attendants. Some have more weight than the ingenue looks of previous eras. As a result, the weight checks have finally been eliminated.

A food obsessive facing the pressure of a weight check will perversely sabotage success by actually turning to food for solace. When I was newly out of graduate school in 1972, I was offered one of the most sought-after jobs in Los Angeles County. Because of my extensive background treating drug addicts on the streets of New York, I was offered the position of clinical director of the counseling program at a newly built women's prison. I was ecstatic.

I was applying for a federal civil service position before hiring practices came under close scrutiny, when the scale still ruled the day. When I went to take the hire-in physical,

I weighed 187—two pounds more than allowed for my height, even if I had a giant economy-sized frame, which I did not (I'm actually small boned). The interviewer assured me that they wanted me. He knew the complete physical with blood tests and other reports would take at least a week He suggested, "Why don't you take this week to get the two pounds off, and we'll weigh you at the end of the week." (Even today weight discrimination still exists in hiring. Employers will explain that it is the insurance carrier that predicts whether the overweight employee will be a bad risk. They will say this even if the employee who interviews is in perfect health.)

Despite my extensive qualifications and background, that spring-driven contraption would determine who would be clinical director for the opening of the new women's prison. Back then, I'd been bingeing and dieting all my life and just knew I could lose two pounds in a week. No problem. This was the early 1970s, when Dr. Atkins first advised people to "eat all you want" of fatty proteins. I spent the week munching dry roasted peanuts. For variety, I also threw in some fried pork rinds. I returned having gained ten pounds. You can't tell someone like myself to "eat all you want" of anything. The tragedy of this story is that I actually went to weigh in. A normal person might have realized she'd gained weight. I instead jumped on the scale and then, surprised, mortified, and humiliated, backed out of the human resources office. A food obsessive believes in magic and fantasy, "I can get away with it." I didn't. . . .

Death Watch

When efforts to monitor the weight of loved ones leave you exhausted, you move into a death watch. The daily bout with their slow suicide leaves you feeling helpless. The feelings are similar to those of someone who cares for a chronically ill loved one. You see the daily sickness and don't dare hope for a cure. This brings on depression. You may isolate yourself from the community. You see no clear-cut end to the suffering; you are in love with someone who is present in body but whose mind has left home long ago. You see a loved one seeking solace in food instead of you. This makes you feel angry and abandoned. But you can't be angry with a sick person. Instead, you live in chronic anxiety and uncertainty, even at times wishing them dead. That at least would be a clear end point with acceptable mourning rituals signaling that the suffering is over. But with food obsessives it just seems like constant pain. Having wished them dead, you feel guilty, so you overcompensate by being excessively helpful and loving. The anger erupts in power struggles and negotiations for control.

The skirmishes often leave other innocent bystanders suffering from the fallout. Children witness couples battling over control of food. By the time I met Cassandra and Elliott, she weighed more than three hundred pounds, and he was addicted to a major tranquilizer that was prescribed to relieve his depression. Their marriage was stormy. From the very beginning each fought for control. Her eating and his avoiding yard work were the overt issues. The power struggle progressed, and she got fatter while the yard became a junk heap. Strangely enough, they came to see me because of their eight-year-old's bedwetting. The bedwetting was presented as the family problem.

As we talked, their depression emerged. Each felt they had failed the other. They were depressed, feeling they should be able to do something. When Elliott finally gave up on helping his wife lose weight, he became depressed. Pills helped him avoid his feelings. Each was watching the other die. The son knew no other way to show how helpless he felt than by wetting his bed. When Mom took responsibility for her own eating disorder, Dad stopped worrying about her and, instead, cleaned up the yard. He now sees hope in his wife's progress and is fulfilling his own responsibilities to his home and family. His depression is lifted. As a by-product, their son stopped wetting the bed.

Healthy Neutrality

While overinvolvement with the sick person does not work, totally ignoring the problem doesn't work either. You can care without taking on the job. You are establishing a compassionate healthy neutrality where you are not attached to the outcome. You must learn to express your concern and at the same time show that your life will go on anyway. While this kind of thinking may seem selfish and uncaring, it's actually a gift. You give up fixing people and just let them know you care no matter what. You are starting to see that efforts at controlling and helping don't work. You need another way. That new way is giving up and letting go. Letting go may sound easy but is almost impossible for a confluent to do without help. You must learn to say no and really mean it. You must give the problem back to the one who really has it. In self-help groups you can discuss your own difficulties with others similarly afflicted. You will extend your family system to learn you are not alone. In later chapters, you'll see how that is done.

I Only Have Eyes for You

The confluent sufferer attempts to become a mirror image of the F-O, but the reflections become distorted. Confluent personalities feel a certain justification in taking over another person's life. After all, they don't even note the separation of the other. In Al-Anon, a self-help group for families of alcoholics, a common joke is told about confluents: "When the confluent person dies, someone else's life flashes before their eyes." This system works because the F-O, in order to keep eating or starving in rebellion, needs or wants to be told what to do. Because confluent personalities assume they understand what the F-O is feeling, they become the only ones who express feelings, while the F-O remains mute. It is not uncommon to hear a confluent personality say, "I know what you're thinking better than you do," while the F-O clams up or just cries. Quiet rebellion with food is not far behind. This reinforces the attitude of the confluent personality that "I must be right; they didn't even answer." Which side of this mirror would you like to be on? Both suffer.

So while one partner promotes the myth of incompetence, the other promotes infallibility. The F-O will silently fail while the confluent keeps trying and recommending new approaches. The confluent can maintain this fantasy indefinitely until the eating disorder eventually brings reality into focus. The confluent begins to wonder why this "well-controlled" person who "I fix" keeps gaining or losing weight. The F-O's body bears witness to the futility of the confluent's efforts.

Why Look at Me?

A confluent's self-image is that of giver rather than receiver. If you are confluent, it is very difficult to accept the idea that *you* need help. Your questions will usually be something like the following:

Didn't I offer to pay a dollar for each pound lost?

Didn't I offer to baby-sit while she went to those Weight Watchers meetings?

Didn't I buy a new wardrobe every time his body changed?

Didn't I gently remind her about the diet when she seemed to be slipping?

Didn't I help prepare all those special meals?

Didn't I support the gym membership that cost so much?

How could someone suggest I'm the one who needs help?

What does this eating disorder have to do with me?

Wasn't I only trying to help?

Well, your situation is confusing. Why would anyone want you to look at yourself? You wonder, *How can my self-examination in any way help the F-O?* That's a valid question, and by the time you finish this book, you will see that by becoming interested in your own life and taking care of yourself, the F-O will in turn assume more responsibility for his or her own life. You will both develop healthier mutual dependence and, in turn, interdependence.

Developing Confluency

Let's take a look at how your involvement developed. Just as no one asks to have a food obsession, you didn't ask to have a confluent personality. No one questions that you came by it honestly. You did the best you could with what you knew. You tried your best. Your intentions have been well-meaning and your efforts genuine.

Whether you are a spouse, friend, mother, daughter, sister, brother, father, employer, concerned professional, or just interested observer, your experience has a certain recognizable pattern. You have watched someone you care about become more and more obsessed with food and thus more removed from you. You have been affected. You are another victim of the disease. Your interest in the problem has become an obsession in and of itself. The following list shows the gradual progression of a confluent personality.

---■---

Progression of Confluent Personality

Use the following as a checklist to monitor your own progression.

Early Stages

☐ Early learned to care for others as measure of self-worth.

☐ Failed to cure parents so will cure F-O.

☐ Finds an F-O who is needy and controls him or her.

☐ Begins doubting own perceptions and wants to control F-O's eating to show decisiveness.

☐ Social life affected. Isolates self from community to help F-O.

Obsession

☐ Makes pleas and threats related to the eating behavior.

☐ Judges self and feels that he or she caused the eating/starving.

☐ Hides food.

☐ Attempts to control eating by hiding food, making idle threats, nagging, and scolding.

☐ Shows anger and disappointment regarding F-O's promises.

Secret Life

☐ Becomes obsessed with watching F-O and covering up for F-O.

☐ Takes over responsibilities for F-O.

☐ Takes pivotal role in communications, not permitting contact between F-O and others.

☐ Expresses anger inappropriately.

Out of Control

☐ Makes violent, often physical, attempts to control F-O's eating.

☐ Lets self go physically and mentally.

☐ Has extramarital affairs, starts working longer hours, or becomes obsessed with outside interests.

- [ ] Becomes rigid and possessive. Appears angry most of the time and careful and secretive about home life.
- [ ] Develops medical conditions such as ulcers, rashes, migraines, depression, and obesity, or starts abusing drugs such as tranquilizers.
- [ ] Constantly loses temper.
- [ ] Becomes sick and tired of being sick and tired.

———————■———————

Let's explore more deeply the larger categories of developing confluency.

HEREDITY. Those who are food obsessed learned to use food to relieve stress long before they have any choice about it. Similarly, you learned to become a caretaker long before having any conscious choice. As a confluent personality, you may have been born into a family whose members abused alcohol or other substances. You learned early to feel responsible for the pain of those members. This mistaken sense of responsibility is a prevalent aspect of confluency.

You learned this sense of responsibility early. Young children feel omnipotent, and consequently, responsible for the well-being of their parents. They feel they have created everything that happens around them. Children see themselves as the center of the universe (some carry this perception into adulthood). In an addicted family, parents are suffering, and children, of course, take responsibility for the suffering. You may have even heard parents complain, "My life would have been much better without you kids." Or a mother, after she is beaten by her husband, cries to her daughter, "I would leave the SOB if it weren't for you." You can see how a child would automatically take on guilt. If you come from such a family, your mission was programmed long before you ever thought about it.

CARETAKER ROLE. In such families, you rarely learned to expect nurturing for yourself. You never learned how to receive. You learned to take care of others. From your perspective, the degree to which you demonstrate caring and helpfulness is the measure of your own self-worth. You have not cured your parents' lives, so you're a failure. Their problems continued and progressed despite your best efforts. With your mission still unaccomplished, you need to find suffering persons and help them. This will be your redemption. Many people who become doctors, psychologists, social workers, and nurses do so to try to make up for childhood "failures." You've just got to fix someone. Then you will feel okay.

MARRY TO FIX. Failing to cure your parents, you found a needy mate. The agenda then is to cure your spouse. You are still trying to win that merit badge by fixing someone you love. Taking on this mission keeps you feeling somewhat in control. In truth, however, you can't control them at all. Obsessions with food have nothing to do with you, just like in the situation with your parents. It doesn't matter what you try or don't try. You keep choosing fixer-uppers. Marrying a needy mate keeps you from ever having to face your own needs. You say you want to be the receiver but really don't know how. You may complain, "Why isn't it ever my turn to be the 'falling apart' person?" This lament is easily voiced where you know you won't be heard. Your relationship with an F-O keeps you deprived but safe.

CONTROL IS THE KEY. As the eating disorder progresses, you have usually escalated your attempts at control. Initially this brings about gentle pleadings to cut down. When these attempts fail, the next step is subtle threats or promised rewards: "I'll pay you five dollars for every pound you lose" or "Get into that new bathing suit and we'll go on a cruise."

When such efforts produce no new results, you begin

seeing yourself as inadequate. Since you took on someone to fix, your ego and identity are very much tied to that person's success. If they fail, you fail. Fearful of the impending failure, you may escalate your threats, even threaten to leave. The F-O may turn the tables on you and also threaten to leave. At that point, you may beg him or her to stay. You are re-creating the same scene your parents acted out—making a stand and then backing off. You are at first helpful, then punitive, then guilty. Efforts escalate and now include hiding food, locking cabinets, nagging, and scolding. But no matter what efforts you undertake, the food obsession continues.

PIVOTALLY PISSED OFF. The F-O has made and broken innumerable promises. Despite whatever appropriate, caring, "helpful benefactor" feelings you'd like to effect, the truth is that you are *angry*. Often you have taken over many of the F-O's responsibilities. Initially you took on these extra burdens as a labor of love. It felt good to be giving. However, you expected this would be temporary, and you later began to resent the permanence of your benefactor role.

You may have become the family message center and are now overburdened and involved in everyone's business. You have seen the F-O through inappropriate and widely varying mood swings based on whether he or she is on a binge or in withdrawal. You wanted to protect others from some of this, so you became the communication hub for everyone, interpreting and rephrasing all conversations so no one would be hurt. "Mommy's having a bad day. She didn't mean it." Unfortunately, this role hurts you. If you are busy analyzing and heading off others' emotions, you will never have a chance to acknowledge and feel your own. And while this role may have given you a sense of importance at first, you now wish the F-O would handle his or her share of problem communications.

Sometimes your rage comes out in the form of ulcers, colitis, migraines, or other physical complaints of your own. You take in all your own anger and express it within your own body. However, as time moves on, you will have to express your pent-up resentment about this role. After brewing underground for so long, your anger may surface inappropriately in a way that is embarrassing or humiliating. Confluents often look angry all the time, but no one knows why. After all, the F-O has been walking around partially sedated, perhaps even entertaining others with a jolly-fat-man exterior while you have faced all the family problems coldly and soberly conscious. You haven't had the comfort of food abuse. You may use the silent treatment for a while, only to eventually falter into loud and hostile outbursts when least expected.

Embarrassed and guilty from such outbursts, you may become excessively apologetic and walk on eggshells to smooth over your recent behavior. In this way, the C-P and the F-O mirror each other. Both feel guilty, out of control, frustrated, and angry. Both compensate by becoming overly conciliatory and apologetic. Such behavior merely perpetrates the problem. All these adjustments will have to be renegotiated.

WHO CARES? Caring, not caring, raging, being silent, hinting, cajoling, nagging, scolding . . . *nothing works.* You hang on precariously as your pendulum swings between rigid silence and maniacal ravings. You live with insecurity and without hope. You don't know what kind of behavior to expect from your F-O or yourself, and all the while you have an image of yourself as being able to keep things in control.

The only solution is to give up trying. Often you have let your own grooming and personal care slack off. *If my loved one doesn't care, why should I?* you think. If you can't beat 'em, join 'em. In Al-Anon, old-timers often comment on a new member, "She got here at the stage where she's still combing her hair."

Or you may decide to join your F-O and develop your own form of substance abuse. In an informal survey, I discovered at least 40 percent of the spouses of alcoholics were obese. There's that mutual suicide pact. Confluents also become addicted to sedatives and tranquilizers (all doctor-prescribed) as alternatives to anxiety.

RUN AWAY FROM HOME. The runaway problem in such homes is not merely packing up and moving on. The confluent leaves by withdrawing emotional investment and finding outside activities to gain satisfaction. This is actually a healthy survival adjustment. Although it weakens the family structure, leaving is the only way to endure a situation in which you have no effect. You have run away because you can't stand how helpless you feel.

Tests done with monkeys have dramatized this feeling of helplessness. Monkeys were alternately shocked and rewarded with no possibility of figuring out which response would come when. No matter what they tried, there was no escape. Eventually, the monkeys stopped trying at all. Later, when new options were offered, they sat in a helpless, hopeless huddle, refusing to try. This is termed "learned helplessness" and aptly characterizes the confluent personality. You withdraw to survive.

If you don't withdraw and close down completely, you may decide to gain personal satisfaction outside the home. Since your own self-worth is tied to helping someone, you will have to become a helper away from home. At home you still feel like a total failure. You may become a workaholic. As you work excessively, you can finally say, "I've done enough." You may decide to become president of the chamber of commerce or PTA or become a Scout leader, thus gaining recognition and approval from others. The more the home situation fails, the more you throw yourself into these outside projects. Often the F-O may suspect infidelity, but that is rarely the case. Actually, you don't even feel good enough about yourself to allow for an affair.

SICK AND TIRED OF BEING SICK AND TIRED. You passed through being fed up long ago. When you are sick and tired of being sick and tired, you are ready to take positive action to effect some change. Here you reach the same crisis point as the F-O, where you say, "My God, this is really my life, not a drill. It's not a dress rehearsal. I have to listen and learn a new way." Some think of a quick, runaway solution such as divorce. This is rarely effective. Guilt lingers, and the mutual nature of the disease is never addressed. More than likely you would remarry into the same situation. You must learn about your own role in such a predicament. It is imperative that you address whatever personal needs you have in this type of relationship. If you don't, you will continue the cycle yet another time. You may as well work through your problems here.

Triangulation

Family systems sometimes break down into power triangles. As each person fulfills his or her role in points on a triangle, power bases are formed that keep all members locked into certain characteristic roles. When one part of the triangle begins to move, shows a little vibration or some new life, the reverberations move others as well.

The most significant base of a triangle is between the mother and the father. Often, as couples fail to negotiate the changes they need to make, children become too powerful, and this wrecks the family system and hurts the child. Family therapists have seen this so often that they recognize a commonly held theme: *the acting-out child is acting out the unresolved conflict of the parents.*

With food obsessions, the acting out happens in eating behaviors. The child is unconsciously eating or starving to form a diversion from issues the parents need to face. We learned this most clearly in the early days of treating alcoholic families. We saw that when the alcoholic's drinking stopped, someone else in the family took on the role of IP, or Identified Patient. When a couple in early sobriety attends marriage counseling, children sensed that the parents were really talking about serious business and might actually break up. This was much more threatening than the earlier drunken tirades, physical abuse, and idle threats to leave. This was *real.* Children would automatically act out to divert the parents from their own problems.

By the time you enter treatment, you need to become more aware of your automatic behavior patterns that might have served a purpose in your family of origin. They helped you survive but have outlasted their usefulness. Remember, I warned that giving up food obsessions is about growing up and into your own life. This doesn't mean that your parents' problems are the cause of your problems. You don't need to place blame here. You are just investigating to uncover what might be your unconscious motivation to be self-destructive.

You have carried self-destructive childhood diversionary tactics into your adult life. You need to identify what your motivations and intentions have been so you can *choose* to continue your behavior or change course as a grown-up. You may have had the sense to get out of your early family system without abusing yourself. But if you suffer from food obsession or confluency, you were probably deeply enmeshed before you began to have a clue about what was really going on. Your pain became the repository for all the family's pain.

When two people unite and collude to lock a third person out, it's called "triangulation." The third person is viewed and treated as an object of either scorn or pity. The locked-out person works to keep him- or herself in that place, all in service of maintaining the family status quo. In anorexia, it is usually Mom and Dad locking the daughter out. They have a common problem in having to fix their poor, dear suffering daughter. This gives them a mutual project. If the daughter is obese, it's usually Mom and daughter locking Dad out. They gossip about "how men are." Two people stay focused on a third to keep from getting angry with each other. They don't see how absolutely necessary the third person is. The objectified problem person provides a diversion so the other two don't have to look at their relationship.

Sometimes we mask anger with excessive worry and concern. For example, parents may show grave concern by vigilantly monitoring a daughter's eating. Parents may be consumed with worry and use this as an excuse not to get involved with anyone else in the family, namely each other. Maybe Mom and daughter are united by worrying and raging over alcoholic Dad. The problem person serves to unify the other two. The family system needs the family problem. We need the eggs.

As we investigate triangulation, we can see how Mom's pain and anger was shunted into the daughter, who stuffs it down with food and later pukes it into toilet bowls or garbage bags. Most of the time, family therapy shifts to couple therapy. Mothers getting their own mating life in order, whether by staying or leaving, will help daughters separate and grow up. Daughters who take on their mothers' sorrow are secretly enraged, because they're fighting someone else's war. Their souls know they're in the wrong arena, and they must decide which war is really theirs to fight. Addicted daughters serve as substitutes and salves for their mothers' loneliness, as they try to make it up to Mom for all she's been through.

Jenny's Story

Seventeen-year-old Jenny's story so classically illustrates the concept of triangulation that I've used it in my Fat & Furious™ seminars for years. Hazelden has also produced a film documenting her family's recovery called *Dark Secrets, Bright Victory.* Jenny's bingeing and vomiting came on at a very critical developmental stage—when it was time for her to grow up and leave home. Instead of making that difficult transition, she vomited twelve times a day, starved herself most mornings, collapsed into compulsive bingeing after she got home from school, and finished off her stashes in midnight raids that ended with a solemn oath to fast the next day. She was thirty pounds underweight and ashen. You'll later see why treatment for her vomiting was such a necessary rite of passage for her eventual maturation and separation from her family.

Jenny's mother, Aggie, said, "I thought she was feeding the neighborhood." Trying to control her daughter's bingeing, she found herself rummaging through kitchen cabinets, counting bread slices, measuring jam jars, and doubting her own experiences, wondering whether she had ever shopped or stocked shelves. She was distracted from her own life, watching Jenny's food consumption and spying on Jenny's chaotic relationship with a drug-addicted boyfriend who held wild, raucous parties on weekends. She just knew if she could get her daughter away from "that boy," she'd get some control back.

Jenny spent weekends at the boyfriend's house, where his mother was usually drunk and allowed all the youngsters to do whatever they wanted. Often, when a daughter is trying to separate from Mom, she takes on a surrogate who is less judgmental and fearful—but one who may encourage obsessional behavior.

During initial consultations with Jenny and her family, treatment staff members sketched a brief outline of her history and our possible directions as a team. Her parents, Aggie and Rod, had separated and divorced when Jenny was five. Whenever Jenny asked about the divorce, she was told it happened because Mom's work moved to a new location, an hour away.

Jenny would later tell us in group therapy that she thought this was the weirdest reason she'd ever heard for a family to break up. But her parents were so upright and straight that Jenny was sure this had to be the reason; they'd never lie, and she must be evil for even questioning it. For Jenny, like many others, initial doubts left unexplored eventually led to compulsive behavior as a way to avoid further questioning. The failure to pursue these initial rumblings of confusion and doubt provides a fertile ground for food obsessions. Instead of trusting their instincts, children see Mom and Dad as perfect and themselves as evil. They choose to punish themselves instead of questioning further.

Upon receiving our evaluation that Jenny qualified for treatment, both parents sighed with relief. They expressed gratitude to our treatment team that at least she wasn't "an addict or something." Even though they'd been divorced for twelve years, the Barrows continued to function as a family unit. It was as if the couple had never really acknowledged the reality of their divorce. They couldn't face their pain. We'd later learn even more about their family situation. Dad visited every weekend "to see Jenny," often staying over "as a friend," with the three of them going on outings together and operating as a commuting triad. When they learned we'd want both parents in family groups three nights a week, Rod admitted it would be a hardship, but he wanted to do all he could to support Jenny.

Family nights lasted for three hours, during which time each family member attended separate groups where they could share any secrets, practice any new approaches, and generally let their hair down without loved ones present. Aggie would be with other moms, Rod with other dads, and Jenny in groups with other inpatients and recently discharged patients returning for aftercare. After a short break, the families would reorganize and come together in multiple family groups.

Counselors and fellow patients from the first groups would also be in these later groups to help advise families on which issues needed confronting and which were best left for individuals to handle separately. These decisions are extremely important with any addictive disorders because it's so difficult for sufferers to establish boundaries and determine which is their private territory and which is the family's domain.

An early aspect of treatment is learning the concept "We're as sick as our secrets." During the initial psychosocial evaluations, patients are asked to tell the counselors any secrets they harbor that they feel may get in the way of their recovery. They are assured of confidentiality and that we will not pressure them to divulge what might harm them. We let them know, however, that we are required by law to report to authorities our knowledge of child abuse or incest, past or current, and are also bound to warn possible future victims of any threatened injuries.

We do caution them that because we are family therapists, we will want to protect some individual secrets as necessary, but our patient is the entire family system, and we will want to proceed in a manner best for the health of all. We can't keep secrets within the family system. We will encourage eventual, careful disclosure. It might be enough just to say, "I've got a secret." You won't necessarily have to say what it is. But if you pretend you don't have a secret when you do, that makes others around you feel crazy. They know.

Jenny's biggest secret was about her own victimization

when she was twelve. She'd stayed late at a schoolyard with girlfriends, playfully taunting some older boys. She had dressed provocatively and flirted unconsciously. We'd later learn that this was in marked contrast to the starched lace collars of her mother. In this schoolyard, Jenny was raped. Her mother, though horrified and devastated, felt an eerie responsibility for what happened and swore Jenny to secrecy—they must never let her father know. Aggie feared that if Rod knew, he'd declare her an unfit mother. She feared he'd use that to take Jenny away. Instead of helping Jenny heal her own wounds, Aggie enlisted her as co-conspirator against poor Dad's supposed inability to understand or handle the situation. Mom's primary concern was making sure Rod would not find out. She couldn't focus on her daughter's pain. So it was sent underground.

A common theme in treatment circles is women disrespecting and distrusting the strength of their men. Even if his career brings him great accolades in the work world, he is often berated at home for being emotionally unavailable or unable to handle feelings. As women voice this amongst each other and to their daughters, they don't face their own difficulties in seeing and feeling their man's pain. Despite all the fantasies played out with macho men and dollhouse marriages, addicted women don't expect much of men or have much faith that they'll be there when the going gets tough. Aggie and Jenny effectively froze Dad out. They created a triangle of dishonesty and secrecy, and I'd later learn how much this protected Aggie from facing and remembering her sexuality and the causes of her divorce.

In treatment, Jenny wanted to clear up that bit of subterfuge. Sometimes we find patients in early recovery wanting to deal with past trauma as a diversion from current work. They make an unwitting deal with themselves and a therapist to work on the wrong issue. Some eat right through such explorations. But their inner sensors know they are on the wrong topic; their souls know it's the wrong war.

We had to make sure uncovering this past pain was the work Jenny really needed to do at this time. Too many think that catharsis of past pain heals food obsessions. This is not necessarily so, especially if the past situation is not germane to the current situation. We had to also make sure that Jenny would work on her own true dilemmas—not Mom's or her counselor's. We decided to focus first on getting Jenny painfully aware of what she was currently doing with food.

The rape would have to wait. We call this "bracketing." We decide to put certain issues in brackets and deal with them at a later date. We want abstinence first and then we'll see what's needed. We'd help her develop a support system at Overeaters Anonymous (OA) and wait until she'd had a few months of abstinence from vomiting. We knew she'd probably gain weight in recovery, which would be difficult for her, and she'd need a lot of support.

Jenny did quite well in early recovery. Eating moderately, cutting out junk foods, and stopping vomiting, she started to gain her weight back slowly, and she negotiated this change well enough. She even relaxed into it, giving up some of the characteristic perfectionism of many anorexics and bulimics. She dressed more casually, was able to leave her work assignments imperfectly completed, and even told sexy jokes with other residents. However, her mother's collars got starchier, her eyes darted ever more fearfully, and she tried to get Jenny into conversations alone between groups to form a pact about what could and couldn't be discussed.

Rod showed up semiregularly to groups. He came across as so many men in food-obsessed families do—as an unnecessary appendage or, at best, a foil for the women—generally ineffectual in the feeling realm. He had a rather cold, scientific demeanor and seemed not to be in any way needy or even aware of sadness or other feelings. Some evenings Rod called to say he couldn't attend group because he'd had to work late, and the hour drive in Los Angeles rush hour wouldn't get him there on time. Months later we'd get to see how well timed and less than coincidental those absences were.

As Jenny's recovery began to stabilize, she got a sponsor in OA, an older woman to present yet another competitive surrogate for Mom. She was eventually discharged from treatment with a fair prognosis if she could just learn to be a little less perfect.

Aggie had mellowed out some and was going to Al-Anon. She was learning how to keep her eyes off Jenny. As she started attending more to her own life, she didn't even know or care what was in the cupboard. Eventually she even started going away on business trips.

Six months later, all hell broke loose. Jenny started continuous bingeing and vomiting and came back to treatment thoroughly depressed. She'd had a smattering of feeling good, knew what recovery felt like, and trusted us enough to come back when the going got rough.

She was readmitted as a relapse patient, and the treatment team moved to make decisions about what was missing or not working in her recovery plan. We looked at what paths we'd taken in the past that might possibly be changed for the present course of treatment. We asked Jenny to make the same evaluation.

After initial consultations, we decided it was now the right time to discuss the rape. We also wanted assurances of perfect attendance from Rod so that he could assume his rightful place in his daughter's life. Even though Jenny was more into dating and moving away from the family, she didn't know how to negotiate that separation. They needed to talk. After a few weeks in this second course of treatment, Jenny shared that during the past family groups, just as she was mustering up courage to talk to her dad about their relationship, the freeways seemed too crowded for Dad to get to group. (Some of the "coincidences" we learn about in family therapy are so bizarre that we hear strains of *The Twilight Zone* theme echoing in the background, "doo doo, doo doo." There is so much more communication going on than our little pea brains can dream of.)

Investigating her relapse, Jenny decided the guilt of not telling Dad about the rape was weighing heavily on her conscience. Notice it was not the rape itself, but the secrecy. She didn't need his counsel at this point; she just didn't like keeping secrets. When it had happened, she was too young to fathom all the choices she had in the matter. Also, her mom was making most of the decisions and shutting down any discussion of what had happened. Now with more maturity, Jenny realized that she had bought into her mother's fear and effectively colluded to lock her father out.

Recovery involves a lot of forgiveness—of yourself and of others. Jenny felt she wanted her father's forgiveness. She decided to tell him about her lies. These issues are not easily decided. They need the guidance of sponsors, counselors, and others outside the family because family members might advise you to hold secrets and spare loved ones. Or, conversely, family members will advise confrontation and attack as a way to stir muddy waters and get you to do their work. When you run your options by a therapist or spiritual mentor, he or she will most likely advise you to try to share secrets without hurting anyone, including yourself. It takes some work to make sure whether sharing or hiding is the more painful route. For Jenny, it was time to come clean.

Work began on preparing her to tell Rod the truth. She wrote out scripts in the form of dialogues, emphasizing what she wanted Dad to know and how she'd help him understand it wasn't his fault that the rape happened or that she chose to hide it from him. She practiced in psychodrama sessions with her peer groups, setting the proper stage and experiencing all her fear and trepidation. By the night of this "come clean" family group, Jenny was superconfident and prepared.

As many patients have found, if you do enough homework and preparation, nothing you'll experience in real life will be half as difficult as you've imagined. An important value of treatment programs is the opportunity to practice and get feedback from uninvolved, caring others. All fellow patients and staff were primed for the family group, and everyone was prepared to help Jenny and Rod weather the truth. No one was prepared for what happened instead.

It was Aggie who threw a giant monkey wrench into these well-laid plans. Before Jenny could get her throat cleared, Aggie jumped in with "I've got something to share." This was not offered as a request; there was none of her usual hesitation or pause. She raced on with, "I know Jenny has been curious for years about our divorce, and I think it's about time I cleared up any confusion." Aggie had never mentioned this as a dilemma in any of her groups with the other moms. As far as we knew, the divorce was a minor inquiry on Jenny's part. We had no idea it was a strong issue for Aggie.

Counselors stared, dumbfounded. I must admit I felt somewhat usurped as I'd felt so in charge. The whole treatment team was primed, ready to move toward mending the father/daughter split. We even had cameras rolling and were filming this family group. Didn't this woman know we were on a timetable? We'd been rehearsing Jenny all week. Too bad. As we hear so often, life is what happens when you're making other plans.

Aggie continued on without waiting for any sign from the counselors. She addressed her daughter with, "Jenny, I think you should know your dad and I divorced because I was having an affair with another man." She then burst into sobs.

Why now? Why had Aggie chosen this moment to spill the beans about long-past, unrelated events? Unconscious and unknown to her, she was operating from deep confluency. She was also setting up new triangles between herself, her daughter, her ex-husband, and the group. Sensing her daughter had major pain to share, Aggie decided to divert attention and any strong emotion toward herself so her daughter could be spared the pain.

This is also a form of triangulation. From my early drug-counseling days, we called such behaviors "throwing a bone." Aggie thought she could throw out some interesting material for the group to chew on. If she could get us interested in this long-past topic, perhaps Jenny would give up on talking with Dad about the rape. On some level, Aggie sensed that her daughter was going to share her secret. So she tried to distract attention onto herself. It worked for a while—but not for long.

Jenny exploded with anger. "You mean YOU, lily-white, perfect Miss Virgin Queen, always impressing me about being a good girl? You had an affair? And here I was trying to live out some kind of bullshit morality that had nothing to do with reality. Why couldn't you tell me the truth of who you are?" Jenny raged on for a full five minutes and then fell in a heap, sobbing. Her mother's composure was certainly bent as she sniffled quietly, staring holes into the carpet. Finally she offered, "I'd like you to forgive me. I hope you can. I'm sorry I misled you. These are things I tried to deny even to myself. I hope someday you'll understand."

Jenny wasn't ready in that moment to engage with Mom. Their healing would wait for later. Perhaps Jenny's strong motivation and direction toward health would not let her be deterred by this unconscious tactic of her mom's. She turned instead toward Rod and said, "This side of the family has been dishonest too." With that, the tears flowed freely and Jenny sobbed about being raped and how badly she felt that she'd hidden it all these years. It was not the rape but the hiding that caused her pain. She hugged him, gulping, "You've always been there for me, and I didn't come to you. I'm so sorry I closed you out."

Rod's immediate reaction was to question Mom, as he asked Aggie, "Why didn't you let me know?" Before she could respond, Jenny answered for her, "We were scared, and we were afraid, and we're sorry." Jenny, in answering for her mom, didn't yet see that she was unable to separate her own feelings from her mother's. She was accustomed to operating from Mom's fear, not her own.

Rod glared at his ex as he hugged Jenny to him. His own pain finally welled up as he thanked his daughter for being able to trust him now. They both cried. Then he reassured her with, "We'll work it out. I love you." Jenny then broke down into bigger sobs and said, "I love you too." Mom sat quietly on the other side of the room, huddled and alone. This time she was locked out.

But we don't want to create such triangles. We don't want to lock anyone out. We want each family member to occupy his or her own autonomous space and not be pivoted to react to someone else's pain or power or energy. Healing progressed gradually over the next few weeks. In private sessions, the parents began to talk with each other about how inadequately they'd handled their divorce and how they still genuinely care and feel committed to each other but hadn't known how to talk. With all the family secrets out in the open, there was room for a lot of talking. The dam of emotions for all three family members couldn't be plugged. They got to see what they'd been avoiding. The parents didn't want to face the pain of their divorce. Jenny saw how she stayed Mommy and Daddy's sweet little girl so they'd have ample excuses for seeing each other. Despite their divorce, to care for Jenny, Dad visited every weekend, and their family outings resembled a perfectly content intact family system. Divorce was ignored. Sex was also.

This couple loved each other, but they'd had no ability to weather the crisis that had entered their relationship. As long as Jenny stayed their little girl, they never had to confront their pain. If Jenny were to grow up and leave, they'd be left alone with each other. They'd have to face their past. Jenny had dutifully developed a food obsession to keep from growing up, to bring attention to all this unresolved pain. Working on Jenny's food problem had brought that pain back into the spotlight.

But as a natural rite of passage, it was now time for Jenny to grow up and leave the family nest. How could Rod and Aggie continue to spend weekends together without her as the ostensible excuse? They'd have to face past hurts to become ready for future joys without Jenny as the central character. They'd have to acknowledge both love and hate for each other so that they could move on into their future.

Once that pain was unleashed, there was no more need for Jenny to be center stage in her parents' lives. When I show the video of their story in training sessions, I still cry at the end when Jenny looks straight to camera and says, "I'm really growing up. I really am." I am still amazed that she was so prescient and knew how important that family session was for her future.

This was a watershed moment for her parents as well. In separate sessions they started realistically looking at their divorce and were later able to heal the pain. They started going out on dates without Jenny. No longer the central diversion and focus for her parents' attention, Jenny was now free to grow up and leave home. Within three months she moved out to live with a friend from school. Six months later her dad moved in with her mom.

Rod and Aggie had needed an honest way to face how they'd mutually hurt each other and to admit they still loved each other. They needed to find a way to live a full life without their daughter between them. Mom had to face who she'd been and how she'd survived. She had to forgive herself, and then she ultimately asked for her daughter's forgiveness. A year later the couple remarried on what would have been their twenty-seventh wedding anniversary. The triangle was broken so a new dyad could emerge.

CHAPTER 4

Why Are We Together?

One F-O keeps fifteen to twenty confluents busy. While the F-O falls apart, the C-P tries to put things back together. You are each an extension of the other. You each take on opposite sides of the same personality structure. Both together constitute one fully functioning, almost adult human being. Trading off the roles presents problems, but roles will alternate. Food determines who fits where in the equation. When food makes an F-O superachieving and functional, confluents benefit from the energy. Other times, food creates self-loathing, depression, and angry, irrational outbursts. Then the C-P becomes comforter and rescuer.

As the F-O's obsessive relationship with food progresses, predicting the effects of eating becomes more and more difficult. Giving up food often creates a total personality change. At this point, food no longer works as a coping mechanism. Returning to it continually gets you nowhere, and you can't predict what effects are in store. You do know, however, that you are ready to find a new way out. This is the beginning of recovery.

As-If Personality

To give up obsessive eating you must renegotiate your place in the world. It is no accident that you have taken on an illness that allows your physical body to change size continually.

Your psyche is doing the same thing. Your inner self is trying to establish its own place, and it is confused about how large or small it wants to be and how much space it needs to take up. Your honest self is looking for its true home. When you take on unrealistic roles for yourself, your body signals your personal deceit. *The body doesn't lie. The head does.*

You fashioned yourself in such a way that you thought you could achieve love and closeness and instead lost yourself in the process. Fat is the price paid for dishonest love. Most often, this trade-off for love occurred first in the mother-child relationship. You took the patterns you learned there with you into adulthood. Needing love as well as needing independence, you struggle with a fear of being trapped as well as a longing to be swallowed up. You can avoid that struggle—*you'll do it by yourself*—as long as you keep swallowing up every piece of food in sight. When you eat, you keep yourself trapped and fearful. No one else is involved. When the food obsession stops, you will start to see how much of yourself you have traded off in order to play the roles that would win you love.

Prisoners of Childhood

Psychiatrist Hilde Bruch conducted research on obese families as early as the 1940s. Her data still holds up today. She found very strong connections between overeating in children and their mothers. However, in recent years, many therapists and the general public have moved away from examining these issues. In the early days of psychiatry, writers seemed to be blaming mothers for how their children turned out. In schizophrenia we used the term "schizophrenogenic mother," indicating a certain personality of the mother and relationship with the child that might result in schizophrenia. With the women's movement and advances in psychiatry, many referred to these early writings as "mom bashing," and the pendulum of this investigation swung so far the other way that the mother-daughter relationship has often been ignored. We so feared blaming moms that we didn't investigate some important imprinting that had transpired.

In my years of treating over- and undereaters, I find no other relationship as important as what I termed the "mother-daughter wound." I wrote an entire book about it—not to blame moms, but to show how a mother's disowned power creates her daughter's struggles with power and how food as a power source, a fuel, becomes the vehicle for expressing the struggle. The main theme in my book *Fat & Furious* is that daughters are bingeing and purging their mother's disowned pain and anger.

In the early research, Dr. Bruch found that mothers of obese children were often insecure and ambivalent regarding the child. Often the child was born in the mother's later life and wasn't really planned for or expected. The mothers weren't sure whether they really wanted the child. Even today it is still taboo for mothers to express anything less than exultation at having a child. There is great fear the child will be damaged emotionally, as if the child doesn't know already.

Upset at their own mixed emotions, these mothers over-compensate by excessive feeding and extreme overprotectiveness. They want to ensure that the child feels loved. The food offers the security and satisfaction they fear they cannot give. Even though early feedings are an infant's chance to assert independence by both refusing and grabbing for food, mothers of children who were later obese reported that these eating episodes were "uneventful." We can assume that either the mothers were not paying much attention, or else the infants became hypervigilant to mom's needs and quickly adapted to fill them. Even at that early stage, infants can respond to their mothers' needs rather than their own. This adaptiveness could surely later grow into food obsessions or confluency or both.

To prove how much they love these children, the moms expressed grave concern and fear about the outside world. This made the children clingy and dependent. The moms inhibited the children from risk-taking and muscular activity. And whenever the children presented needs the mom hadn't planned for, the mom voiced her own complaints, usually competing to show who is sicker.

The fathers in these homes were either absent or weak and unaggressive. Their wives treated them with a great deal of contempt and reproach. The wives, being sickly types, did a lot of blaming of Dad and berated him constantly. The message to the child was "No matter what, don't be like your father." This dynamic operates in overeating women. Many have great struggles with men's strength and their own. They want a strong man but also fear him. Even more, they become fearful when showing their own strengths. They don't want to intimidate anyone.

Growing up, these children were not very close to their fathers. They felt like possessions of the father. He was more interested in work or business activities. Despite business acclaim, his efforts never got him rewards within the family system. Even if Dad was successful in his work, it was never enough. Mom continued to complain that her needs are not met.

Further research revealed a number of fathers' occupations that often produce fat daughters. The top three occupations were dress manufacturer, movie producer, and specialist in metabolic diseases. It was almost as if the daughters decided not to compete. If what Daddy wanted was thin model types, beautiful movie stars, or great successes from his medical practice, the daughters absolutely insisted on being the opposite.

Dearest Mom

Even though fathers do have influence, clearly the most important relationship to investigate is between mothers and daughters. Significantly more women than men suffer food obsessions. Women naturally have a tendency to gain more weight because of hormones. Then they are subjected to the media's bias of punishing the rounded female body. Then there are mothers who have been abusing themselves by fighting to keep weight off and who seek to control their daughters' bodies the same way. There are mothers who even teach their daughters how to vomit.

While women can struggle with food obsessions all of their lives, most eating disorders emerge in adolescence, just when the daughter experiences herself growing into her mother. Though I've written an entire book, *Fat & Furious,* about the mother-daughter struggle and how it affects food obsessions, here you can simply compare your obsession for excess or minimal food to your enmeshment with your mother. Your relationship to nurturance is unnatural. Whether you are addictively drawn toward it or powerfully repelled from it, it's got ya. Are you smothered, getting little air or light? Are you weighted and stuffed? Or are you totally estranged, feeling cold and alone? Most anorexics are truly hungry all the time. So estrangement doesn't work. It also doesn't work to give your life over to your mother, creating no autonomy for yourself. You must learn how to develop a more distant intimacy that allows you to breathe and dance into your own life.

Breaking the Tie That Binds

Even though you've had such strong early programming, you'll still have to struggle to grow up and leave home. People with food obsessions are like overripe fruit rotting on the vine. It is time to get plucked. When you truly reach an adult commitment to live your own life, the food obsession will take on a whole different character. This is true whether you have moved three thousand miles away from home or live around the block. It is true if you are a teenage anorexic struggling to grow up in high school or a forty-year-old mother of four who presents herself as "earth mother" to everyone but herself. Recovering from the eating disorder is a definite statement that you will begin to live your own life for yourself. This is it.

The emotional struggle to separate from previous programming and live your own new life of possibilities is crucial for your recovery. If your separation plans don't work out well, attachment to food often results. Often the marriage contract is a new commitment to the same old struggle you have with leaving Mom's home. You may have married your mother. You marry the same struggle you had with Mom. For example, if at home you usually felt guilty, as if you had never done enough, you may well marry someone who helps you feel guilty, as though you don't measure up. If, at Mom's home, you felt superior and special and spoiled, you will marry someone who keeps that fantasy going. If you felt inadequate and competitive in childhood, you will likely marry into the same situation. In any event, you will need to find new ways to relate in order to recover. You will have to explore and get acquainted with your opposite side.

Mutual Dependency

Though F-Os and C-Ps complain about each other, you are more alike than you are different. You are, in a very real sense, mirror images of each other. One takes on one extreme and the other its opposite. There is nothing inherently wrong with this. The personality dynamics are common to many people, whether or not they exhibit any form of addiction. In fact, many people thrive on this interdependency. With food obsessions, however, the addition of food into the equation upsets the balance.

In other words, we're not all that weird and different from other families. It's just that we *must* get more honest and conscious in every area of our lives and face things in our relationship patterns that other people can get by ignoring. They just blithely continue along with expressing frustration in some other less self-destructive way. Most people can function quite well without examining their relationships. F-Os and their C-Ps, however, *have* to look at relationship patterns. The only other alternative is to keep food obsessions in the picture.

You have been using food to avoid risk. You have failed to explore and own all parts of your personality. You stayed with what was safe. In choosing partners, you gravitated toward people who could fulfill the parts of you that you feared. If you feared being too loud and arrogant, you chose someone to be shy for you. If you feared being too shy, you appreciated someone more aggressive. You'll have to develop a way to play all the parts for yourself. Your partner can't be your other half. Whatever you are avoiding will have to be faced in recovery. You must become whole. You've been eating or starving to fill that vacuum of the unknown, disowned self.

From time to time you may undergo role reversals as you each try on new parts. As you both recover, you will each become more functional as separate individuals. As your relationships with people become healthier, your relationship with food will also become healthier. Food was used to avoid the risk of growing into full adulthood. Now let's see what emerged and what was left behind in your adult personality.

Extremism

As I said earlier, F-Os and their C-Ps gravitate toward opposite personality traits, becoming rigidly fixed in one mode or the other. These people are both attracted to, and repulsed by, their opposites. They work well together to keep conflict and control in the foreground. When they are busy trying to change the other, they have no time left to experiment with a more moderate position for themselves. By focusing on the other person, they ignore themselves.

Healthy recovery involves developing your personality so you have options about which behaviors to take on and when. With new behavior options, you will move closer to your center. It is not always worthwhile to be the outgoing life of the party, nor is it always essential to be neat and well groomed. You will practice becoming your opposite.

In treatment centers, patients are often given assignments to try on the opposite. They will be asked to take a full day of trying on behaviors the direct opposite of their normal behavior. In fact, when I created the HOPE House residential community, we actually gave people job assignments that had them accomplishing tasks totally outside their normal purview. For example, someone who worked as CEO of a company might be given the job of gardener. We'd ask a shy person to lead a meeting or go on a flirt assignment. We'd put a talkative person on silence. Taking on such a change acquaints people with a part of themselves they may have denied. This kind of change is difficult, especially when certain learned behaviors seem to work well and help you survive. You don't want to give them up. When trying on new behaviors, you risk and melt a little. When you are at risk, you feel more alive. You won't crave excess food to refuel a tank that is sluggish, nor will you need excess food to sedate yourself into upholding a false front. Natural cells constantly fuse and separate, and human behavior needs the same fluidity. By staying fixated and obsessed, you became unable to weather movement and change. Recovery is change. You grow or you go.

Reactors

F-Os are more responsive to external cues than internal motivation, or messages from their own bodies. In studies, obese and "normal" subjects were asked to go into a room and then report what they saw. Normal people reported seeing a chair, a desk, and a lamp. Obese subjects reported elaborate details of a blue-tweed chair, a Victorian desk, a picture on the wall with an autumnal scene, blue-speckled wallpaper. F-Os are highly sensitized to the environment and react to what comes toward them.

In doing math problems, the F-Os' performances diminished when music was played. Normal people continued at the same level despite external stimuli. F-Os are thrown off base by externals more easily than normal subjects. Similarly, F-Os tend to respond to external expectations. Placed in a room with no windows but with a clock, F-Os reported hunger and expected lunch when the clock showed noon. Normal people reported with dismay that they didn't feel like eating even though it was lunchtime. They responded to internal stimuli, listening to and trusting their own bodies.

Confluents, though not as responsive to food cues, are very sensitized to the feelings of others. This trait is an asset in helping-professions but can be anathema in a personal relationship. Constantly reacting to the needs of another allows little chance to develop a sensitivity to one's own needs. Remember how confluents tend to come from families with addictive parents? They develop an ability to watch closely and gauge another's feelings. This quality of surveying the outer landscape is known as hypervigilance. They have learned to walk on eggshells, to be overly helpful and sympathetic as a way of warding off criticism. They learned little in the way of making positive, assertive stands for themselves. Both F-Os and their confluents are highly responsive to others and too little in touch with themselves. Therefore, each needs to have the other around as a base from which to react.

Passive/Aggressive Struggles

In the relationships between F-Os and C-Ps, if one is the tough guy, the bully, the other will be fragile and dependent. "You wear the white hat; I'll take the black one." Two fairly typical patients in hospital treatment are Passive Pauline and Aggressive Angela. The passive one wants to lie back and say, "Wake me when it's over." She wants no active part in her recovery. "Just fix me," she says. She may warn the treatment staff that her case is so difficult that there is actually no cure possible. With "terminal uniqueness," Passive Pauline presents passivity and dependency as a challenge. "Prove to me, Doc, that you will make the difference." If the doctor has not closely examined his or her own needs to be a helper and fixer, both can have their problems perpetuated.

Passive individuals challenge a well-meaning confluent to try and make the difference. While the helper assumes the rescuer role, Pauline stays rigidly locked into passivity. Both are convinced that one is a failure and the other a fixer. Without a C-P, the passive person can't reach rock bottom. It takes two.

Aggressive Angela is just the opposite. She enters treatment aggressive and boisterous. She explains to everyone that she knows what works and what doesn't. She tells the counselors how to fix her. She begins with a highly critical and judgmental evaluation of the treatment team and then moves quickly to become a cotherapist and colleague of the therapy group leader. She has great difficulty receiving and being in a nurtured position. Eventually, she has to give up control and grieve. As much as she longs to be cared for, it is safer to be giving. (Often such patients are nurses. They have found a profession that helps them maintain their giver role but keeps them fat.)

Aggressive persons usually attach themselves to people who are needy. They will avoid people who want to give them something because these people are a much greater risk. When they give up the food obsession, they become needy and must learn how to receive. They will also start expecting more from the people they once helped.

Ego Struggles

Often called egomaniacs with inferiority complexes, F-Os and C-Ps have little sense of real personal worth. It is easier and safer to reflect others. It is a constant comparison game. Who am I? Compared to what? You seek out better-than or less-than relationships but can rarely tolerate one based on equality. Food gets abused in the process of maintaining the power balance. If, as an "inferior" person, you start feeling too good, you use the food to get back down into a degraded position again. If you were in the superior position, you may need to fall apart a little. You will expect your opposite to rise to the occasion.

Recovery involves assuming an image of yourself that has nothing to do with someone else's success or failure. You must gain a realistic picture of yourself. Then you will be free to love without a power struggle. In healthy relating you will exalt in being ordinary.

Anger Blockers

I have not met an F-O yet who was not raging within. F-Os use food to push down anger. Perhaps you saw inappropriate expressions of anger in childhood and are afraid to repeat the pattern. You judge anger as highly inappropriate. Rather than confronting an angry situation directly, you smile ingratiatingly and seethe within. C-Ps often exhibit the same avoidance of anger and quietly withdraw rather than air legitimate grievances.

Recovery involves acknowledging your anger and then telling someone else your feelings. You don't necessarily have to confront the object of your anger directly. You might vent enough by confiding in others. If you are an anger blocker, you may choose angry friends to talk for you. An F-O may express a C-P's anger so that he or she can maintain a nice-guy image. Food supplies energy to be angry. Giving up excess food may make you less willing to fight the old battles, whether yours or those of another.

Hopelessness Cycle

Why be angry? Food obsessives and confluents have years of failed attempts at controlling. You have lowered your expectations and have lost your motivation to take on anything new. This hopelessness must be expressed and acknowledged before recovery can begin. You both played out an elaborate game: one sad, the other happy-go-lucky. This works as long as each stays in character. But what happens when the long-suffering fat housewife says she will "go for it, no matter what" and is genuinely motivated and energized to develop a new life? What happens when she takes over the happy role? Where does that leave the confluent? Getting happy will upset the system. Often people don't want to hope again because they are afraid of change.

Magical Thinking

One surefire way to remain hopeless is to believe in magic. Magical thinking helps you remain a victim of the weight-loss, diet-fad mentality. You buy all the books and pills that promise an instant cure. In a way, you desperately want to believe they work, and they sometimes do—for brief periods. Because your body changed form so rapidly, it is easy to think your life could change just as easily. Even though thinner, you found problems you couldn't solve. So you returned to the abuse of food and made that your problem again. That at least has a magical solution.

Perfectionism

Well, because we can't control food, let's at least make sure everything else is perfect. It seems easier to be perfect in business, housecleaning, and child rearing than to deal with the food obsession. Both F-Os and confluents run co-workers, friends, and family ragged trying to maintain standards of perfection. You hope to mask your feelings of failure with regard to food. If not playing "perfect success," you may play "perfect failure." It takes just as much effort to fail as it does to go for it.

Low Frustration Tolerance

Perfection means "do it my way faster." You maintain highly ritualized standards of how things should operate, especially when it comes to how others should perform. To keep control of the situation, and especially the outcome, you devise elaborate scripts detailing where, how, and when people should speak, move, or breathe. When others don't perform to expectations, this is extremely irritating to you.

Many tell me, "You're wrong here. If there is one thing I can endure, it is frustration." They brag about the business and professional situations in which they keep a cool, corporate exterior. Of course, they were cool with food in the mix. Without the abuse of food, irritability rapidly rises. Excess food has enabled you to maintain serenity while others panicked. Without food abuse, you may become the captain of chaos. However, if you can keep your head while those around you are losing theirs, perhaps you don't adequately understand the situation.

Moralistic Attitudes

Another aspect of perfectionism is to maintain an impossibly high standard of morality for yourself and others. F-Os and confluents can carry on fierce philosophical discussions about morality. You can maintain excessive standards as long as you keep shoveling the food in. I continued to date alcoholics and excessive drinkers as long as I wanted to maintain a superior position in relationships. This kept me eating and drinking. I lectured them constantly for their behaviors while I took the moral high ground. When I was no longer comfortable berating them, I instead chose men I could respect and not put down.

Perhaps the C-P is living out the opposite side of this equation, balancing immorality to the tune of the F-O's morality. Maybe the F-O is a secret seductress and afraid to get thin to find this out. Many feel that, if let loose, they will go raping and pillaging through the streets.

Sexual orientation is another aspect of personality that must get renegotiated. If you don't address this issue, you may stay fat and celibate and leave the runaround role for others. You might feel more satisfied to sit in judgment.

All-or-Nothing Mentality

Nothing gradual or moderate gets attention in F-O relationships. The complaint with recovery is "Serenity is boring." To reach higher highs and correspondingly lower lows, the F-Os and C-Ps keep extremes neatly balanced. Either you are rigidly stuck on an abusive, restrictive food plan, or you eat the refrigerator bare. You turn your perfectionistic expectations to food and use any deviation as an excuse to binge. The dieting mentality feeds right into this problem. Ritualized prescriptions of what to eat create dogged adherence followed by rejection of the whole plan with a return to bingeing.

I am constantly amused to read that one cup of air-popped popcorn contains fifty-five calories. F-Os don't eat one cup of anything. How about the calorie count for a tub of buttered popcorn? Why bother doing anything unless done to excess?

Workaholics

You might hope that if you work hard enough and succeed, your professional accomplishments will camouflage your food obsession. This is surely the wish of many young career women—rapid achievers in a competitive world who binge and vomit nightly. Success in one area makes up for lack of control in another.

Often, the workaholic will be a confluent personality who, failing to cure a spouse or child, tries to prove him- or herself in other areas to feel accomplished. In recovery, many workaholics become just average, so-so workers. No longer needing to prove themselves or cover up food obsessions, they begin to put in an honest day for an honest dollar, no more and no less. This can present problems at work where the employer enjoyed the fruits of the obsession. That boss may try to re-create the old system.

People Pleasers

To prevent others from saying anything about your weight problem, you might decide to be the nice guy at all costs. If others enjoy your company, they will excuse your appearance, or so goes the rationale.

F-Os and C-Ps both learn to anticipate the needs of others in order to fit in, becoming chameleons, adapting to the needs of others. In relating to each other, one may take on the role of sweetheart, while the other plays the sullen grouch. The people pleaser keeps excusing and explaining the behavior of the grouch. Unfortunately your true feelings in the situation get pushed down with food.

Fear of Success

Despite being excessive workaholics and superachievers, F-Os and confluents fear success. (In chapter 8 you'll learn more about how this fear manifests itself.) Some of it has to do with leaving your suffering family behind, and some has to do with the fear that when you achieve success, you'll have to *maintain* it. Remember your standards of perfection? If your true capabilities are known, you fear you will be expected to perform at maximum efficiency at all times. Since you can't possibly meet your own standard, it's easier not to succeed at all. This fear of success holds true with weight loss. Many get down to within ten pounds of goal weight and start back up again. In recovery you learn to tolerate *progress, not perfection* and accept the fact that, even though successful, you *will* have bad days. Big girls *do* cry.

Fear of Intimacy

You fear intimacy for the same reason you fear success. You can't endure the expectation that you might have to *maintain* it. Trained through film and TV, you think true intimacy involves eyeball-to-eyeball seriousness and deep catharsis or sharing. Who would want to stay locked in that? It's fine for TV, but even on TV, they cut to commercials. Even the most dramatic intimate scenes in a movie last but a few seconds. Who could tolerate more? Just as cells in nature come together and divide, your closeness needs the same ebb and flow. You might feel cuddly and close one day, and the next, each go to separate rooms to read the paper. What's wrong with that? In *The Prophet*, Kahlil Gibran advises, "Allow for spaces in your togetherness."

Isolationists

With so many conflicts about intimacy, distance, achieving, failing, working, quitting, anger, and pleasing, it is no wonder

F-Os and C-Ps would rather be alone. At least when alone you have no one's expectations but your own. Unfortunately, as your food obsession progresses, it becomes less and less tolerable to be alone. There is too much guilt and self-loathing and worry. Food becomes the only relief from overactive self-loathing. Eventually, however, food also stops working and turns on you.

The way out is through people, but not just anybody. It is easy to win friends and influence people by being helpers and people pleasers. You can find people who will "like" you very much when you say and do what they want. But that's not what you need. If that had helped, you wouldn't be obsessed with food right now. You've actually been winning friends through presenting a false front, a chameleon-like adaptation rather than who you really are. To "relate to recover," you need a way to talk and be heard by people who honestly want to know the real you. You need to be able to show the real person inside instead of the "self for others" you played out with food.

That can happen with other people who have been where you've been and found a way out. In Marilyn French's *The Women's Room,* she explains, "Loneliness is not a longing for company. It's a longing for *kind.*" F-Os and C-Ps find their "kind" in Overeaters Anonymous. This is where you can talk and be heard. With your "kind," you can share the pain of suffering a food obsession, find comfort, and then move on. You will also want to listen as you hear from others who've been there and are now finding ways to live without obsession.

Trading Roles for Realities

There's more to lose than fat. There's also much more to gain than just a fleeting thinness. When your relationships change, you won't want to go back to the old system. You won't even be able to. The new you can't act on the old stage. Those old stereotypical roles will seem boring to you. Let's take a look at the old roles and the new approaches that lead out of addiction.

THE VICTIM. This is the starring role for our fat family's drama. Without the continued suffering of the F-O, everyone else is quickly displaced. This is partly why the F-O has to keep suffering. By suffering, you are ensuring that those around you remain secure and protected. The victim, though hurting, is a subtle blamer. "You made me this way. You have to fix me."

There is a great deal of strength in failing. Just by the law of averages, you are bound to succeed 50 percent of the time. If you continue to fail regularly, you must be working at it. Thus, the victim holds great unleashed power and energy. The victim's blaming is never too direct, as that would reveal too much strength. Instead, the victim shows continual self-loathing and guilt as a way to deny personal possibilities for happiness. This also keeps everyone else in the family working to fix him or her. Thank God our loved one stays sick. In this way, he or she is the family scapegoat. All can complain, "We'd be happy if only _____ would get it together."

If the F-O does not continue this role of victim, someone else in the family will take it on. This person is actually a family hero and serves as the excuse for all to stay grounded instead of soaring.

As long as the F-O continues to suffer, those of you who are confluents won't have to test your own capacities for happiness. To recover, you will have to find your own way, whether you cured the F-O or not. You will have to risk trying on new happy-face behaviors. You will have to take personal responsibility for yourself.

The former victim used to complain, "I'm a hopeless failure and just won't ever make it."

The recovering victim now declares, "Today, I'm doing the best I can. At least I'm getting started, and that's all I can manage today."

THE ENABLER. If the victim holds star billing in this drama, the enabler is certainly the most important supporting actor. Enablers wear the white hats while F-Os don the black ones (in the mind of the enabler, of course). As an enabler, you provide stability in an unstable system. You are great organizers, workers, and successes in business. You promptly do chores or whatever else is asked. As children, you do well in school, exhibit strong leadership qualities, and are usually highly goal-oriented, known as having realistic, rational minds.

Outwardly, you espouse feelings of high self-esteem, but you rarely develop intimate personal relationships. In that area, you don't quite feel worthwhile. If asked to give up rigid control or open boundaries to others, you become fearful. It's safer to control by helping. With only slight encouragement from the F-O, you move in to take on the whole job of recovery. You will need to move out of the way so the F-O can fall apart if necessary. Let the F-O sink or swim alone.

The active enabler says, "I refused the party invitation because I knew you couldn't handle the food."

The recovering enabler declares, "Your friend Jane phoned about the restaurant party. I figured you'd know how you want to handle it. She's waiting for your call back."

THE PERSECUTOR. The persecutor role is usually played by a parent or spouse. This role serves the dual function of helping the victim remain sick (enabling) and, at the same time, blaming him or her for being sick (persecuting). It is a double message. You rescue and cajole the F-O for a certain amount of time. Then patience runs out, and you begin to criticize and demand perfection. Like the buzzards perched atop a dried cactus branch, you finally scream, "The hell with patience. I want to kill something!" The one you want to kill is the F-O, and though you're not actually killing, your rage lies just below the surface.

The angry feelings are usually masked with a thin veil of "helpful" manipulations. Though critical, the persecutor, in the enabling part of the role, is also the constant pusher, encouraging a binge "just this once." Persecutors suffer great pain in this dual personality.

As a persecutor, you have to find a way to express anger directly. You must first reject the eating disorder. Your message to the F-O will be, "I love you but hate your disease. I won't support this self-destructive behavior any longer. You've got your troubles; I've got mine."

Once you voice this position, be quiet. You don't need to keep haranguing, and you don't need to move in to help. Speak your piece and back off.

You will also have to find a way to forgive yourself for your old punitive stands. You really don't like yourself that way, but you have responded to the frustrations of your own powerlessness. The best way to forgive yourself is to begin immediately to change your behavior. No elaborate speeches are needed. No declarations of future perfection are called for.

The active persecutor says, "You are a weak-willed glutton and you disgust me."

The recovering persecutor says, "It hurts me to watch your suffering, but I know you'll recover without my help."

Persecutors and enablers want some appreciation for all the effort they've expended. You had hoped you could shame the F-O into shaping up. Instead, the illness got worse.

One of the saddest families I've ever treated involved an overeater/alcoholic mother who was admitted to our hospital's emergency room with lacerations to the face and neck. She lived down the block and was brought in by her twelve-year-old daughter, Emily. Upon later investigation, we found that early that morning she had promised Emily she was beginning a diet and going on the wagon. That afternoon, upon returning from school, Emily found her mother passed out in the kitchen atop cracker and chip boxes along with an empty bottle of bourbon. In her rage and frustration, Emily beat her mother's face with a shoe. Imagine the pain this daughter feels from both loving and hating her mother. In this case, the daughter needed help in accepting her rage and forgiving herself as another victim of the illness.

Part of Emily's victimization was that early on she adopted the parental role of managing the household. Emily saw Mom as too nervous and suffering to handle her own responsibilities. Daughter Emily was the enabler as well as the persecutor. Emily likes managing but hates it too. She will have to learn to be a child again rather than Mom's mommy. She'll also have to forgive Mom for not being well enough before. She has to give up wanting to be paid back. She may spend a lifetime in abusive relationships to try to get paid back, but it will never work. She will only be free when she finds a way to nurture herself and get what she needs from surrogates—people other than Mom.

THE CLOWN. Both F-Os and C-Ps would love to be clowns. They want to laugh to avoid crying, and they also believe, "Laugh and the world laughs with you. Cry and you cry alone."

As a clown, you see the family's suffering and develop a sense of humor as a form of diversion. You are quick, witty, and fun to be around. You laugh and play and pretend life is light. You espouse a devil-may-care, *c'est la vie* attitude but are actually closely tuned to the suffering. You are a reactor rather than an actor. Joking or distracting, you pretend you are irrelevant, just hanging around for comic relief. You rarely ask to be taken seriously.

As a clown, you have seen the chaotic addicted family system and decided not to play. You create distractions to help the family avoid intimacy. Acting uninvolved, you approach a heated family battle and ask innocently, "Are we going to the beach next Saturday?" You hope such distractions help others avoid pain. You see intimacy as death. Denying intimacy, you don't know how to take yourself seriously. Often developing your own alternate addiction is the only way to relax or be taken seriously. You have spent so much time distracting that you have become distracted from yourself. You often think the following:

Let me make a joke of myself before you do.

At all costs, let's keep things light.

Why make a big deal of everything?

Why is everyone serious?

The active clown spoofs, "I'm such a tub o' lard I know I'll break the chair."

The recovering clown says, "I feel badly about my situation. I need to talk and be heard."

THE HERO. Often a sibling, fellow worker, or spouse, the hero decides to excel and achieve to prove that all is well. You try to cover up suffering. You appear sensitive and insightful and aware of others as well as feeling extremely responsible. You push to achieve and accomplish in order to make things better for everyone. In recovery, you may have to learn how to fall apart. When you move aside, you create room for the "failing" F-O to show his or her stuff and measure up. When the hero dominates the success spotlight, the F-O stays sick so as not to displace anyone.

The active hero brags, "Don't worry, Scarlett, I'll be here ever-ready to solve your problems."

The recovering hero says, "It's really up to you. Frankly, Scarlett, I've got better things to do."

THE RECLUSE. At all costs, make no waves. The quiet and shy recluse senses the anxiety and fear of the family and decides to withdraw to avoid contributing to the family's suffering. You feel the family suffers enough and want to shrivel up to have no effect. If you withdraw, you feel successful. Often the recluse is a child who spends much time alone, demanding little attention, inviting comments such as "At least this is the one child I don't have to worry about." You learned that family involvement revolves around sickness. Not knowing how to play sick, you'd rather not play at all. In recovery, you will have to discover new personal excitement and learn to have fun. You have to release the energy you've been holding back and risk having an impact on others. You can't avoid it. You *do* exist, and you *do* have an effect.

The active recluse withdraws, saying, "Don't consider me. I'll make my own way."

The recovering recluse takes action by saying, "Count me in. I'm to be considered also."

THE SURVIVORS. All members of this enabling system have learned to adjust and survive. Some have even turned suffering into a badge of courage or martyrdom. You all know how to adjust. You've learned to be compliant and amenable to others. Great at following directions, you may also seek employment that offers constant uncertainty (commission sales or publishing deadlines). You know how to anticipate the needs of others and adapt with chameleon-like rapidity. Underneath all the surviving is deep depression and loneliness because you never learned to represent your true self. You try at all costs to avoid expressing feelings. Expressing feelings rarely got anything but criticism. When sad, no comfort was available. When angry, you were punished. When expressing yourself, you were usually ignored. You learned to adjust and manipulate others, but ultimately lost yourself. In recovery, you will have to learn how to express your feelings honestly and not be overly burdened by the needs and troubles of others.

The active survivor says, "I'll take on whatever burdens I have to and won't make waves. Phew! Look at all I've overcome."

The recovering survivor says, "Even though I may be able to handle this, I really don't care to—thanks. It's not my job."

Serenity Is Boring

Without help, family members drift farther apart into their separate isolation and loneliness. The system survives as long as the addiction is operating. Everyone has silently, and often unconsciously, made compromises to the disease process. Often, the family has become isolated from the community. Party invitations have been refused, public functions are avoided, and children's school activities aren't supported. Family members have developed the attitude that it doesn't matter. Husbands tell themselves, "I really didn't want to go to the party anyway." Children sigh, "It's really not important if Mom comes along." Sexually frustrated husbands surmise that perhaps they are too demanding and need to give their spouses rest. Family members even begin to doubt their own perceptions:

Did Mom really promise to take me to the park, or did I make it up?

I thought for sure she said she wanted to go to the store.

Why is she just sitting there eating?

Family members have adjusted to such chaotic, unpredictable situations. They live in constant uncertainty. They do not know how to live calmly. Violent contact is seen as an expression of caring and involvement. The calmness that comes in recovery is seen as withdrawal and lack of love. Family members sometimes try to re-create the old conflicts so that they will feel involved and close again. They sometimes complain that the situation has become boring at home. What do they share in common now? The opposite situation can also exist. If, while eating, the overeater tended to withdraw from contact, others learned to live without her. In recovery they may secretly resent her "returning home" and upsetting the system.

Remember Emily who beat her mother's face with a shoe? How does young daughter Emily give up her homemaker role when Mom returns sober? She has to give up her premature power and responsibility. Children often complain that they liked it better when Mom ate because she noticed fewer of their misdeeds. Even though "Dad yelled a lot," they could get around him because Mom was really in charge anyway.

Family Message Center

Ralph had alcoholic parents and felt bad about not being able to help them. So he married obese Katherine and tried to help her. Ralph, Katherine, and their seventeen-year-old son Bernard eventually came to family group therapy. Their first night in family group was early in the mother's recovery. The father started the session by yelling at his son, "Your mom is upset and feels like you are ignoring her." They conversed about this for a few minutes while Katherine watched silently. Ralph had been the caretaker for his alcoholic parents and showed his value by being in the middle of family interaction. His wife, Katherine, had known how he needed to be needed so had early on given most of her power over to him. Thus, he could feel valued, and she could secretly eat.

When I asked her to address her son directly, Katherine

began accusing him of never paying any attention to her and of always being self-centered. She really needed something from this boy, but rather than ask directly, she had developed a style familiar in addicted families. She began blaming. She would rather accuse him than share her needs with him.

In the family group session, I asked Katherine to try to find another way to get her needs met.

I started by saying, "After all, Katherine, there is clearly something you *want* from this boy. Let's see if you can go at it in a way to get your own needs met."

At this point, Katherine began to cry. She faced her son and through her tears said, "I am so scared that you are angry at me because I need this help. I am afraid you are saying I am a fool and why wasn't I strong enough to handle this on my own."

Instead of judging, Bernard leaned over, hugged her closely, and said, "No, Mom. I'm really glad you are finally asking for some help. It's clear you've really been trying on your own but not getting results. I'll support you in any way I can." They hugged silently while Katherine sobbed. Dad tried to intervene. He needed to break up some of the closeness so he could feel important again. I reassured him that he was a good father and that his best effort would be to let them work it out alone.

In this particular family situation, Mom was a secret eater. But it wasn't her eating that needed review, it was the family's relating. In this family, Mom was anesthetized. This father and son fought out her grievances. She was never expected to stand up for herself. The two males were kept distant from each other by fighting Mom's battles or fighting over Mom.

Now, Mom and son fight their own battles directly, and the men can have their own relationship, separate from Mom. Mom and Dad can also get closer. They don't complain about Bernard so much. They find other things to talk about. If Mom has complaints, she goes directly to the source.

Katherine eventually became very assertive with both her husband and her son. When Ralph tried to talk for her in a subsequent group, she reminded him, "Don't speak for me. I can take care of myself." As he stopped being the disciplinarian in the family, he and his son got closer. They even allied with grievances against Mom. Katherine began confronting her husband directly rather than demurely sending her son in. This produced a more conflicted marital relationship for a while but also a renewed sexual appetite for both partners. As her weight dropped and her insecurities lessened and she fought her own battles, a long dormant energy emerged, and Katherine felt a new interest in sex. She started taking Ralph to bed instead of sending him into the ring.

Please Mom, I Don't Wanna Go

Even though there have been at least two generations of women who have entered the workforce since the women's liberation movement, there are still quite a few traditional mind-sets that linger. Some mothers who have cherished being stay-at-home moms want the same for their daughters. When some of these daughters decide to pursue careers and rewards outside the home, Mom may experience this as a slap in the face. As a daughter chooses a lifestyle different from her mother's, the mom feels rejected. Painful partings can result, and if not addressed honestly, the conflict comes out over the plate or the toilet bowl.

This was true for Elvira and her mother, Vanessa. Elvira found that her mom had built an entire identity around being a mother. Jim and Vanessa Ferguson married because both were graduating college, and it seemed the thing to do. Vanessa had majored in home economics and knew her calling was mothering. Relating with Jim was not a priority in her

131

life; she saw him as an instrument on her way to her higher calling: motherhood. She flowered into motherhood and focused all her attentions on her daughter. She really didn't like talking with Jim all that much anyway. She made her entire identity around raising and grooming Elvira for her eventual marriage and motherhood. Even after Elvira moved away to college, her mother believed she'd just stay long enough to get an "MRS" degree. She believed that then Elvira would get married and have kids, and they'd have mothering in common and a lot to talk about.

The high point of Vanessa's life was Elvira's weekly call from the dorm. But as Elvira moved into her sophomore year, Vanessa sensed a change in her daughter; a change she didn't like. Elvira started really liking some upper-level classes and talked about majoring in physics and going on to graduate school. When they had weekly chats, Elvira didn't have much to say about decorating, dressing, or makeup—all the things her mother enjoyed. Vanessa felt left out. When Elvira talked about joking around with dormmates, sometimes sharing an off-color joke, her mother felt particularly resentful. Her daughter was learning too much from other people, people whose values Vanessa didn't accept. She didn't like her daughter's choice of interests or friends. It seemed like her daughter was having too much of both freedom and fun and like she wasn't keeping herself focused on the "right" goals: marriage and motherhood. Elvira wasn't even a good confidante and companion anymore. She was no longer interested in hearing about Mom and Dad's arguments. Once she responded, "Mom, my friends and I aren't ready to take men all that seriously. We just want to have fun right now."

Elvira was shocked when her mother shot back, "Sure, just hang out in those college dorm whorehouses." The statement was so shocking; there was no way for Elvira to understand how displaced her mother felt. She was being attacked because she was becoming less attached. Her mom didn't know how to weather the parting. Elvira started to see that she had never felt like a real person on her own. It seemed every breath she took and every thought or action had to somehow be referenced back to her mother. Her mother worked hard to keep her accountable and responsible. It was as if Mom was out of her own mind but inside her skin. The only time she felt alone and independent was after she vomited. Exhausted and spent, she felt a euphoric separateness come over her.

By her senior year, Elvira registered at the campus guidance center to see a counselor for a few sessions. She was having panic attacks, vomiting incessantly, and very afraid to go on to graduate school. She didn't feel like she was living her own life. She found that even if her mom needed children, she herself needed to grow up and be her own adult.

She began to understand that her mother had wanted to be a better mother than her own mother had been. With her own daughter she could play catch-up ball. Elvira had to become a good mother. That would make Vanessa feel like she'd done a good job. Elvira saw that her mother's agenda and needs were about proving something to herself. That task was established long before Elvira came on the scene. Elvira wanted to separate herself from her mother's programming.

Elvira had to face a painful picture: that of leaving her mother behind to solve the problems in her own life. Many recovering daughters have faced this painful crossroad. *Fat & Furious* is a whole book about this struggle. These daughters have to walk away and let their moms figure out and fix their own identity struggles. Elvira knew she had to create some distance; her mom's agenda was so powerful, there was really no way to exist without following the established program.

She wrote a painful letter of separation:

Dear Mom,

I don't really expect you to understand how I feel. You really don't even notice how definite you are about what you think is best for me. Quite honestly, it feels somewhat insulting as you don't seem to question or care to find out what I really think or want. It's like you've already decided what you know I'll like. You say so definitely, "All women want children, and if they don't have them, they feel incomplete." I'm not sure I buy that, Mom. At least for now, I feel very content with my lifestyle, and I am more interested in learning than in caring for someone else. Quite frankly, I don't want the responsibility, and I do want the freedom to come and go and develop my life as I please. You made different choices. I'm glad you decided to have a child, and I'm glad I'm here. I can't say for sure I want to give another being that gift of life. I'm not sure I want to raise any children. I'm just not sure, and until I am, I need to shy away from some of your discussions. There just seems to be too much pressure to do things your way. I'm busy trying to find out what is "my way." So I hope you will understand if I remain silent or even leave the room if some of that talk starts up. I love you but have to love my own choices as well.

The letter was sent, and Mom didn't respond. It took three separate occasions of Elvira leaving the room when her mother started ooing, aahing, and cooing about some neighbors and their new babies before Mom started to change. Eventually she stopped emphasizing those things when Elvira was around. Elvira then felt safer to visit, as she knew she could leave if the going got rough. She also stopped vomiting and went on to graduate school.

"We've Only Just Begun"

How poignant it is to close this chapter by quoting one of gifted singer Karen Carpenter's greatest hits. She was a pop singer of the 1970s and one of the first public figures to admit her anorexia. Because she'd gained and shed so much weight with the world watching and let us in on her bouts with starvation, there was a media frenzy after her death. I attended her funeral, which was a painful day for thousands of fans lining the streets of her small Los Angeles suburb.

Even though many in the crowd protested that "it wasn't anorexia; it was a heart attack," Karen died of anorexia nervosa. She had just regained twenty-five pounds with induced medications. Her heart could not stand the strain. Most people think the cure for anorexia is to get patients eating. Not so. In fact, the refeeding stage is the most dangerous part of anorexia because life-threatening edema and heart problems can surface.

Refeeding is also the time during which patients are at the most risk of committing suicide. (Anorexia has the highest suicide rate of any psychiatric illness.) While patients are feeling stronger and depression is lifting, they may have more faculties to gather the wherewithal to carry it out. Also, let's not forget that the patient sees suicidal starvation as a "solution." The only way to take that "solution" away is to offer something in its stead. If there is no alternative offered, patients can feel quite anxious without their former comforting, though destructive, behavior.

Karen, though loved by millions of fans, could not find a way to get her neediness filled. Her personal relationships were unsatisfying, and she suffered an F-O's loneliness in a crowd. Actually, F-Os do die of heart failure. We die of the inability to find a way to get our hearts filled.

· THE WEIGH OUT ·

CHAPTER 5

Accept That It's Difficult

Now that you've examined how you got this far, it's time to face and truly accept living with a lifelong chronic illness. Personality change is the only reprieve. To give up the love affair with food, you will learn new ways to love and be loved by people. That's scary. It seems easier to remain judgmental and tease yourself with so-called "willpower" and "firm resolve." The rationale to remain aloof and judgmental rather than turning to others seems to have validity. You have been disappointed by other people so often. You chose the secure comfort of food over the unpredictable comfort of other people. Battered and disillusioned, you really can't raise your hopes anymore. Hope itself is threatening.

Even though I'd been an international expert in addiction treatment and even though I'd sent hundreds of alcoholics to AA and even though I'd cried in hospital staff meetings about how fat I was and how I saw us treating all these alcoholics and how I'd wished there was something similar for me, I still could not believe I'd really have to take such drastic measures. This was only a food problem after all. At that time, we didn't even know such help existed for me. Even though we were in Los Angeles, the birthplace of Overeaters Anonymous (OA), we didn't have a clue. I worked with world-famous psychiatrists who saw me bring Tupperware containers of salad into our lunch-hour meetings who answered my cries and pleas with, "There is no hope for people like you. You've always been that way, and you're always gonna be that way." I cried some more.

When I finally found out there was something similar to AA for overeaters and resolved to get help for myself, I didn't tell anyone I was planning on going to the meetings. I didn't want anyone to see me fail again. I felt I could take it, but *they* couldn't. I didn't tell my husband. I didn't tell any of my colleagues, other addiction counselors. I knew it wouldn't work, and I couldn't put them through any more pain. My confluent personality convinced me that I could handle pain that others couldn't. I see today that I may have wanted to reserve my right to fail. I didn't want anyone else involved. I also didn't want to accept for myself how the obsession dominated my life.

When I treated an aged skid-row alcoholic, he growled in group, "I'm John and I'm no alcoholic. I'm a drunk." He didn't want to acknowledge having an illness but instead wanted to judge himself. He later came to realize that derogatory name-calling could keep him drinking. But once he confessed to being an alcoholic, he saw possibilities for help in doing something about it. The recognition leads to recovery.

That same awareness is vital to an F-O's recovery. You must accept that you are different from "normies," or normal eaters, and have different struggles with food. Often I am asked to explain the difference between food obsessives and normies. The simplest difference is that when the server brings the meal, normies finish their sentences. If you don't understand that answer, you are probably a normie. Every normally neurotic American is into dieting—Monday through Friday and alternate weekends, right? That is not an F-O's situation. You have an *obsession* with food. It dominates and rules your life. You already addressed the evolution of this obsession to its chronic stage. Now is the moment to admit you can no longer play around with this substance casually. You can't join those cocktail-party discussions. The latest fad diet is not for you. You obviously won't stop eating altogether, but your old obsessive relationship with food has to go.

It isn't easy to admit you are sick. I'm not suggesting that you make yourself a buffoon, telling the old jokes you told, ridiculing yourself before anyone else could: "I'm such a sickee." I'm talking about truly admitting to your innermost self that you actually have done your best over and over and still end up in obsession. You will have to admit over and over again that, despite your best efforts, you're defeated and are in serious trouble, needing serious intervention. You have surely felt this way before, even if only for a fleeting moment. Then you quickly and conveniently forgot how bad things were.

Really negotiating a lasting recovery involves a constant, continual, and deep acceptance of the seriousness of this affliction. This is not easy for you or for those who love you. It is especially difficult without the comfort of excess food. Let's begin now to accept the fact that you have spent a lifetime being powerless over food. All of your previous attempts at control have landed you in this spot right now.

Accepting Powerlessness

"Yes, it is that bad . . . and without help it will get worse!" By picking up this book, you took the first essential step to recovery. You already leafed through most of the quickie books and easier, softer ways and found them to be anything but quick and easy.

The old line goes, "There's good news, and there's bad news." So, first the bad news. Every F-O and C-P must face the fact that they are suffering from a lifelong illness, an illness that requires extreme measures to overcome.

Now, the good news. Just because it is difficult doesn't make it impossible. And as soon as you accept that recovery is difficult—once you understand the disease and the necessity for dramatic change—recovery is no longer so difficult. Amazing as it may seem, saying "we know how hard it is" makes it easier. No matter how many doctors handed you twelve-hundred-calorie diets across big brown desks, not one of them has ever said, "I know how hard this is to follow." You were just handed a piece of paper with an implied expectation that you certainly could follow directions without any further help. But if you could have followed those directions, *you wouldn't have been in that office in the first place.* You already know what to do. If you could have, you would have. The truth is, you can't do it alone. This illness must be treated with respect. I have tried all my life to control myself, and I can't. It's embarrassing but true.

It is not easy to reach this stage of profound acceptance. I'm sure you have probably come close before, or you wouldn't be here now. In the past, you probably felt sure you could mobilize all your willpower and fight as long as needed. You reached a goal weight and clenched your fists to begin. The problem was that you assumed the mobilization would only be needed for a week, a month, a year at the very most. We get this idea from the false notion that once we have handled our weight, we have handled our problem. This is not true. Despite your white-knuckle resolve, you ended up holding on to the following false beliefs:

- I want to believe that it's just a weight problem.
- I refuse to pay attention to my eating for the rest of my life.
- I promise, "When I get thin, I'll never gain it back."

What you end up with are the reasons for failure rather than the results of success. For any result to last, you must continually acknowledge and attend to having a lifelong chronic illness. This must be considered in all matters at all times. You cannot put it on the back burner and forget it, as much as you might like to. This illness permeates life's every moment. Think about how many of your waking hours are spent obsessing about what you will or will not eat, wear or not wear, achieve or not achieve. You must make recovery permeate your life as much as the suffering used to. Instead of living a dress rehearsal, you must begin today accepting life where you are now and who you are now. This is not a drill. This is not a dress rehearsal. *This is your life. This is it!*

In this chapter you will see where you are on the road to acceptance. The stages are fluid. You may jump back and forth and could be in two or three stages at once. By the end of the chapter, you will find where you are on the road and identify your own major coping mechanism. Let's begin.

The Road to Acceptance

You are being asked to recognize the seriousness of this disease and the uselessness of simple half measures. I learned this through my own self-observation as well as from sessions with patients who minimized. Later, when I read Dr. Elisabeth Kübler-Ross's description of her work with patients facing imminent death, I was struck by similarities. Her dying patients traveled through five distinct stages to reach acceptance: denial, anger, bargaining, depression, and finally, acceptance. In *On Death and Dying,* Dr. Kübler-Ross concludes that her patients are actually accepting their powerlessness over a force that will soon dominate and ultimately end their very lives. I see my patients travel through these same five stages in accepting any serious illness. This holds true for an overeater, alcoholic, blind person, paraplegic, quadriplegic, or anyone. The issue for every one of these persons is that life has dealt them a hand they did not expect or appreciate but one they would ultimately have to accept.

You do not have to accept this all at once, nor do you even have to feel accepting all the time. "The only way out is through," states Fritz Perls, father of Gestalt therapy. As Dr. Perls puts it, "Once we accept fully and completely exactly who and what we are, we have then given up the struggle to 'be someone else.'" In accepting ourselves, we automatically become someone else. In other words, we move from being a self-hater—a person who says, "I should be different"—to a person who echoes Popeye the sailor and says, "I yam what I yam and that's all what I yam."

Radical Self-Acceptance

Are you really ready for radical self-acceptance? Can you take the necessary steps to accept where you are right now as the best of all possible worlds? Even if you don't like it, can you accept that it must be the correct consequence of all you've been and done to this point? Can you accept that where you are is where you should be? You may have to face a lot. See how much of the following you can buy:

- Your best friend, food, has turned on you.
- You have tried everything already and ended up right here.
- Your obsession with food fits right in with how you have been living your life.
- No guru out there is going to fix your obsession for you.
- Your obsession with food has got the best of you.

When Dr. Kübler-Ross began her research, she asked hospital staff whether she could counsel the dying patients. Agitated and fearful nurses told her, "Oh, no one dies here."

The hospitals had elaborate procedures for the care of dying patients and definite courses of action for when a patient did die. They had their own morgue and even separate driveways for hearses. Still, the answer she got was, "Oh, no one dies here."

This is denial most blatant. Thus, Dr. Kübler-Ross's first task was confronting the denial system. The denial in food obsessions is no less blatant and no less difficult to confront. Sufferers may admit they have food obsessions but won't accept that the problems are lifelong and chronic. Facing the severity of the disease is just as hard as accepting death. You're putting to death an old obsessional way of life, trading a life of battling for a life of surrender. You must also mourn the loss of that old relationship with your best friend. You must surrender to the fact that your best friend has turned on you.

In facing food obsessions, the denial stage is probably the most prevalent and definitely the deadliest. You deny the harsh reality of having a chronic and often terminal illness. You desperately want to believe you really have a minor ailment that you will soon treat by yourself —"as soon as I'm ready." You deny that the illness is affecting every area of your life and that its arrest will require major life changes. "I know I can diet whenever I want to," you say. "I'll start tomorrow or next Monday." How many years has that gone on? You would like this to be a simple project that won't require too much effort or too much disruption in your lifestyle. To think like that is to remain self-deluded, believing that the whole thing is "no big deal" and that "I can handle it myself." You don't recognize how pervasive denial has become.

There is another aspect of denial, which is often reinforced by well-meaning C-Ps: "All you need is a little more willpower." This only adds guilt and self-loathing. The truth is that lack of willpower is not your problem. On the contrary, you have an abundance of determination and willpower when it is in the service of others. You may be known as the best worker at your job. You are known as a really good friend, always there in time of need. You typically exhibit a great deal of power and strength. All of which, of course, does nothing for your lifelong terminal illness. At this point it should be obvious that willpower has absolutely nothing to do with this illness.

Yet denial does not stop even here. Many try wearing bright clothing and jewelry or eye-catching hairdos, hoping that no one will notice the fat. You might have great nail jobs, shoes, and hats, all focusing the view out to the periphery so no one will look at your body. But surely, you must be able to see the enormity of your flesh. How can you deny so obvious a problem? Quite easily, and here's how. Whether you are fat or thin, you don't have a realistic sense of your own body image. You have spent many years with a fluid body configuration. One year you wore size eight all summer, and then the next year size twenty-four seems snug. It seems reasonable to think that *the dryer is shrinking my clothes.* Most of you put on and take off weight so fast that you amass great poundage without even noticing. Not seeing realistically is a way to continue the weight gain/loss cycle.

You have gained and lost thousands of pounds throughout your life, so you assume this is normal for all folks. I used to gain twenty pounds in a weekend. You have spent countless mornings paying homage to a flat spring-driven contraption—the Great Scale God. Even this god cannot conquer denial. DENIAL stands for **Don't Even Notice I Am Lying.**

Take the case of Patricia. She is an attractive and intelligent businesswoman with a definite image of herself and an expectation of what her poundage should be. She knew she was overweight, and she was intellectually very clear about the top weight she would never surpass. Her weight fluctuated from 150 to 180 pounds. This was her "hovering weight," the numbers around which she could hover without great distress. If Great Scale God stayed within these figures, all was still right with her world. Life worked. After each bout with a newly published diet, or before a social event where a dress size was the goal and fasting the method, Patricia expected to weigh in at about 150 pounds. Between Thanksgiving and New Year's, or after a vacation, she expected to weigh close to 180. This was distasteful, albeit predictable, understandable, and acceptable. It fit in with her self-concept and expectations. Patricia knew that if she ever hit 181, an alarm bell immediately sent her to pills or fat farms. Her self-image remained intact and all was right with the world, because she weighed no more than 180 pounds. Then something happened.

Unexpected professional reverses drove Patricia into seeking solace with even more excess food. Bingeing helped her work later hours, trying to recoup her losses. Her food consumption continued unchecked. Patricia did not find time to get on a scale for three months. This is not unusual. It is common for denial systems to help us misplace scales, calorie counters, or tight-fitting clothing. Patricia forged on, oblivious to everything.

Then, when the business crisis was finally over and Patricia once more found her bathroom scale, she weighed 202 pounds. Impossible! This figure would not register with her image of who she was. Denial sprang up like a demon to keep Patricia's self-image intact. "There must be some mechanical error," it crooned to her. Patricia's answer was quite simple—she threw away the scale. Absurd? Maybe. Yet this is not uncommon for F-Os. Many have not weighed themselves for years. First the scale is worshiped, then renounced and discarded. This is denial.

Patricia must first weigh in and face the scale. She must face reality and smash denial. She must take a look at how, using excessive work pressures as the excuse, she keeps bingeing. To say no to excess food, she may have to say no to some of the work assignments. With the great downsizing of our industrial complex, many workers are asked to take on three and four jobs previously done by now-absent co-workers.

The Patricias of this world, people doing three to four jobs, have quadrupled since this book was first published. What if Patricia's job helps her to stay fat? What if her job is at stake? She would prefer to just diet rather than face having to make changes in her daily lifestyle. Many employees call in sick when overworked, when perhaps asking for a longer lunch break, doing some exercise, and taking a moment to regroup during a workday could keep them healthy, productive, and still on the job. Patricia needs to take some risks to recover. When she treats her illness seriously, she is more likely to ask for what she needs. Otherwise, she keeps sacrificing for the employer and bingeing to soothe her worn-out self.

In the same way you deny physical reality, you deny psychological reality. Your life is filled with secrets you keep from yourself and others. You keep your eating behavior secret and live in a private emotional hell. You rarely tell people how you feel. This holds true for the "people pleaser" who is always sweet and charming and the brash, confrontive "tough guy" who never seems to experience a weak moment. Both of these stereotypes, common to the food obsessed, deny the existence of their opposites. You must face the undeniable fact that we are as sick as we are secretive. Without her food, the "jolly fat lady" may uncover the bitch she's been suppressing, and the "tough survivor" may have to spend some time falling apart.

Marnie was jolly, competent, and already successfully losing weight when I confronted her denial system.

"But I've just lost 120 pounds! Why would I need help?" Marnie seemed astonished that I had approached her about becoming a patient in treatment. She weighed more than six hundred pounds. Breathing was difficult. Her chest was so heavy her lungs were unable to expand, and so she suffered frequent dizziness from lack of oxygen. She had heard my lecture to a community group about the opening of a new HOPE Unit dedicated to **H**elping **O**vereaters through **P**eople and **E**ducation. She approached me later to ask whether we had a job opening, mentioning she was an excellent secretary. I smiled and took her number, agreeing to call her the following week. I felt we both understood that she was really approaching me for professional help, not employment.

I was surprised when she again mentioned her secretarial skills at our meeting. Her own personal denial system was so effective that it had walled her off from reality entirely. There is nothing else that adequately explains why a six-hundred-pound woman would deny a need for help. She did indeed want to overcome her lifelong, chronic problem, but wouldn't admit she'd need others. She would do it herself.

Like many who "volunteered" to work at my clinics over the years, Marnie wanted to "bootleg" therapy without truly facing herself and asking for help. She was terrified at the prospect of facing the full dimensions of the problem. She had indeed lost a great deal of weight already and wanted to believe she could make it on her own. Denial sings, "I can do it myself."

As we took on the more straightforward and serious approach of beginning counseling, we discovered that the 120 pounds she claimed to have lost was actually a figure she had made up. Because there was no excess weight scale available, it had been impossible to weigh her; no one ever really knew her actual poundage. She also admitted that the lost weight was returning; her muumuus were getting tighter. Weighing more than can be recorded on a scale has a certain element of personal security—poundage can come and go without record. It is possible to continue to deny the problem without definite evidence. Chronically obese all her life, a weight swing of twenty or thirty pounds in forty-eight hours was normal for someone like Marnie.

At our first meeting, we sat down with a counselor to discuss why she had come to the hospital. She again quickly pointed out her office managerial skills. She convinced the counselor that she was very adept at controlling and managing office situations, but her body attested to her inadequate self-control. We gently directed the conversation away from office proficiency and toward psychological pain. The counselor, a compulsive overeater in recovery, told of maintaining a weight loss of more than one hundred pounds and that she remembered her own attempts to show off at work so that no one would notice she was fat.

That helped melt Marnie's denial system, and at last she opened up. She admitted to hoping she could get some help by working with me. Later she saw how she was hoping to "bootleg" therapy and gain help by working with us rather than painfully admitting her own desperate neediness. She wanted to help others as a way of staying in denial.

With addictive disorders, an essential ingredient for success is that you face your own denial and admit within your own heart a personal need for help. The help may be professional but doesn't have to be. Families and friends can sometimes help, or new friends in Overeaters Anonymous can help. To recover, you have to become vulnerable and *ask*. Then someone else can have an effect.

Confluents Also Deny

The same hopes of clearing it up "next Monday," of minimizing the seriousness of the obsession, also happens for C-Ps. In fact, many times the C-P is in even more denial than the F-O. The C-P denies the seriousness by pretending the obsession will clear up soon. The C-P denies his or her own powerlessness by either deluding or continuing to harangue the F-O. This denial helps the F-O keep bingeing. For example, the following is a common scenario between F-Os and C-Ps.

F-O: Dear, do you think I'm as fat as that lady
     over there?

C-P: Oh, I don't know. It's really hard to tell.

F-O: Well, please take a look. I just want to know
     the truth.

C-P: Well, er, no, you're not. I think she's *fatter*
     than you.

F-O: Thanks, I really wanted to know.

I can't recall ever hearing such an interchange with the more truthful answer, "Well, you are actually fatter than that lady." When F-Os know that answer is coming, they will not ask. They only ask when they know someone will help in maintaining denial.

Another way spouses help in denial is when they assume a punitive parent role with the F-O. In this case, they are telling the truth, "You are fat," but they do it in a way that minimizes how difficult recovery is. They deny the seriousness of the problem by cajoling or manipulating with hints of diets or controlling food. They may yell and threaten, all as a way to keep believing willpower will fix things.

C-P: Why don't you do something about your
     weight?

F-O: I'm really trying. I want to do it for you.

C-P: Bull! You don't care about me.

F-O: Yes, I do. I want you to be proud of me.

C-P: Sure. If you really loved me, you'd take care
     of it.

F-O: I can't help it. I want to but can't.

C-P: I don't believe you. In fact, if you don't
     get it together, I'm going to leave you.

In this exchange, the C-P has become punitive as a result of hurt and disappointment. This person is denying that the F-O is actually trying but still failing. C-Ps don't want to believe how powerless everyone is. As a C-P, you take the F-O's behavior personally with the "if-you-loved-me" approach. The F-O's problem is not a slap in the face to you. The F-O is not doing it to *you*. This person is continuing the behavior because he or she is sick. Denying that this is an illness keeps us hammering away at symptoms rather than causes or cures.

Many food obsessives suffer with other lifelong chronic illnesses such as alcoholism, diabetes, or tuberculosis. A symptom of untreated alcoholism is that people *must* drink. A symptom of tuberculosis is that people *must* cough. A symptom of a food obsession is that people *must* eat or starve compulsively. We do not approach the tubercular patient and say, "If you loved me, you'd stop coughing." Why do we think stopping eating has anything to do with love?

A healthier response to the weight question is, "Dear, I am very happy you asked me for my opinion. I know you love me but hurt yourself. I have noticed you suffering about your weight, that you feel guilty and scared. It seems like you really are motivated and trying. I can offer you my love and support if you are willing to get help. I really don't think you can keep tackling this thing alone. I also see that I can't be the one to help you. I certainly don't want to be involved in evaluating your body as if you were an object. I love you as a person but hate your illness."

How the F-O gets help, then, is none of your business. He or she may seek hospital treatment, work in partnership with a friend, join a diet club, or, as I suggest, attend Overeaters Anonymous. In any event, strange as it may seem, you can't include yourself directly in the helping system. You will need your own help in letting him or her quit alone. You will find you need even more help as your loved one truly begins to recover.

As an F-O or C-P, please don't be hard on yourself. You can't *know* until you *know*. Remember DENIAL means **D**on't **E**ven **N**otice **I A**m **L**ying. Let's take a look at all you haven't noticed. See if you can trace your own denial stages.

———————————■———————————

Dealing with Denial

Check to see which of the following statements
you have said or thought in the past year.

☐ I can't find my scale.

☐ I'm still within "hovering weight."

☐ My hairdo gives me height.

☐ This food in my mouth has nothing to do with the fat on my body.

☐ The scale is broken.

☐ The dryer is shrinking my clothes.

☐ It is a minor ailment that will clear up as soon as I am ready.

☐ I can go on a diet and lose weight whenever I want to.

☐ I'm going to start tomorrow [or next Monday].

☐ This is a simple project.

☐ This won't really require too much effort or disruption in my life.

☐ This is no big deal. I can handle it myself.

☐ All I need is willpower.

☐ I am so accomplished in other areas that I should be able to do this easily.

☐ It's not my fault; who wouldn't eat with a husband [wife, mother, father] like mine?

☐ I have to eat this way to maintain my job.

☐ I don't really eat very much at all. I eat like a bird.

☐ I am really not my body; I am really something else.

- ☐ I can lose weight as easily as I gained it.
- ☐ I like "slenderizing" clothes.
- ☐ I guess it is slight water retention.

———————◼———————

If you recall thinking any of the foregoing three or more times during the last year, denial may be your major coping mechanism. You probably avoid acceptance by staying in the denial stage.

I'm Mad As Hell

"Why me? It's just not fair!" Of course, you're right. "Look at that skinny thing over there; she eats anything she wants and never gains a pound. Why was I dealt this rotten hand? Why must I live so stringently? Why am I so deprived?" The lament goes on.

F-Os are angry at God, fate, and a society dictating a body standard that borders on painfully thin. You are angry at the kid at the beach yelling, "Hey, Mom, look at the fat lady" or "Gee, look how fat that man is." You are mad for all the lost years, the proms not attended, the outings refused. Anger is probably the most prevalent underlying emotion an F-O knows, yet it is also the hardest to express. It is no accident that I titled my second book *Fat & Furious*. You have spent so many years practicing the art of people pleasing so you could fit in. You overcompensate so no one will notice the fat. However, buried many layers deep, you are very, very angry.

Suppressed anger must be brought to the surface. It would be unrealistic to expect someone who has spent a lifetime in self-abuse—to say nothing of abuse from others—to immediately feel serene, self-satisfied, and content. You have to vent anger first. Usually, very little work is required for this anger to emerge. When you stop eating compulsively, anger automatically erupts within days. These raging feelings have been boiling under the surface and have only been kept under control by the sedation excess food provides. Have you noticed how irritating everyone at home becomes the day you start a new diet? Is it the food or them or you?

Anger should not only be allowed but actually promoted and encouraged. Family members, take cover! The anger is often vented against those nearest and dearest and especially those trying to help. As an F-O, you know your food is being taken away. Whoever is close seems to be the one who is taking it away. You have to strike out. There is absolutely no reason you should like the idea of facing life without comfort from food. You don't know any other way to get comfort yet. You are still scared of people. You bet, you feel threatened and angry.

As a C-P, if you want to stay around, you will need to develop a fairly thick skin at this point. The F-Os will need to express all kinds of rage. You must decide whether you want to be the one to listen or whether you want to suggest they turn to others instead. You don't have to be the garbage can. In ancient Rome, when a messenger brought bad news, his tongue was cut out. Romans went directly to the source of the information. That is exactly what F-Os feel like doing to anyone who tries to help them. They will strike out blindly like a wounded animal as they face how hard it is. You don't have to be the one to bear the brunt of these tidings. The anger is not necessarily at you. If you step out of the way, the F-O will find others who can help in sorting out where all the rage belongs. Often, treatment professionals are better trained at receiving and holding the pent-up emotions. Family members do best to get out of the way.

You might be like many who assume that all this anger really applies to someone else. You think your case is different and you will come through with flying colors and without showing the menacing dark side. Sorry, the anger must be expressed, or it will only be drowned again with food abuse. *Be angry now and healthier later. . . .*

---■---

Agitating Anger

Check the phrases you have said or thought in the past year.

☐ It's really not fair!

☐ Who says I can't eat that?

☐ How the hell can you help me?

☐ You are an incompetent helper.

☐ That skinny bitch can eat whatever she wants.

☐ Clothes are made cheap to rip.

☐ Those models are fanatic in showing off bodies.

☐ I know they're out to get me.

Add whatever angry responses you've noticed from yourself. (Because so many are hidden anger blockers, you probably masked anger while you smiled and kept still.)

_____

_____

_____

_____

_____

_____

---■---

Don't worry if you don't feel angry now. All you have to do is cut down the eating and believe me, anger will emerge. It's been drowned by food and is just waiting to get out.

I have seen one patient who did not go through this angry irritation stage. I was concerned and uneasy about her treatment. She never got irritated about anything. It didn't fit. Eventually she cleared up the confusion. She admitted in group therapy that she had been secretly stealing food out of the refrigerator late at night. Her rage had been kept in check through a well-practiced and familiar means—bingeing.

Vomiting is often a way to express rage that seems inappropriate. This was certainly true for fourteen-year-old Cindy, who vomited ten times a day rather than talk with her family members about their excessive secrecy and anger with each other. Cindy became the family symptom-bearer. As she sought help to stop vomiting, the whole system came into the full view of health care professionals.

Cindy's father, Mel, a middle manager with a West Coast firm, enjoyed a prominent position and was highly respected. Attractive and stately, although somewhat pudgy, he looked appropriate for his years and position. He and Janelle had married when both were developing careers, and she became his able companion as they raced up the corporate ladder. Her alcoholic parents had separated when she was nine months old, and she grew up living out her mother's worries about abandonment and financial insecurity. She resolved she would marry success. She would work to cheer up her somewhat stodgy husband and make him happy. Instead, by the time Cindy was negotiating her adolescence, Mel and Janelle were approaching divorce. No one talked, but all raged within.

Her mother, Janelle, was wraithlike thin. Her drawn face framed piercing eyes, and her body contorted rigidly, signaling pent-up emotions within. Sitting motionless was her way to mask the rage she felt, but her right hand contorted into a fist on her lap. Her knuckles showed white, and her fist could not unlock. She was holding on for dear life.

Cindy accommodated her mother's need to express rage by bingeing and vomiting. Obsessed with carbohydrates, she also wanted to be as thin as her mother. She didn't know how to eat away at herself from inside as Janelle did. (Janelle had previously been treated for ulcers and colitis, physical responses to blocked emotion.) Cindy had to juggle a love of food with a desire to be thin. She felt all her mother's feelings and didn't know what to do with them. Vomiting became a workable solution.

When I approached Janelle about the necessity for treating the whole family, she balked. "I am on my way out of this marriage. I don't want to be talked back into it."

I didn't know then that Janelle had been saying this for the past nineteen years. Later she explained that she was staying just long enough to get some financial security so she wouldn't suffer like her own mother had. (Actually Janelle had already suffered her own mother's pain and her own. Cindy would suffer her mother's pain in the same way.)

Mel had been having an affair, which caused him extreme guilt and anxiety. His secret relationship with his secretary had been discovered, and he had vowed to fire her and end it. He later secretly rehired her, hiding that fact from everyone except fourteen-year-old Cindy. He was using Cindy as his confidante but at her expense. He couldn't talk with his enraged wife, so he sent messages through Cindy: "Tell your mom we'll all meet over at the club later." This gave Cindy an unnatural and overly important role in her family. At a time when she would naturally be working toward separation and independence, she was instead used as the family message center. She was in a double bind for which vomiting proved the only outlet.

As family members became more honest in recovery, secrets came into the open. Mel talked about his guilt and self-loathing and desire to do whatever it took to end the family's suffering. His daughter's food obsession brought them to treatment and gave them an opportunity to uncover hidden turmoil. He later stopped blaming himself so much and realized that he had not been able to open up in the marriage but did deserve to get love and support for himself. Janelle later revealed that she knew that the affair had resumed but was waiting around until she amassed enough money. She didn't see that this man was not like her father and would make a fair financial settlement in divorce. (They also lived in a community property state where assets are legally divided fifty-fifty.)

In other words, no one really *had* to stay in this suffering, except Cindy. When mom started expressing her rage directly, Cindy was displaced from her job as the family secret-bearer. When all the secrets came out, Janelle had to admit that she really stayed for other than financial reasons. She had to admit that the only model she had ever known was of a woman angry and complaining about a man. She was playing out the only role she'd ever known. When Janelle honestly admitted this, Cindy's vomiting stopped. Dad's secret affair was disclosed. Mom's plans to leave were exposed, and Cindy was refocused to care for herself. Her illness became her first priority. She saw that her parents had their relationship and intrigues long before she was around, and it was not her job to worry about them. With that, the parents entered divorce mediation counseling, and Cindy got on with the business of growing up. Her parents had to find a more appropriate avenue for their anger with each other than routing it through Cindy. Everyone benefited from treating the food obsession.

Let's Make a Deal

You will want to maintain some sense of power over this illness. You want to feel in control. You want to change the results without changing what you're doing. But it can't be done. You can't keep "the same old me" and gain recovery. Old-timers often quip, "You won't have to change one single thing. . . . You have to change *every* single thing." Your life must change, and then a change in the obsession will follow. Now, no one really wants to hear that, so you will search after easier, softer ways and busy yourself with half measures. That's exactly what dieting is all about. You want to chide yourself that this is purely a physical problem: "It's my glands" or "It's low blood sugar; a high-protein diet will take care of it." You bargain with the disease and, in the process, deny how serious it really is.

Similarly, you try to bargain with the time and effort required to recover: "I only want to attend meetings once a week" or "I don't see why I should give up my vacation plans just because they happen to fall smack in the middle of a treatment program."

You want to bargain not only about how seriously you need to invest in recovery, but also about what personal changes are needed: "I'd like to change my relationship with my sister, but I don't want to talk to my mother," or "My spouse and I can benefit from this, but there is really no need to involve the children," or "I wouldn't want to ask them to help me."

In the angry stage you rebelled: "Why me? I don't want this. Give it to someone else." In the bargaining stage, you accept that you have this affliction and that it will not be easy to overcome. But you still want to go it alone. This stage is both comical and devastating. Here is where you try the various diet fads, pills, shots, acupuncture needles, meditation, hypnosis, protein drinks, health foods, and so on.

In Alcoholics Anonymous's Big Book, chapter three itemizes the "methods we have tried" to give up alcoholic drinking. For example, it lists, "not drinking in the morning, drinking only after five, using no hard liquor, taking a trip, *not* taking a trip." If food-obsessed dieters ever wrote anything like this, it would be so voluminous that you couldn't even lift the book. All of these are short-run solutions that give us the false hope of personal, individual, and self-sufficient mastery. Each new plan helps continue the delusion. You want to believe in the myth of self-sufficiency while dying inside.

In the bargaining phase we often try to avoid looking at the basic underlying personality structure and instead focus solely on the physical. That's when we resort to shots and pills; diet clubs, gyms, sanitariums, health spas, and fat farms; surgical procedures; shock treatments; nutritional counseling; and bibliotherapy. These approaches let us believe that we don't have to change. The ego and false sense of self can stay intact. We truly want to believe that our bodies can change without our heads. Many continue on with the bargaining and undergo none of the major relationship changes that could bring a lifelong, stable recovery.

Conversely, some try changing relationships without giving up the obsessive relationship with food. Many of my therapist friends are constantly involved in their own growth programs or with helping others in order to hide their own neediness. However, they continue eating compulsively. They go to weekend workshops and retreats and learn psychological interpretations, meditations, Sufi dancing, and Reichian explosions—all the while bingeing on nuts, fruits, and "healthy" grains. Some binge for weeks and then seclude themselves in health farms for a few days of fasting, only to begin again. They are pretending that personal insight alone can lead to cure. They do this bargaining while still bingeing. Insight without abstinence is not enough. It's a head full of knowledge and a belly full of food. Also, abstinence without insight is not enough. It is a physical *and* psychological illness. You can't treat one half and not the other. It's a package deal.

Essentially, bargaining addresses isolated aspects of your life. You compartmentalize yourself and assume an unrealistic power of the mind over the body or vice versa. These approaches fail to integrate the mind, body, and spirit. You will need to address all three aspects of the illness to gain lasting recovery. Most of these other methods promote the idea that recovery is time-limited and that you can undergo a certain treatment and thus achieve a cure. You want to believe you can do something and be finished once and for all. You see it as a kind of exorcism. Such a deal has been a lifelong wish. It only serves to keep you fat.

Morris was just such a bargainer. He was tall, blond, and gigantic. He was thirty years old and weighed 594 pounds. As he entered the lecture hall where I was speaking, a number of people moved aside. His size alone intimidated most. He was accustomed to people getting out of his way and being somewhat fearful around him. Later, in recovery, he admitted this was a puzzle to him, as he felt so tiny inside. When he eventually stopped eating compulsively, he felt like a little boy, not the giant he had become. Because everyone else had viewed him as big and tough, he was only acting out the part for his audience.

No seat in the auditorium was big enough, so he slouched against the back wall to listen. Before I finished with introductory remarks, his questions boomed loudly from the back of the room. "Why do you talk about this being an illness? Don't you think that's discouraging to people?"

As I tried to explain that accepting it as difficult made it easier in a sense, Morris boomed again, "Well, isn't it a matter of willpower, and if a person really wants to, they can?"

I asked him whether he could answer that based on his

own experience. He was quick to reply. "I've had a weight problem for years, but I've never really tried to diet. My weight has not really been a problem for me. I am energetic and personable; my friends call me the life of the party. I don't see why you refer to overweight people as sick."

At this point, others in the audience asked Morris to be quiet and allow the lecture to continue. I was, admittedly, intimidated, but went on.

Morris remained quiet for the rest of the hour. Later, when others approached the podium to ask personal questions, Morris disappeared out the side door.

A week later he called. With no greeting and no mention of his name, he blurted out, "I want to find out more of what you're about."

"In what way?" I asked.

"What kind of treatment are you suggesting?"

At this point, I recognized the gruff voice and asked for his name. "You don't need to know that yet. I want to know first if you have anything to offer that could interest me."

"Didn't you say you have never tried to diet and have never seen your weight as a problem?" I replied.

"I still don't see it as a problem and really don't think I need help. It's just that the coach of my basketball team is bugging me."

I was shocked to discover that a man of this grotesque size was capable of playing basketball. Imagine what he might have weighed without such strenuous sports activities. I proceeded to outline a typical regimen undertaken by most successful patients. This included attendance at group therapy sessions three nights each week.

"Well, that is ridiculous. I can't make that kind of commitment. I have my basketball practice. I'm certainly not going to give that up. I know the coach wouldn't want that." He thanked me and hung up.

It was two months before he called again. With no intro-
duction, he barked angrily, "The coach is becoming a real
pain in the ass." I knew right away who it was and didn't ask
his name this time. "So, maybe, I could get involved with
your program if I could come once a week and still make
practice regularly."

"I'm sorry," I said. "We've found that this particular plan
works best for the greatest number of people, and I think you
deserve the benefit of full treatment." I have found that if we
keep everyone committed to the same plan, they all usually
do well. Our saying is "Routine patients do well." The special
cases where exceptions are made produce more complications and mistakes. Surgical teams in most major hospitals
can attest to this. When they admit a doctor or doctor's wife
for any type of surgical procedure, the incidence of compli-
cation is statistically higher. Instead of treating them like a
routine case, everyone works to put in special effort to ensure
the finest quality care. What often happens is overzealous-
ness, which leads to incompetence, and this can result in
more problems. As I tried to explain this to Morris, he hung
up again.

His next call came within the month. As I answered the
phone, he began, "Surely you can understand that a person's
physical activity is important for their emotional and physical
well-being. Don't you believe in exercise for healthy bodies?"

"Sure I do," I replied, "but your exercising has not really
helped you cut down on compulsive eating."

"How do you know how I eat? That's really none of your
business."

"I do know that for anyone to get as big as you are, even
while playing basketball, they certainly have to pack in a lot
of food. Your exercising may be serving as a perfect excuse to
keep you bingeing."

He hung up. I didn't hear from him for three more

months. When he called again, he sounded forlorn. The fight was out of his voice. The hurt was there. "I've really been trying to handle this thing on my own. I seem to go along fine for a week or more, but then end up running from one 7-Eleven store to another. My apartment is strewn with straws and wrappers. There's a three-foot pile of garbage around my bed."

I responded with, "Sounds like your experience is common to many of us. The more we try to control it, the more it dominates our lives. I'm really happy you are calling. Could you tell me your name?"

"Morris," he replied gently. Then he quickly pointed out that his case was "quite different." He wanted me to know that his being a young and brilliant engineer coupled with his athletic ability made his situation special. He tried to convince me: "Since I am very intelligent, I pick up information and learn much more rapidly than most people. Don't you think I could get along with coming to therapy less often than others?" His tone had turned from hostile to pleading, but I still had to say no.

"I assure you I am giving you the best recommendation I can, based on my own professional experience. Why don't you give yourself the full chance you deserve and jump into recovery with both feet?"

His curt response was, "You won't be hearing from me again!" And he slammed down the phone. Following the progression, you can see how Morris moved from denial that he even had a problem to bargaining with the schedule recommended for his recovery to anger at me for bringing the possibility of help to him in the first place. Morris's negotiations with me to help him get away with doing less are all part of the bargaining stage. We call his position "terminal uniqueness."

Terminal Uniqueness

"If the other guy had to pay a dime for it, let me pay
a nickel."

"My case is different."

"I need special handling."

"I'm not as bad as all that."

"Give me a good deal."

"Nobody gets the better of me."

"I'm not a nerd like everybody else."

Unfortunately, the food obsession brings all F-Os to their
knees facing human fallibility. No one is better than or less
than anyone else; we're all in the human race together.
Morris was using basketball as a way to set himself apart from
others. His ego ran rampant across the basketball court, but
his need for human closeness was submerged in his bed with
a TV set and a bag of Oreo cookies.

Four months later, Morris was kicked off the team. He
had gained twenty more pounds. For Morris, the basketball
coach had been his enabler. He liked having Morris as the star
player. He had tried to get Morris to accept help but didn't
feel secure enough to be forceful about it. The coach had a
lot to gain from Morris's skill on the court. Morris was his star
player. Morris ran harder and pushed himself more than anyone on the team. His spirit and drive motivated the other
players. The coach was willing to keep Morris, even fat, rather
than risk losing him completely. However, when the twenty
extra pounds came on, the coach was terrorized every time he
watched his star player move down the court. Morris became
so red and winded that a heart attack looked imminent. The
coach had no choice, and Morris's bargaining proved expensive.

Morris never did say "I need help" out loud. When he
called, he simply said, "This is Morris. Where do I sign?" In

his case, he had to lose the very thing he was bargaining to preserve before he was willing to commit himself to recovery. Sometimes, the thing we are absolutely, resolutely unwilling to give up becomes the very thing we have to let go. That applies whether we are striking the bargain for basketball, homes, jobs, husbands, wives, cars, or children. We have to contemplate that we'll *lose to win*. We have to be willing to give up.

Morris ultimately recovered much more than he gave up. He was back on the team within three months. He has let go of more than three hundred pounds. He's newly married and expecting a baby. He still plays basketball, but he can take it or leave it. It doesn't own him. He doesn't need it to fulfill ego needs to overcompensate for his physical deformity. People don't move aside when he enters a room. In fact, he's become so warm and cuddly that many reach out to hug him. What a deal!

———■———

Bargain Poor

Check the statements you have said or thought
during the past year.

☐ I will diet Monday through Friday but binge on weekends.

☐ I will change to eating only at mealtimes and not in between.

☐ I will eat smaller portions all day long.

☐ I will only eat in the kitchen.

☐ I will spend three hundred dollars for this exercise gym.

☐ I will go to a health spa for two weeks.

☐ I will buy an exercise bike.

☐ I will go to a steam bath.

☐ I will wear sweat suits.

- ☐ I will go for cellulite therapy.
- ☐ I will have an intestinal bypass operation.
- ☐ I will have a stomach staple.
- ☐ I will take diet pills.

Add in some more of your own "unique" bargains.

_____

_____

_____

_____

_____

―――――■―――――

It's Okay to Feel Bad

American society frowns on feeling bad about anything.

"Keep a stiff upper lip."

"Let a smile be your umbrella."

"Oh, you're just feeling sorry for yourself."

"Eat something. . . . You'll feel better."

And yet, despite all the cultural taboos, it is essential that the F-O feel the pain and hopelessness of the condition. You must face the tragedy of the illness and experience mourning and loss. You must give up the lifelong delusion that you *don't* have an illness. It will make you sad. You must face the fact that life is not a dress rehearsal but that this is it and it stinks. It won't get better on its own. Recovery won't be easy. All other life projects will pale in comparison.

The past was undertaken with the comfort of a lifelong friend and faithful companion—food. Now you will face losing this friendship. You must look at the wasted teenage years and all the other time lost in trying to control this illness. Only by facing these things can you muster the energy to recover.

Seeing the lifelong wish for easy answers shattered invariably results in deep depression and mourning—mourning the loss of a dream, mourning the hope that the easy thin life is right around the corner. Every F-O has offered up the secret prayer "God, let me make it this time, and I'll never be fat again" only to face the despair of another weight gain later. To recover, you must mourn the loss of a simple cure.

Most of us have lived in a dress rehearsal, preparing for that ever-elusive time when we get thin. Without drastic measures, without a total life reorganization, you are doomed to repeat the same cyclical patterns. One of my telephone patients, a bedridden woman in Philadelphia, told me that she is Greek and cannot give up her feta cheese. A 425-pound Hispanic man in Los Angeles, hospitalized in a diabetic coma, once told me he could not give up his burritos. Be careful. Whatever you say you'll *never* give up may be the very thing you'll *have to surrender.* Sure, there might be some cultural food rituals to renegotiate, but there are even greater changes in store on a personality level. To accept recovery, you must first mourn the old way of life.

Noted psychologist Carl Jung said, "There is no birth of consciousness without pain." F-Os who truly accept recovery must lay old patterns to rest and give birth to a new life. There is pain, and you need to cry. You need to mourn the loss of comfort through food. The relationship as you knew it is gone forever. A new relationship with food will take its place. It has to become fuel to stoke your engine.

Those of you who are confluents are vitally affected in this stage. You must release with love enough to allow F-Os to experience their own pain. You may want to try to shelter and protect them and encourage avoidance of pain. You want to offer some diversion to keep the F-O's mind off the problem. Even if you were superjudgmental and critical before, you may now become supreme rescuers. Please be aware of what you are doing. You may be trying to soothe your own pain. You are depressed that all your efforts have not succeeded in helping your loved one. You are facing your own powerlessness.

One husband became quite upset when his wife cried in group therapy. His first offer of solace was, "Come on, dear; let's forget about all this. I'll take you out to dinner." He needs instead to find a way to offer tough love and respect her enough to let her cry her own tears.

The best way to help an F-O with depression is by being an example as you face yours. When you see that recovery involves changing relationships, you will anticipate losses for yourself as well. You will have your own mourning to go through.

Lose to Win

There are losses for all family members in recovery. You have actually been too close and will need to develop some breathing space. Remember Kahlil Gibran's enjoinder to allow for spaces in your togetherness? This new way of relating is a space from which there is no going back. You can't go home again. You will be facing the pain of growing up and leaving home. You will be leaving the security of all you've known and stepping out into a new way of life.

This growing up and leaving home takes a much longer time in the United States than in any other culture. This may account for why we are so much more obese than the rest of the world. Primitive tribes negotiate this rite of passage at the onset of puberty. Instead we remain childlike and emotionally infantile, sometimes until death. It is no accident that food obsessions flower in adolescence. Sure there are a myriad of hormonal changes, but perhaps we have not learned effective ways to grow up and leave the nest.

Other animals have a much easier time with this than humans. Perhaps it is because they're willing to suffer the pain of separation. A Canadian TV documentary shows well how the natural world negotiates this phenomenon. The film *Cry of the Wild* shows a den of red foxes in which the mother has died. The father was left to raise the pups. As they approached a year old, it was time for these babies to leave the nest. It was Dad's job to kick them out. This resulted in a knock-down-drag-out fight with blood all over the snow. These young foxes did not want to go. Winter was approaching, snow was falling, and they wanted to stay home. Dad didn't care. "No, you gotta get out," he growled. They fought through the night. Smaller and weaker, by daybreak the babies whimpered away.

The scene was quite sad, especially for Dad, who was left alone in his empty nest. His mate was gone, his kids were gone, but it was something he had to do. He had a natural instinct to help his children suffer the pain of growth. With no therapy and little thought, he just did what he had to do.

When winter came, he and they stalked the woods alone. He was sad, but he'd done the right thing. With the spring thaw, all the little pups came back to visit. They returned as totally new entities. They strutted up to the den, proud and separate. Their walk was different. They were in a whole new relationship with him. Some brought a mate along. It was clear that this was *Dad's* place, and they were coming to visit awhile and then be on their own way.

Daddy fox had done his kids a favor. He helped them learn about differentness. He almost had to kill them to teach them, but it was something they had to learn. When they returned, there was mutual respect on both sides.

Although it was painful, he helped them separate and become themselves.

In particular, this pain has to be weathered by mothers and daughters, or the daughters will have to keep amassing flesh to feel grounded and separate. When mothers ask me, "How can I best allow my daughter to separate and move into her own life?" I answer, "Grab her around the knees and yell and scream, 'Don't go; I need you.'" That is usually what they'd honestly like to say. The daughter knows it anyway. It is best to say the truth and let them deal with it. Each will have to consider the pain of growing up as an alternative to the pain of food obsession.

Losses for the C-P

Most of the time, family members plead with a treatment team about how much they want to see their loved one give up food obsession, and they say how ecstatic they will be as a result. Rarely do they anticipate any loss or disruption for themselves. I feel it is the job of treatment professionals to emphasize that there will be disruption and sometimes chaos, and if this is not expected and dealt with, it can be dangerous. If you, as a C-P are not prepared to set up some preventive strategies, you may secretly sabotage whatever recovery is set in motion. This won't be done wittingly. You will just be trying to return to old familiar patterns. Let's look at some of the losses you can anticipate.

LOSING PREDICTABLE PATTERNS. Before, when the food obsession was in power, it was all quite simple. You knew exactly what to say that would make them mad or quiet them down, and they knew the same about you. You might prefer the old system. You used to know exactly how to push the right buttons to light up their keyboard. Maybe life was a pile of manure, but you knew what it smelled like. There are many surprises in store now. Maybe you won't like such risky business. But as you mourn the loss of the old, predictable response patterns, you can get turned on to the excitement of meeting a new person and developing a new relationship.

LOSING SECURITY. You once felt secure in the attitude that "I'm the best thing that ever happened to her. She certainly can't do better." You may find it difficult to be in a relationship where the other person is with you out of choice. Ultimately though, you'll feel more secure later when you see that this person is still around because he or she wants to be.

LOSING A SCAPEGOAT. It was once quite easy to blame problems on the F-O, but who do you blame now? What if the F-O gets better, but you uncover other problems? It might seem safer to keep the food obsession as the focus of your discontent, but it's not. When you face real problems during recovery, they can heal in the open air rather than festering unattended.

LOSING MARTYRDOM. No longer can you represent yourself as the one who is sticking it out despite all obstacles. You won't get any more praise for endurance. In fact, you may see the F-O praised for abstinence and feel jealous. You must find a way to get your own strokes for yourself. Instead of praise for suffering, you'll be encouraged to go for even more happiness.

LOSING A CARETAKER ROLE. When the F-O takes full responsibility for his or her own recovery, you may feel like your child has been snatched from your arms. Who will you care for now? It's hard to be out of a job. You may want to seek out another sicker F-O to fix. Don't. Try to face just being happy without fixing anyone.

LOSING FALSE ESTEEM. Your identity has been closely linked with the F-O. You established your personality based on comparing yourself with someone else. You used to be able to say, "At least I'm better than that." What do you say now? Now you can find out who you really are.

LOSING RETRIBUTION. If you truly accept that the F-O behaved in certain ways because of the sickness, then you have to stop blaming. That's a lot to give up. You may want him or her to atone for the past. What do you do with your vengeful feelings?

As a C-P, you will also have to accept that you chose to endure and live the way you have. No one is responsible for your past but you. Just like the F-O, you did the best you could with what you knew then. You may want to mourn for some of the time you wasted. You, too, have invested years in wishing and waiting. Now that there is hope of recovery, you may feel safe enough to let the pain out and cry for yourself. You'll cry about who you've become. Like the classic fairy tale, you thought that with your kiss, a loved one could turn into a prince or princess. Instead, you turned into a *frog!*

Delve into Depression

Check the statements you have said or thought in the past year. (F-Os are often C-Ps as well. All have felt depressed. So every family member will benefit from doing the following checklist.)

☐ This is hopeless.

☐ It seems like I just had to keep eating like that.

☐ I can't continue like this.

☐ I really screwed up my whole life.

☐ We're both failures.

☐ I'm afraid you won't need me anymore.

☐ I haven't been able to talk to you.

☐ We both missed out on a lot.

☐ Why didn't we see this sooner?

☐ There's no comfort without food.

☐ There's no comfort with food.

☐ It's not worth it.

☐ It's not fair.

☐ I'm afraid if I change, people won't like me.

Add more of your own.

_____

_____

_____

_____

_____

——————————■——————————

Acceptance at Last

When depression is allowed, it passes. When it is denied, it festers. It goes underground through use of food and other drugs and serves to help deaden every other feeling. You need help to weather the depression. You can then move into a meaningful acceptance of the illness. The only way out is through.

In acceptance, you may be quiet and even somewhat withdrawn, almost passive from time to time. Your calmness may inspire serenity and tranquillity in others. You won't have answers. Instead, you will be open to following new directions and asking for help. You won't be embarrassed. At this stage there is actually little to do or say. Just sit back and enjoy the ride.

When you begin to accept the disease concept, your mind

is open to new ideas, and you will show a childlike receptivity. You will come to know on a very deep level that your own efforts got you to exactly this place. You will find yourself willing to accept help from someone else. You'll know you can't do it alone. You'll ask for help. People with broken legs can ask for crutches. With this disease, your prescription is to turn on to people. That is acceptance. You will become willing to live your life one day at a time. You will give up previous fantasies. Realistic recovery is now fully under way.

As mentioned above, when first accepting the serious nature of obsession, you may appear void of feelings and closed off. You must allow yourself this space. Your loved ones might become alarmed. They will need guidance and comfort to keep from rescuing. At first you will only be interested in recovery and nothing else. If you are lucky, that singleness of purpose will last for a while. You will see that as the eating falls in line, other aspects of your life do too. Your attitude must be "Abstinence is the most important thing in my life, without exception."

You do not necessarily go through acceptance or any of the other four stages in any particular order, nor do you finish with one stage, never to return. It is a continuing and fluid process. Actually, the analogy to stages traveled in accepting death is not really far-fetched. In reality, you are laying to rest an old way of life and giving birth to a new personality. The process is often slow, but the timing is accurately paced for each one of us. You needn't worry about getting on with it or pushing too quickly. You have the rest of your life to travel these stages. Acceptance is not achieved once and for all. It is a process of surrender. It is not a destination.

---■---

Accepting Acceptance

Check the following feelings to see whether you are in acceptance

☐ I really don't have much confidence that this can be cured.

☐ I think this will go on forever.

☐ I'm sort of removed from all talk of food and diets.

☐ I really don't seem affected anymore by whether they like me or not.

☐ If I don't keep my abstinence, all else feels miserable.

☐ I see how much of my past emotion was generated by food.

☐ I certainly won't waste my time in therapy if I'm still eating.

☐ I see food has been my major tranquilizer and coping mechanism.

☐ I wonder what my real life will be without bingeing.

☐ I wonder what I'll do with excess time.

☐ I feel somewhat withdrawn and quiet.

☐ I don't have a clue whether I will really make it with this illness or not.

☐ I do not seem as jovial as I used to be.

☐ I am feeling serene and quiet.

☐ My feelings seem cut off, and I am void.

☐ I need to feel quiet.

☐ What used to seem important now appears trivial.

☐ I am not interested in anything but my recovery.

☐ My abstinence is the most important thing in my life, without exception.

---■---

Often, at the acceptance stage, other people become angry with you. They will see you experiencing a significant change and feel threatened that they are left out. They may be jealous that your recovery plan is working. As an F-O, many of the new ideas you learn from counselors or other guides are the very same things your loved one has been saying for years. He or she may wonder, *Why are you listening to* them *when you wouldn't listen to* me?

As a confluent personality, you'll see your loved one listening and hearing but moving away from you. As close as you are, you are least likely to be the helper. Confronting behaviors around food is such an intimate issue that sometimes an F-O can only hear it from someone outside the family. Each of you must work it out separately. You will each need a helper outside the family. You can get close again later. Let yourselves cry over the brief separation with the knowledge of a closeness beyond your imagination later on.

In the next chapter, you will see how all family members can turn to groups such as Overeaters Anonymous and Al-Anon for help. All must accept the need for outside mentors who've been through the process. Once there is true acceptance of the need for help, you will see how to get it. This will help you extend the family system and develop some individuality so you can come back together healthier, closer, and stronger.

CHAPTER 6

Extend the Family System

To start a diet at this point would be again bargaining for control. Remember, your life experience has already demonstrated that diets don't do it. Instead, you must find a way to work with someone else to "relate to recover." Recovery will involve moving away from an obsessive relationship with food and your loved one and toward nurturance from others outside your immediate system.

In this chapter you will find a way out of enmeshment and failed attempts at control and into a more relaxed self-acceptance and ability to give and receive help from others. Your enmeshed family relationships will be traded for a more distant intimacy, which will ultimately prove more healing.

Macho Myths

Many of us live with the myth of total independence, that is, "self-made man," "pulled up by your own bootstraps," "stiff upper lip." Each boastful proclamation can cost five to ten pounds. Instead of seeking mutual support, interdependence, and reliance on our friends, we eat. Sometimes we pay a therapist two hundred dollars an hour to listen. We really show the dependence we fear, but paying helps ease the shame and thus makes it more acceptable. We can also control when the sessions end. We withdraw the cash.

However, there is another way to gain effective support, nurturance, and understanding totally free of charge on a 24-7 basis. You can extend your family system and get support outside the home. That support can come from Twelve Step groups—Overeaters Anonymous (OA) for the F-O and Al-Anon for the family and friends, the C-Ps. Ideally it works best if you each attend your own meetings. When C-Ps go to Al-Anon, they will fit right in, as their relationship patterns are similar to those involved with alcoholics. The F-O is addicted to solid sugar, while the alcoholic is addicted to liquid sugar. If you choose to get involved with therapy as well, choose family therapy with someone trained in treating the addicted family.

The Twelve Step meetings address not the substance, but the *relationship*. You will develop a new relationship with food and your loved ones. I need to provide a warning for all you C-Ps. Please don't set up a situation that will deny you the help you need. I have heard so many report back, "Well, I told them I wasn't there for an alcoholic but just for my daughter's eating disorder. Then they told me I didn't belong." Please don't go to an Al-Anon meeting and immediately tell the group the reason why you *don't* belong there.

If you really want to find help for yourself, you won't set up such a scenario. Please, just sit quietly and find a way to fit in and get what you need. If you must talk, tell them you are there to look at *yourself,* to deal with *your* need to control and *your* pain while watching a loved one suffer. That's what you share with the other members there. You don't have to give information to exclude yourself. The meetings are helpful no matter what your situation. Most meetings will address your own personal issues about wanting to control a loved one's behavior and the difficulty in letting go and waiting for help. Other members will provide guidelines for what to say and how to say it and when enough is enough, when to go forward and when to back off. Use the meetings to enhance all areas of your life.

I once used a phrase from Al-Anon in one of the most important business meetings of my life. A jealous mentor was upset with me about my newfound confidence in my work. He'd been accustomed to my ingratiating behaviors, begging for crumbs of his approval. At one point, he screamed, "You've got to be humbled, and I'll humble you!" Then he proceeded to read me a list of demands for our future working relationship and told me I must consent to them or leave. Some of his demands were legally unethical, and all were engineered to degrade me in front of my newly trained staff. It was clear the new working rules were fashioned to humiliate me. As I'd come from a family of knee-jerk reactors who immediately blurted out answers before an interrogator even finished a question, I had no training in contemplation and quiet deliberation before responding. I needed to learn effective tools for holding my feelings and giving myself time to gain perspective. Luckily my time at meetings had provided me with a solution. I quietly answered his rage with a lovely phrase I'd picked up at Al-Anon: "I'll think it over, and I'll get back to you."

Whew! What a blessing that was. I was able to stay calm, give myself some time to think, and not injure myself or anyone else. It was a shining moment. I walked away, not necessarily a winner but feeling like a winner, because I liked my behavior.

Attend a meeting, humble yourself, and admit the need for help. Realize that you've already asked for help hundreds of times before with doctor's visits, shots, pills, or fad diets. Now you are asking for another kind of help. You are actually finding a way to gently join the human race. You need to accept yourself and your plight as part of the human condition. You are not a weirdo or a freak. You have been trying to negotiate the difficult human dilemma of seeking nurturance without violation. You chose the safety of food and now need to learn there can be safety with people.

The people in any Twelve Step group are fallible human beings like yourself. These groups are actually a leaderless outpatient program. People there may, from time to time, fail you. Because you will be extending your neediness to a large group rather than one or two individuals, you will be able to weather these disappointments.

We Know How Hard It Is

There is nothing easy about asking for help. Even some of the most motivated, open, willing people I've seen were scared to death to show vulnerability. After all, you wouldn't have chosen a food obsession if you were secure and open. This time you'll take a risk without your best friend. Just going to a meeting is a very risky proposition. It is both an admission that you can't fix it all alone and a plea for help. What happens if they can't fix you right away? You want the quickie. What if they won't understand? The greatest fear is "They wanna take away my food." The truth is they do want your former relationship with food to change.

You may fear someone will actually take your "self" away. You sense that you have to change, not just your food. Don't worry, you won't give up more than you can surrender. Any change is a gradual shedding of the old way of life as you slowly learn new behaviors and attitudes. There is no hurry. You have the rest of your life to recover.

One member told me that when she thinks of her experiences at OA, she wants to echo Gladys Knight and the Pips crooning, "You're the best thing that ever happened to me." This member knew the program had changed her on many levels. It might be too soon to expect so much for yourself, but please read on so you can give it a try.

Empathy and Sympathy

Your own family members felt too responsible to let you sink or swim on your own. Whether enabling or punishing, they implied it was their job to fix you. Because OA members understand how hard it is, they can show you the way out and warn you of the pitfalls. But the work is still yours to do. They will not do it for you. At the meetings you will get support and guidance, but people there are each committed to finding their own way out. They seek solutions rather than reasons or excuses. Because the group comprises people who have struggled out of the depths of degradation, they know from first-hand experience that it is difficult but not impossible. In this new family system you will get support and encouragement and many necessary pats on the back, but no one will do your work for you. This is your chance to be reborn psychologically within this same physical lifetime.

Twelve Step groups will become your powerful extended family. When you struggled to be born physically, your mother helped, but you struggled and pushed to move yourself out into this new life. Now you'll take on a new psychological birth. Group members will give you a lot of push and cheer you on, but the work is yours.

Getting to a Meeting

One advantage enjoyed by hospitalized patients is that they are actually transported to meetings. It would certainly be easier for counselors to just recommend they go and leave it up to them. My experience has shown, however, that people will rarely follow that suggestion. Even with my private practice clients, during the first visit I recommend attending at least one meeting. I assure them that if they attend meetings, the process with me will take less time and thus be much less costly. I tell them how they'll have access to helpers by phone whenever needed. I tell them that the process of changing behavior will be much more painful without OA. They assure me they think it's a good idea and that they have every intention of going, but it is often months before they finally do go. Don't let that be your situation. You are not hospitalized, and there is no one hauling you to a meeting. You will have to push yourself to go. Don't sit at home reading this book and agreeing that it is a good idea. You won't know until you go.

"Where do I go?" The easiest way to find your first meeting is by calling your local information hot line and asking for Overeaters Anonymous. Overeaters Anonymous has meetings for overeaters, undereaters, bingers, vomiters, and any brand of eating you like. In large cities, there are more specialized meetings for different eating patterns. Don't worry about finding the right kind of meeting. No matter what styles of food obsession you hear about, you will identify with the feelings presented. Each type of eater is still food obsessed, and that is what you are going there to treat. When you first call, you can also find out about Al-Anon for C-Ps.

If you have trouble finding a meeting, place a long-distance call to the world headquarters of OA in Rio Rancho, New Mexico, at 505-891-2664 or visit them on the Web at www.overeatersanonymous.org. They maintain an updated directory for the entire world and can give you a local meeting place as well as names and telephone numbers of people to call in your community. You may call these people to get directions to your local meeting and even transportation should you need it. The people who have their phone numbers listed are offering to help newcomers and will gladly get you to your first meeting. You can also call your local OA office and ask them to send you a directory of local meetings. The directory will give addresses of meetings, times, and contact persons with phone numbers. *Let's go!*

Let's take a look at the kinds of discussions that are heard at a typical meeting. After the preliminary introductions are out of the way, Marva says, "Last night I saw how much my mom uses me for a garbage can. She dumps on me all the stuff she really needs to be saying to my dad. She's been doing it since I was sixteen, telling me about her affairs and attractions to other men and stuff, because Dad is supposedly so 'closed up.' I wish she'd tell that to him instead of me. I'm the one who gets all her venom and deceits, but with Dad she pretends and makes nice. She complains about their relationship, but she sure seems to like it this way. I can release the tension I pick up from her by bingeing my brains out and then vomiting. I'm tired. I've got to tell her we can't be confidantes anymore, and I can't listen to her stuff. It's not my job. Let her deal with her husband, or go see her own therapist. I've got my own life to live."

No one responds. There is no cross talk at the OA meeting. Members use the group as a forum to go public with their private thoughts and feelings. They realize their food obsessions are diseases of isolation, that by sharing their innermost selves they can stop turning to food for solace. No one is asking for advice, just a witness. They need each other to witness their own personal growth journey. The presence of others is comforting. During sharing, each person gets to hear a personal echo. They hear themselves as they share with others.

At meetings, people talk about things they would not mention elsewhere. Each has made a commitment to try to stop compulsive eating or starving. When not practicing your food obsession, you will need to let out feelings that bubble up.

Annette speaks next: "It's really hard to tell my husband I'm bored. He lets me make all our party and social plans. I carry on all the discussions with our kids and manage our entire lives. That was great when I was eating compulsively. It was my perfect excuse for overeating. After all, I'd say, I have to care for all these other people. I want my reward. My reward was food. Now that food is out of my picture, I want more from those I love. I'm finding out they're not there for me. The only place I feel nurtured is when I come to these meetings."

Arthur, a very obese young man, pipes up angrily from the back of the room. "My fat mom is a perfect earth mother, and I love her. I wouldn't want her coming to these meetings. She'd get her head filled with new ideas about taking care of herself. As it is now, she pays my bills when I get in a jam, she gets my dirty socks out from under the bed and makes sure they're washed and matched. She likes it this way and so do I. I'm just here to lose a little weight. Why change a perfectly workable family situation? What's the difference who manages whose life?"

These last two people represent opposite sides of the same coin. There is no one right solution for all situations. Arthur doesn't expect an answer. He knows it's okay to blow off some steam and express himself. There are no judgments. Feelings are neither right nor wrong. They just are. By hearing himself speak, Arthur is free to dig in his position, change his mind, or simply do nothing. This is the ideal family environment. Members get heard with no lectures back.

The members do care about what happens to each other. They have a common illness and know how hard it is to open up and also how crucial that is for survival. It would be terrible to criticize or judge each other for speaking openly. Each is there to witness the other. If they want feedback or further discussion, they can ask specific people after the meeting or confide in their sponsor, the person they've chosen to be their guide through the recovery process.

Before getting to OA, they had all tried changing their eating instead of their lives. Their best efforts walked them through the doors of their first meeting. Some had dieted their way up to two hundred or four hundred pounds. Some are thin or normal-sized and eat and then vomit or abuse laxatives. By the time they got to that first meeting, most found they ate for any reason. Whether in celebration or mourning, there is always a good reason to eat. They now come to these meetings for an experience that often can't be explained. That's okay. What they get keeps them from abusing food. Though they can't explain what they get, they know it works. Satisfaction with self lasts while the compulsion to eat drifts away. Their slogan is "If it works, don't fix it."

In the early days of alcoholism treatment, it was often said that you could not help people in trouble until they had hit bottom. Once they'd hit that bottom, it was assumed they had exhausted all denial systems and were ready to listen and receive help. Even then, there were people who said, "Well, you can lead a horse to water, but you can't make 'em drink." Father Joseph Martin, a famous lecturer in the alcoholism field, had an excellent answer: "Yeah, but you can make 'em mighty thirsty." Hopefully, by listening at these meetings, you will become attracted to this new way of life and get thirsty for recovery.

When alcoholism treatment programs were established, those administering the programs hoped to provide enough training, education, and confrontation so that even if the patient was not yet at bottom, or not yet even "thirsty," he or she could be convinced of the prospect of a joyful turnaround into recovery. That is why I created that first Obesity Recovery Service at San Pedro Hospital in Los Angeles in 1975, which eventually became HOPE units, then Hollis Institutes, and then spawned a national wave of eating disorder units.

There was a distinct difference between hospital treatments and OA. The primary difference was pushiness. We didn't wait for people to be ready. We made them ready. We took them in vans to the meetings. We talked back in group and confronted their "stinkin' thinkin'." We practiced new behaviors in psychodramas and encouraged them to try new things in their lives. We even brought in their family members and made the family aware of what was happening so there was no fertile ground of negative behavior to return to. Since managed care has swept the country, I closed all my units, and many others have vanished. Now we are left with food obsessives needing to make OA work for themselves without hospital help. They have to be more ready. It's not easy, but it can be done.

What is the healing process and what can you as a reader gain from attending these meetings? The meetings offer a forum for self-expression and an opportunity to open up and be *seen*. The avoidance of that visibility is what hiding in food is all about. Instead, meetings bring you out. Meetings work as a form of reparenting.

Children need a witness. Little Johnny plays on the slide and shouts, "Look, Daddy, watch me go!" Daddy doesn't know what to do or say. He responds as his father did, "That's a great slide." This scenario certainly meets all the guidelines for effective parenting. We see Dad providing positive support and encouragement as well as praise. However, we miss one crucial point: *Who asked him?* No one asked for his praise, encouragement, or evaluation. Johnny only asked for a witness. "Watch me, Daddy." That's all.

Unfortunately, most of us don't know how to be good watchers or listeners. We feel we have to offer something. We have *to give* in order to feel adequate and valuable. Who asked? At OA, you will get witnessed. You will be seen and heard. Members have learned how to *do* less and *be* more. As you get witnessed, you get healed. The meeting provides you the audience you need in order to come out. That's the new relating.

OA members celebrate the anniversary of their first entry to the program, referring to this date as their birthday into a new way of life as opposed to their natal birthday. They celebrate these as program birthdays.

Conduct of a Meeting

These meetings will be your place for *you*. You will eventually come to see this group of people as an extended family. Therefore, go to a meeting with an attitude of making it *your* place. Here, as nowhere else, will be a place you can be totally yourself. Whatever you say or do will be okay. Above all, don't try to make an impression or influence others. This is your place to be cared for and nurtured. Save your impressive stuff for the rest of the world. Let your little self emerge here. I suggest you attend initially as an observer/listener. Save your questions until you have attended at least three meetings. Try to go at first just to listen and learn. And try not to judge.

Most meetings run for an hour or two, depending on the format and local preferences. There is usually a written procedure for conduct of the meeting. This provides structure for the leader for that day. Most groups do not have established regular leaders but shift this role to different people each week.

There are few dos and don'ts about behavior at meetings. Meetings are intended as a place for you to be spontaneous and be yourself. There is only one cardinal rule suggested at most meetings: *no cross talk*. Members are encouraged to talk about themselves and their own experiences but to offer no advice to others about what should or shouldn't be done. In other words, you and others are safe to express your own feelings without anyone telling you what to do. Do not offer advice or feedback. Just listen. Those who talk are talking to hear their own echo. The purpose of self-expression is self-expression. Often, by hearing what comes out of your mouth, you gain an understanding of how you really feel. Then you'll instinctively know the right actions for you.

You may drop in late and leave early. You can do whatever works and fits your life. There will be no demands made on you by OA. The best advice is "take what you can use and leave the rest." Don't get attached to many questions. Let them all pass for now.

Types of Meetings

Meetings are different in different parts of the country. They are composed of different types of people with varying attitudes. You will find the same cross sections of people at almost every meeting place, but a specific meeting can change from week to week. Therefore, I recommend you try one meeting at least three times. See the variations. Inspect, don't reject. After all, haven't you given food a second chance? Remember when something tasted slightly moldy? Didn't you cut off the green stuff and take another taste just to make sure? Only then did you reluctantly toss it out. Give the same second chance to this recovery program that can save your life.

This same advice goes for family members. As a C-P, you have given your own controlling and destructive behavior patterns more than a second or third chance. You doggedly held on to the old behaviors insisting that just one more time would work. Try to develop the same type of faith in meetings. It's a way to help you detach from the F-O and to get help for yourself. It's a way to come back home.

Most locales have either closed or open meetings. An open meeting is open for all to attend—friends, family, or anyone interested in learning more. Closed are only attended by overeaters, anorexics, or vomiters—someone who has the illness. The closed meeting is open to anyone who wishes to stop eating compulsively. Following is a brief outline of the types of meetings you can expect.

NEWCOMERS MEETING. In many cities, especially large metropolitan centers, special meetings are organized for beginners, where specifics of the program are explained. A member introduces basic concepts about the treatment plan and the tools and is then available to answer questions and offer suggestions to the newcomer. Remember, OA is not run by professionals. A group therapy session has cross talk and feedback and confrontation and resolution. In OA, some statements just hang in the air. Other recovering members can say what worked for them, but no one comments. Your witnesses lovingly listen to you, and this is a call to your soul that it is safe to come out.

At your first meeting, you can pick up a local directory, which will explain meeting locations, types, and focus. There are now meetings specifically geared for anorexics and vomiters. There are some for one-hundred-pound weight losers. There are some for gays only, or women only, or men only. Some have a specific focus, like sexuality, maintenance, or meditation. Some have child care available, most are non-smoking, and each will have a contact phone number listed to obtain further information. Anyone can attend any of these meetings, but some will have rules about who can speak. This will be outlined at the beginning of the meeting.

Notice this book does not provide elaborate detail or explanation about the treatment plan of OA. It is instead suggested that you go to the meetings and then use this book as an adjunct. You will learn all you need to know as you attend. Bring the body, and the mind will follow.

SPEAKER MEETING. Speakers vary from meeting to meeting. At a speaker meeting, one member presents a twenty- to sixty-minute talk about how they've been helped. These are not professional speakers, simply group members. They are advised to talk about what their lives had been like, how they found a way out, and what their lives are like now. Some meetings allow for question-and-answer time, but usually the speaker stops and then others can speak for themselves.

You will be amazed at the clarity and insight voiced by some of the speakers as well as the wry humor of some of their stories. They often present the results of all their work by taking an honest look at their behavior and discussing it in ways that are palatable and give everyone attending a chance to chuckle at themselves. It's sometimes a humorous evening's entertainment and often a growth experience.

PITCH MEETING. In these meetings, anyone in the group can volunteer to speak, but no one has to speak. Sometimes people raise hands and are called on, or sometimes the attention goes around the room from one to the next in what is called a round robin. If your turn comes and you don't want to talk, you can simply say your name and "I pass." Each speaker talks for three to five minutes. They may talk about anything; usually topics are current activities or something they are learning about themselves or others. There is no cross talk or commenting.

DISCUSSION MEETING. Members sit in a circle and discuss a specific topic decided by the group or the leader. Even if a topic is named, members can still talk about anything they like. The format is relaxed and open, and each member can talk as many times as time allows.

BOOK STUDY. A number of books recommended by the OA fellowship are read at specific meetings. Sometimes these are books from Alcoholics Anonymous. Members are asked to read a paragraph and then discuss how it applies to them. Each person's opinion is her or his own interpretation. Sometimes all members at the meeting discuss how the same particular paragraph applies to them.

WRITING MEETING. The group agrees on a specific topic, and then members write about it. Sometimes there are specific workbooks with questions that are authorized by OA to be used at meetings. Later, some may read their written work to the group. At some meetings there are responses from other group members, and at some there is reading with no comments invited.

I must take a digression to share with you one of the highest points of my life. It occurred at a writing/book study meeting in Long Beach, California. I'd been visiting my brother and his family and decided to pop into an open meeting. During the "business break," one member announced a meeting forming to study a new book (my book) *Fat & Furious*. I got hot, and my heart started racing. I picked up the flyer and anonymously got to the meeting the following Sunday.

As the meeting's format instructed, we each read a paragraph and commented on what we'd read. Then we were instructed to turn to the exercises I'd provided in the book and to write our own answers to the questions proposed. We all wrote for about twenty minutes. Then those who wished were invited to read their writings. I read mine along with everyone else. I had such a strange sensation. Even though these were exercises I had originated in my hospital programs, seeing them implemented from the book without further directions took my breath away.

I struggled as a fly on the wall wondering whether I should let them know who I was. Instead I sat quietly and so warmly proud. At the meeting's end, I couldn't contain myself. I raised my hand and sobbed, "I'm Judi, a compulsive overeater, and I wrote that book." I boo-hooed with such joy and elation, and they did too. It was remarkable. I felt like the mother of Moses, like I had sent my baby down river in a reed basket, and it had developed a life of its own. I had launched it, but it didn't need me anymore. It was a natural high and an opportunity few get a chance to experience.

You can learn about meetings in your area by calling a local group and requesting that a directory of local meetings be sent to you. You can also pick up a directory at your first meeting. These will list the types of meetings offered as well as the name and phone number of a contact person should you like more information before attending. *Go ahead and make that call.* You have nothing to lose but your obsession with food. If you don't like the meetings, they'll refund your misery.

Talking the Talk and Walking the Walk

Over the years since this book was first published, many changes have occurred within OA. While the growth of treatment centers brought many new members to OA, these members also changed the character of some of the dogma.

As the meetings were flooded with patients who were still in treatment centers, the discussions started veering more toward psychological causalities; sometimes people blamed others for the mess they'd created. Patients were bringing to OA the things they were discussing in group therapy. These are not the same kinds of directions taken in OA groups. The OA philosophy is more about "Let it begin with me. Let me see what I have to do to be part of the solution instead of part of the problem." Unfortunately, in my opinion, many OA groups lost that focus and became oriented more toward psychology and less toward spirituality. I believe this has contributed to a decline in OA membership over the last two decades. Even though you do have to search harder to find the spiritual direction, I encourage you to try to find the spiritual element in what you hear at the meetings.

One crucial change at OA meetings has nothing to do with spirit but everything to do with body. There is sometimes excessive attention given to food plans. A number of fringe groups have split off from OA proper because they are upset that the larger OA organization does not support or recommend any specific food plan. Wouldn't you just know it? We come to these programs because of an inability to handle food, and then we let arguments over food divide us.

The great divide started in the mid-1980s. Interestingly enough, though OA's membership is predominantly female, two men engineered the split. Various OA groups asked successful members to come in from other locales and speak at weekend retreats or special seminars to share what had worked for them. They were disclosing what OA had done for them and what they found that worked. One guru traveled from Florida and told groups around the country that he felt nothing had worked for him as well as a rigid focus on a weighed and measured food plan with strict physical guidelines and strict writing and calling assignments. Any deviation from the plan was cause to start over. His groups spawned this rhetoric, were quite militaristic in their philosophy, and split off into many factions known as HOW groups (**H**onesty, **O**pen-mindedness, and **W**illingness), gray sheet groups, Cambridge groups, OA Plus, and even a totally new group called Food Addicts Anonymous. You will find these groups mostly in large metropolitan areas. New York City has many specialty groups.

If you find that you have come upon one of these groups, please know that the spiritual path recommends more of a moderate middle road. We are told, "Wear your recovery like a loose garment." However, many in early recovery are still fearful and want the security of rigidity. They honestly feel that people who aren't following their rigid path are actually self-deluded and almost drunk in denial. Thus, they practice the more ascetic, controlling path. I have never discouraged a patient from trying these groups, as it is a good way to get started. I often recommend people try it for thirty days as a jump-start to their recoveries. It definitely gets your attention and lets you see how the food obsession has controlled your life and what a secret eater you've become. All of those new insights are worthwhile. It's just that if your identity once again is formed around controlling food, then you are still in food obsession and not in recovery.

The other guru traveled out from Los Angeles and took the opposite position. He taught that the focus should be on spiritual principles and off food. Even though he'd lost his weight by rigidly dieting, he proposed that others lose weight by reading and doing writing assignments from the Big Book. Members so wanted to believe that prayer and meditation and reading and writing without food restriction would miraculously zap them thin. Alas, most of the time this did not happen, and these groups are sometimes called the "fat serenity" groups. They had what some members refer to as "heads full of program but bellies full of food." You will ultimately need to find a middle path of gentle personal discipline coupled with placing faith in others and asking for help.

The New Family System

Whatever type of meeting you choose, you will come to see the people there as a new family for you. Many have proclaimed after attending a meeting:

"I've come home at last!"

"No one ever understood me like these people."

"I can talk about anything I like, and someone else feels that way too."

"Whatever I say, I am accepted and feel worthwhile."

"I love how no one tells me what to do."

"I'm not alone as a freak anymore."

The most important healing ingredient of the OA program is the meeting. This is what cures the loneliness and isolation. F-Os and their loved ones are needy people with fluid and changing ego boundaries. Each needs support and encouragement. You can't depend on just one other person to fill those needs. You need the group. You need to spread around those needs so that you can tolerate rejection. At some point, someone will always fail you. If one person is busy or can't be there for you right at that minute, there is always someone else in the group. You won't have to be alone. Loneliness leads back to food; including others leads out of addiction. You will find it becomes more fun to be with people than with food. The choice will be very clear and much less painful. As people get closer, food will become boring. I can assure you, attending meetings will really mess up your relationship with food. You just can't eat in the same old way anymore. Sorry.

Science Catches Up

In October of 1983, research projects reported at the International Congress of Eating Disorders in New York City showed that two crucial elements of the OA program also prove most effective in professional treatment. The research recommended treating people in groups rather than individually and with peer counseling, that is, one fellow sufferer helping another. Every research project mentioned showed that people did much better in a group than individually. Even when treatment consisted of dispensing a placebo pill, those who took the pill in a group setting had more success than those who took the pill alone.

A study at Vanderbilt University showed that when one group of advanced patients was asked to work as counselors for a second group of less advanced patients, dropout rates were practically eliminated and weight loss results were 85 percent higher. In 1985, I wrote, "As medical science continues to catch up with programs like OA, we will see more research explaining why these methods work. For now, we can just take it on faith that if it has worked for so many others, it can work for you too."

I am sorry to say that because of the rapid proliferation of Prozac prescriptions and the changes in OA, we as a nation have come to believe in the old TV commercial extolling better living through chemistry and have put such research onto the back burner.

Reparenting

As an F-O, you came by your behavior and feelings quite honestly. You did the best you could with what you knew then. What was missing was a chance to remain a child. You grew up too quickly, sometimes parenting your own parent. Now it's time for you to collect on the parenting. You need parents who understand and respect you and expect nothing from you. Both F-Os and C-Ps need a place to become children again.

In your new OA or Al-Anon family, no one really expects anything of you. It's up to you to give what you want. You don't owe anyone anything. Actually, for quite a while, the only expectation is that you be the receiver—the baby. Newcomers in OA are referred to as babies, pigeons, or sponsees, as they follow recommendations from a sponsor. Remember, members actually celebrate birthdays on the day they entered OA and essentially were born into a new way of life. You are expected to be like a newborn babe. Don't push yourself to learn, grow, or achieve. Instead, relax into your recovery. You don't have to worry about learning it all right away. You have the rest of your life to recover.

Your new parent figure in OA will be someone you call a sponsor. The sponsor is another member who you pick for yourself. You believe you can learn from this person. You must make the first move and ask someone to be your sponsor. Potential sponsors won't push themselves on you; they don't want to violate you in any way. They will wait until you ask for help. Of course, you know how hard that is, and so do they. Look and listen at the meetings, and try to find someone who you think you can talk with, someone who could offer you guidance. Members recommend that you find someone who has what you want. If you admire what this person has done with his or her life, ask for guidance so you can do the same.

Different things attract different people. Some want only to talk with someone who has been as fat as they have. One patient told me, "I don't want to bother with anyone who hasn't lost at least a hundred pounds." Others discriminate by looking for the eating pattern that matched theirs, such as other vomiters or weekend bingers. Some want a specific food plan, social class, or availability. One busy business-woman wanted someone who was home all day so she could make contact whenever she needed. You decide what is most important to you.

Your reasons for choosing a sponsor aren't as important as just choosing someone so you can get started on the journey. You can use one sponsor for a while and then change when you need to. The essential aspect of this relationship is that you *use* that person. Learn from that person. Take from that person. You don't give back anything. As a way of thanks, your sponsor will ask you to pass it on—to help others later as he or she has helped you. That is the healing ingredient. You take and only give back when you are filled.

When you choose a sponsor, you are investing in your recovery. It's a step toward asking for help. That's the hard part. You may change sponsors when you like, and you may end up having many sponsors throughout your recovery. People change and grow and move in different directions. There is a saying: "When the student is ready, the teacher appears." Don't worry about picking the sponsor. You will choose exactly who you need and what you are ready for right now. Choosing a sponsor is an important step toward developing a program of abstinence.

What Is Abstinence?

Because we all have to eat, there is no easy way to define abstinence from either compulsive eating or starving. It's not simply removing the substance. Alcoholics can plug the jug. We can't. My best definition is "Abstinence is guilt-free eating." Finding that path will be ambiguous. You'll have to negotiate your way daily and personally.

In early recovery you will only be assured that you are not guilty by talking with a surrogate parent, a sponsor in Overeater's Anonymous, each day. Once you have negotiated with another sufferer about what and how you eat, you can feel confident that two heads planned the food plan and you can eat without guilt. You won't have to worry about your addictive, self-destructive, punitive self rising up to hurt you. The healing ingredient is letting someone else see into your plate. It starts with getting honest about what you're eating. That gradually expands to getting honest in other areas of your life.

Once you have found a sponsor, you'll be face-to-face with the *big question:* What to eat or not eat? Although a nutritionist can help you here, this goes much deeper than what you put in your mouth. It involves issues of integrity and of honoring personal commitments to yourself. It's not just about knowing *what* to eat—it's about *doing* it. Your sponsor is the witness you will need to help you keep your promises to yourself. This person is not your judge or your jury, just a witness.

Your food choices are never clear-cut, but they'll get easier once you begin to disclose your daily food consumption to someone else. Together, two people can make daily decisions. It's hard for compulsive people to get rigorously honest. You will initially hate this experience. Decisions about food are extremely intimate and can be very problematic. There is no definite right way. It's difficult for us to tolerate such ambiguity. But when you find someone to share your food choices with, you'll be opening a channel to your inner self. This intimate relationship will allow you to let yourself become more visible.

We focus on food first so that later we can give up focusing on it. Having a disciplined food plan is what gets us to the starting gate, gets us feeling a little raw so that our deeper inner signals can begin to be heard. In any event, please don't forget that the food must always be attended to first. First you need the clarity and discipline, and then you can work on the steps and spiritual dimensions. Think of your food plan as footwork, or preparation.

For many years, my Hollywood treatment center had seen many movie-star wanna-bes and a few celebrities. In the movie business you'll hear often, "It's not *what* you know, but *who* you know" or, "You just gotta wait for that lucky break." Well, I've seen many who were given that lucky break, but they weren't ready when opportunity knocked. They hadn't done their footwork. They got a chance at success, but because they hadn't done the necessary preparation, their "actor's instrument"—themselves—had not been developed enough to rise to the occasion. They were soon forgotten. Others had devoted themselves to training and preparation and continuous study. When their lucky break came, they were ready to seize the opportunity. They had something deep, personal, and real to deliver. They had made themselves ready for success. Think of your food plan the same way, as a readiness for diving into your new life after waiting for your lucky break.

I saw this clearly with Jan, an early outpatient who came to group therapy every week, reported a perfectly abstinent food plan, watched many others share great emotion, sat quietly, and disclosed very little about herself. After six weeks, she hadn't lost a pound.

An easy answer would have been that life is unfair or "Jan is lying about what she eats." The truth was that Jan was still lying to herself about who she was. Her food plan was just as she described it. The problem was that her feelings were still dishonest. Thank God, she didn't drop out at this stage. Most treatment programs expect high dropout rates. Many gyms and behavior-modification programs overbook their classes because they know many will leave after three weeks. If all showed up as registered, those locker rooms would be too full.

Jan was brave enough to keep showing up. And as she watched others begin to come out, her own inner self became awakened and encouraged to come out as well. One night, without warning, she came to group unable to stop crying. She'd been watching others, and finally her inner self felt safe enough to come out.

Jan told us that her weight had stayed on because she needed to hold down a lot of emotion. She was conflicted and blocked about the death of her only son in the Korean War. She had very heavy expectations of herself about what kind of a mother and Christian she wanted to be. She wanted to model herself as decent and God-fearing and accepting of God's will. But when God seemed to have turned away from her, she found no way to cope except to eat. In our group she was encouraged not to eat and ultimately to release her sadness. At the time of her son's death, she had taken care of everyone else, made all the funeral arrangements, never cried, and kept making big pots of spaghetti. She accepted it all quietly, subdued her rage with "It's God's will," and then ate nonstop for the next twenty years.

We all spent the evening encouraging her to come out. We reenacted her son's funeral in a psychodrama session and helped her talk to him and say good-bye. The sobbing from all the group members was tremendous as we each remembered our own sadness and supported hers. The next week she had lost twelve pounds. Her body no longer needed to hold the sadness. Much of it got expressed that evening. More would flow out in years to come as she stayed abstinent.

This whole story may seem far-fetched, and it would certainly be difficult to explain to a purely medical audience. It smacks a bit of California, "airy-fairy, fruits, and nuts." I would be leading the pack of doubting Thomases here myself, if I hadn't seen this happen so often.

Wilhelm Reich, inventor of the orgone box and the earliest body-work theorist, believed that we have emotions locked up in every cell of our being. According to Reich, each of our cells and muscles holds memories about our entire life experience. Reichian therapists will work with you to open up breathing and then do Reichian massage to ease and relax and release muscle energy. These techniques awaken and release long-dead feelings. Similar effects can happen with long-term food abstinence and a gentle invitation from others on the same path.

As with Jan, once the emotion is released, your organism no longer needs to stay blocked off, puffed up, filled, and solidly packed. You become open, empty, and ready to be penetrated by new experiences. Jan was doing the footwork, staying abstinent, getting ready for that evening. She was preparing for her lucky break. Once the sadness was ready to emerge, her body was ready to give up the weight. She wasn't sugarcoated or lard-laden any longer. When her psyche got cleared, her body was clear, and the gluing, blocking fat could melt away.

These things rarely happen according to our conscious timetable. I've now seen thousands who were able to follow these guidelines, seeking their inner souls instead of their outer shapes. Each time, as long as the food plan stayed moderate, the body eventually caught up with the spirit.

Mutual Trust and Interdependence

The sponsor/baby relationship is the crucial healing ingredient in recovery. Previously you had been a terminally unique case who aborted treatment. Now you come to this relationship both asking for help and investing yourself in the recovery process. It is clear no one else will fix you or even expects you to be fixed. With the sponsor, you will not have the excessively enmeshed relationship you had in your own family. You were all too close to help. In this new partnership, you are expected to do most of the work. The sponsor will guide you but won't carry you. In this new relationship there will be enough distance to keep it safe, but a new closeness as you share a common undertaking. You will become survivors together. Your reminiscences will resemble GIs who shared the trenches of war. No one else will understand the rigors of hell you suffer as you transfer dependency on food to a new relationship with other people. Nowhere will you get more for giving less.

Nadia, an early patient, had a lifelong dream that richly illustrates the F-O's longing for nurturance. Her dream never became a reality, so she ate instead. This same dream came to her at least eight times a year and upon awakening, she cried. In this dream, Nadia was a one-celled organism, an amoeba. This single-celled amoeba was three feet in diameter, an undulating, fluid body mass. Tiny hairlike growths radiated from her circumference. Her interior fluid was a rich, transparent, gooey green mass, like hair-set lotion. Nadia, a gigantic cell, slithered quickly across the floor, adjusting form as she went. I asked her to recount the recurring dream as if she were the amoeba. Here is what she shared:

> I feel particularly heavy and slow. I am grotesque. When I move, I blob along from side to side feeling listless and heavy. I feel like wherever the weight of my goo pulls me, the rest follows. I blob and slither

slowly into a room full of people. I hear faint murmurs, their reactions as they move out of my way. They jump back aghast with "eeeeeeeeooooooo" and "yech" and "ich, creepy," but I keep on coming. I feel sorry for all of them because they have to look at me, and I know I am revolting. I suck myself up off the floor into one of the chairs. I work hard to get up the chair leg and then feel depleted. I melt into the chair. Parts of me hang over the sides. I heave a giant sigh and settle myself to rest. The people in the room eventually stop staring at me and continue with their own business. Quite unexpectedly, a young woman moves out of the blur of strange figures and comes over to sit in the chair beside me. I am still and scared. I stop breathing. No longer undulating in and out, I remain perfectly still in shock. I want to disappear but know I attract more attention trying to move. I rest and keep still and pray no one will look. The next thing I know, she reaches over and starts petting me on my hairy back. With soft, determined strokes, she continues, not even noticing how slimy I am. I'm shocked. She continues long after she should be repulsed. I start to relax, figuring she really doesn't notice what she's touching. Soon I relax fully into the experience and even feel like cooing, I'm so blissful. No one has ever petted me like that. She seems to be touching me just because she likes me. How weird, I think. What does she get out of this? Shouldn't I be doing something in return? What's the payback? She just keeps on petting. I coo. Then I wake up.

That same kind of experience is what many report from their first OA meeting. They find that same kind of acceptance, nurturance, and support. What's odd at first is that nothing is expected in return. You are accepted for just coming in the door. You long for a place to just have a seat and relax. Like Nadia, you have had a lifelong search for unconditional love. Even if you feel repulsive, you long for acceptance. "Love me, love my fat." In OA, you have a chance to be bathed in acceptance regardless of performance. A slogan in OA is "We will love you until you can love yourself."

The sponsor's message is "It is hard enough to refrain from eating compulsively. You really don't have to put on any airs or act any roles here. OA is where you can come home to fall apart. Have a seat and relax. You can be passive here."

What happens between you and your sponsor is as varied as the members of OA. You will have to trust that the directions your sponsor gives you are given with love and with your best interests at heart. The sponsor will tell you, "If you want what I have, you must do what I do." The sponsor will recommend certain things that have worked for her or him. These are suggestions, not orders. Feel free to argue with your sponsor. That is the way to have a healthy relationship. You must share your resistance. Blindly following won't work, as you will soon slip away when you have a disagreement. Totally rejecting all the sponsor's suggestions is also a waste of time. You must find the middle ground of trusting someone else as well as trusting yourself.

At the meetings and with your sponsor, don't let your criticisms go underground and don't just smile and tell everyone how wonderful you think the meetings are. I have seen many raving about the value of OA meetings and their ultimate joy in attending. Then they just stop going. What happened? They didn't know how to express their criticisms. You are bound to have criticisms. After all, you are facing the reality of turning around your entire life and doing things in a whole new way. All your relationships in the world will change. You are bound to balk. Let's balk out loud.

After each meeting, I advise newcomers to write down their thoughts and feelings. The most common reactions are anger or sadness. The anger response comes when you judge other participants and assume that they will be inadequate to fill your needs. Sadness bubbles up if you relax and let yourself feel the comfort of the group. You face how long you have been operating without comfort and how sorely it is missed.

Trust your reactions. They indicate where you are right now. You may uncover a pattern as your own reactions change dramatically from the first to the fourth meeting. That is why you will hear, at the end of each meeting: "Keep coming back."

Most newcomers suffer an approach/avoidance reaction to their first meetings. Newcomers want what the others have but are also scared to death to reach out. You, too, will appreciate having found a place to feel accepted and understood. But at the same time, you will pick it apart and find fault. This is a natural reaction to the threat of change. Let yourself flow with these feelings. Here are some comments from patients after returning from their first meetings. Notice the broad range of responses and all the variations and contradictions. Check which comments echo yours.

What Did You Learn at the Meeting?

- ☐ One day at a time.
- ☐ Too many rules for me.
- ☐ I feel hostile.
- ☐ I feel like I can open up to these people.
- ☐ Others have it worse than I do.
- ☐ I am not alone.
- ☐ I have feelings like the speaker.
- ☐ I really am out of control.

- [ ] I see how hard it is.
- [ ] It's not about food, but you can't forget food.
- [ ] I see the illness is about relating in the world.
- [ ] These people are a snotty bunch.
- [ ] I think they're phony.
- [ ] I don't like all the hugging.
- [ ] I'm so shy.
- [ ] I learned it's a disease, and I'm powerless.
- [ ] Don't eat, no matter what.
- [ ] This, too, shall pass.
- [ ] I feel very sorry for myself.
- [ ] I don't like the seriousness of all this.
- [ ] I feel uneasy. I've never had it as bad as they do.
- [ ] I hate myself for being here.
- [ ] I applaud myself for sticking out the meeting.
- [ ] I feel like all these people are closing in on me.
- [ ] I'm angry.
- [ ] I want to kick everyone.
- [ ] I don't feel like working this hard on this stuff.
- [ ] I thought one of the guys was cute.
- [ ] A man told me, "You look radiant," and it scared me to death.
- [ ] I've got to keep my eyes off him and on myself.
- [ ] People talk real honestly here.
- [ ] Even though they've come to a meeting, some people are still jerks.
- [ ] I was scared to talk, but afterward felt high.
- [ ] I felt like an observer rather than a member.
- [ ] I see I, too, have something to give, not just take.
- [ ] Recovery is possible.
- [ ] I know I weigh more than two hundred pounds, but when I get around help, I want to deny it.

☐ I'm afraid.

☐ I feel the strength of others in recovery.

☐ I can see how I reject offered help.

☐ I chose a new sponsor today, and I feel excited.

☐ I entered the meeting feeling resentful, and now I leave feeling peaceful and calm.

☐ I see how much I'd rather help others than care for myself.

☐ I get scared to talk in front of the men.

☐ I hate how they see themselves as such givers.

☐ I need to learn to mind my own business.

☐ This is treatment. Nothing is more important.

☐ I thought about tomorrow's meals throughout the whole meeting.

☐ I see how it's a family disease.

☐ I like the small group. It forced me to come out of myself.

☐ We don't know each other, but I can tell they understand.

☐ I see how being married doesn't fix you either.

☐ I like the jokes.

☐ I can see I don't have to play at being a nice person.

☐ I see whether I eat or not, the problem will still be there.

☐ I don't like all those slogans.

———————◾———————

Try to jot down your overall response after each meeting. You will have reactions similar to those above. Let's move on to categorizing the major response trends.

Capitalize the Critic

Most critical comments about the meetings fall into three major areas: Wounded Healers, Disorganization, and Religiosity. Let's take a look at these major blocks to the program.

WOUNDED HEALERS. There is no professional therapist leading the meeting. Some newcomers are concerned that the people at the meetings are just as sick as those seeking help. That's right . . . and that's exactly why the program is so effective. People identify their own strengths and weaknesses by observing others with similar afflictions. This, of course, is the prevalent concept in group psychotherapy: we learn from watching others grow. Another sufferer sees an addict's denial system and self-delusion more clearly than the addict or often even more effectively than trained professionals.

A therapist friend of mine was treating an overeater who she asked each week, "How's your food?"

The client dutifully reported with a smile, "Fine."

This went on for months, but the patient gained sixty pounds. Even professionals in the field might not have the instinctual ability to understand an overeater or starver. An OA member, however, might have sensed the problem earlier. Let's face it, we know our own kind. OA members quip, "You spot it; you got it."

Other addicts are often attuned to each other's delusions and denial systems. They know to ask for more specifics and closer scrutiny of the daily food plan. They help you remove those personal blinders we all have when we choose not to see. This may sound inviting, but it's also terrifying.

Another complaint many newcomers have is that "I'm not that bad. I've never gotten that fat or been that obsessed or vomited that often. Those people are really sickos. It's not for me."

This refrain often comes from a person who has a minimal acquaintance with the obsession and is in the early stages. They don't want to believe that, to recover, they will have to get honest and show parts of themselves they don't like. This is particularly true for the bingers who vomit. They work at all costs to look good. They are, therefore, very judgmental of people who show weakness. To avoid showing themselves, they develop a case of the "yets":

"I haven't done that *yet.*"

"That hasn't happened to me *yet.*"

"I didn't pick food out of the trash *yet.*"

"I'm not that bad *yet.*"

The "yets" help us remain critical of others. (This is outlined extensively in my upcoming book *The Four-Day Diet.*) When you are not invested and doing something, it is very easy to criticize the efforts of others. You can afford to criticize when not taking action. Just realize that whatever judgments you make will come home to roost. You will be just as hard on yourself, judging all your efforts as you try on new behaviors. You may have to go through a lot more pain before you can accept help.

If you notice yourself veering toward the "yets," ask yourself why you have to go that far down the road before you are ready to turn around? Why not get help now? Do you need to have your eyes gouged out before you'll admit that you might not see things clearly?

A well-known treatise by a famous speaker in Alcoholics Anonymous, Chuck C., is titled *A New Pair of Glasses.* He illustrates how we have to switch our channels and take a new view of our old lives. Accepting help from others who've gone ahead might help illuminate your path for the journey. Try to think of those who have suffered before you as scouts warning you of dangers ahead. Maybe if you become willing to participate earlier, you can head off some of your suffering. The yets are just a delaying action. Why not grab on now?

DISORGANIZATION. People who reject OA because of structure problems see things at both ends of the spectrum. They either find the group "too controlling, excessively rigid and demanding, with no flexibility or humanity" or else see it as "too haphazard, not starting on time, with all members doing their own things with no definite structure or direction." It's all true. So what?

As an F-O or as a C-P, you have a lot of conflict over control, aggression, and passivity. You are keenly adept at discovering loopholes in the control and organization of groups. After all, the people in OA have difficulty being disciplined and keeping commitments to themselves, so they would just naturally take these same traits into their group meetings.

Disorganization, however, is not cause to leave the meeting. Instead, it is a good training ground for you to experience living with too much or too little organization. Whether you complain that you want to be ordered what to do or that the group is too bossy, in OA you will learn to follow directions from fallible human beings. Can you give up control and follow directions? Can you trust that this must be what you need right now?

RELIGIOSITY. In my thirty years of listening to criticisms of Twelve Step groups, one stands out above all others. Whether a narcotic addict, an overeater, or a professional in the field, the most common criticism is "There's too much God talk. I'm not religious." These words are often voiced by someone who has never even attended a Twelve Step meeting. (Professional therapists are the worst. They don't realize that the belief in psychotherapy is equally a man-made construct and not that far removed from a religion.) In fact, OA is a spiritual program, not a religious one. Twelve Steppers say, "Religion is for those who are afraid of hell. Spirituality is for those who've already been there."

If you criticize OA as being too religious, consider the possibility that if you are food obsessed, you are actually very religious. You have been worshiping an external substance that you believed could cure your ills and solve your problems. Food was God.

OA members may joke, "The only thing you have to know about God is 'You ain't it.'" Even so, as you progress, you will learn to "be still and know that I am God." You don't need to adopt a God concept. You may instead look and listen for your own still, small voice within. This is your own personal God you've been ignoring. When you keep yourself sedated and self-loathing with food, you can't pay attention to the special messages from within. That is why I say we are as fat as we are dishonest.

The degree to which we have refused to follow directions from our own personal message center is the degree to which we have replaced self with worship to false gods. By attending these meetings, you will give up those obsessions and find a way to live more closely attuned to your own internal voice. Call it God, or call it chopped liver. Whether a rose or a thorn by name, it works.

Commitment

There are a number of suggested and recommended food plans in OA, and I don't believe any one to be better than another. What matters is the commitment you make regarding eating behavior. This works when the newcomer makes a decision in the morning about what will be eaten that day and how it will be eaten. The food plan can depend on natural phenomena like the weather, events of the day such as exercise levels, or personal preferences. Each day is taken anew, one day at a time.

The newcomer "baby" calls the sponsor with the plan. He or she writes down the food plan and asks a sponsor to witness it. Sponsors are not trained nutritionists but rather fellow sufferers who have been successful. They may or may not advise or comment. Their major role is to serve as a witness to your commitment to yourself. They are neither your judge nor your disciplinarian; they are your confidantes, who will listen as you promise something to yourself. You may easily break a promise to yourself but hesitate to break promises to others. With this commitment, you are including someone else in your thought process.

This may be where your resistance will loom up. Of all the recommendations to newcomers, the idea of sharing the food commitment with someone else is often an insurmountable stumbling block. Most people absolutely hate this idea of "calling in" food. Protests range from seeing it as childish, punitive, a waste of time, or an imposition on someone else, to stupid, unnecessary, and generally inconvenient. It is difficult because it involves imposing some control and discipline on your relationship with food. It is an intrusion to bring someone else into that most intimate and private relationship. "How dare they look at my plate. I'm not a child." But you are a child where food is concerned. Remember, your sponsor will be a new parent figure, not punitive, just guiding.

The Day After

Some people who attend their first meeting fall madly in love with Overeaters Anonymous and decide food is no longer an issue in their lives. They get joy from being with other F-Os. They feel miraculously cured and finished with obsessions. They have arrived! Bull.

That is not what really happens. In the therapy field we call this a "flight into health." These people have become so frightened by the amount of work in store that they say, "Everything's wonderful; my problems are over." What they are really saying is, "Thanks a lot, Doc. It's been great. See ya. I'm outta here. Phew. Got out of that one." They are again believing in the quickie. Members of OA call this the honeymoon period. You want to believe you've found the way. You actually have, but there's still work to do.

More usual than the flight into health is the immediate

rejection of OA. You may find a very good reason why this is not the place for you. Rejecting the meetings often happens because, as George Bernard Shaw quipped many years ago, "I don't want to be a member of any club that would have *me* as a member." You may decide the entrance requirements are too liberal. You want a more exclusive club, perhaps one that is more familiar to you. Both F-Os and their C-Ps tend to use the same types of excuses for rejecting meetings. Initially proclaiming it's a great idea, you then decide it just doesn't seem right *for you*. No matter what the excuse, you actually fear being vulnerable and seeking help from other fallible human beings. You will try at all costs to protect yourself from being human and vulnerable. It is healthy to bring these feelings into consciousness and to voice your intransigence and resistance. Following are some of the resistances you might use.

Resistance Checklist

Check those you have thought or said.

☐ I can do it myself.

☐ I am infallible.

☐ I don't relate to those people.

☐ They are too thin.

☐ I don't want to be too thin.

☐ They are depressing.

☐ Those people are much sicker than I am.

☐ They use foul language there.

☐ They are too religious.

☐ They are crazy.

☐ I'm not that bad yet.

☐ I don't like the food plan.

☐ They have no food plan.

- [ ] It's too vague and unstructured.
- [ ] I don't like people telling me what to do.
- [ ] There are no prizes.
- [ ] I live too far to travel to those meetings.
- [ ] Meetings are boring.
- [ ] I'm embarrassed to telephone and bother people.
- [ ] Those people are too demanding.
- [ ] I want more discussion as a group. I like cross talk.
- [ ] These meetings take time away from myself.
- [ ] I went to one and that's enough.
- [ ] It's too simplistic.
- [ ] I've already dealt with all those issues.
- [ ] The meetings cause problems at home.
- [ ] My spouse objects.
- [ ] I don't need to hear other people's problems.
- [ ] It's too scary to look at these problems.
- [ ] The people are more sloppy [dumb, smart, loud, quiet, etc.] than I am.
- [ ] There are not enough direct solutions.
- [ ] There are too many side discussions.
- [ ] They are having too much fun. Get serious.
- [ ] I really don't want to believe there is hope.
- [ ] The times are inconvenient.
- [ ] They don't give enough specifics on what to do.
- [ ] They want to take my food away.

———————■———————

Even if you feel delighted at your first few meetings, eventually these judgments will loom up. It is important that you voice your concerns both to yourself and others and keep going anyway. Some in OA have said that they had tried all other methods many times and finally remained in OA as they saw it as "the last house on the block."

Threats to the Old with Promises of the New

In any system there is a strong pull to keep the status quo. Stability is easier than change, even if change promises something better. That is true for obese bodies. Bodies have a set point at which they've become accustomed to operating. When you starve that body, it takes preventive measures by slowing down its metabolism to maintain the status quo. The body will work to stay fat even if the brain decides to go on a diet. The same commitment to the status quo holds for our individual personalities as well as all parts of the family system. Even if the old ways served to maintain food or people obsessions, there will still be a strong tendency to maintain the old ways.

Many people have the idea that our family problems are our own, and we'll solve them ourselves. But your best efforts got you where you are right now. You must realize that trying a new way will be a threat to the past, an admission that the old way didn't work. The detachment process is threatening.

Support for Sanity

By continuing to attend meetings, both F-Os and their families will learn to detach from one another and to each help themselves. You will each have your own sponsor for support and guidance and will be willing to let those you love take care of themselves. You will find yourself feeling more deserving and less guilty. You will realize that by keeping your eyes on yourself and your own plate, your whole family will develop separateness, so later you will be able to move back together stronger and more assertively.

CHAPTER 7

"No" to Food Is "Yes" to Life

In giving up the security of excess food and the enmeshment of smothering relationships, you are moving to a new flexibility and excitement about life and yourself. By attending meetings and sharing, you will begin to discover the self you drowned with food. You will move from a static existence to one that is more open and expanding. Confluents will grow to respect themselves whether they are fixing someone or not. All relationships will become more honest. You have to relate honestly or return to the food obsession.

The Body Doesn't Lie

When you are neither bingeing compulsively nor starving obsessively, your body will be a perfect barometer for your own true direction and proper course of action. In fact, wanting that clearly resonant, wisely indicating body is a good reason to stay free of any substances that cloud over or muffle out the signal. You will want to keep your body a little less than full so that the signal can vibrate effectively. You want to put down your dinner fork to become your own personal tuning fork. Self-doubt will evaporate as you begin to listen for internal cues. Your body will not lie. You will find an ability to gauge situations intuitively. Many people find that this has profound effects on all relationships, especially intimate ones.

The profound issues around intimacy in eating and loving

are explored extensively in my book *Hot & Heavy*. After first drawing the connections between eating and intimacy and boundary penetration, I teach women to keep a "vulva vigil" so that they are only available for "conscious coitus." Little did I know that the seeds for that book were already germinating when I wrote the following words in this book in 1985:

> How many have had sexual relations just because they seemed to have started something and weren't able to admit that the mind is willing, but the body is not. Men have a clearer indicator of this deceit as their bodies just won't operate when they're not ready. Women, on the other hand, have developed a keener ability to mask their ambivalence. For example, let's say that Prince Charming has just taken you to dinner at a fine romantic place where you'd always wanted to go. He's terrific. You just feel all close, warm, affectionate, and "ready." You're at home and alone, and he picks up your signal, and he's ready too. As the clothes fly, the bed turns down, and you continue to embrace, your mind wanders innocently to a preoccupation with difficulties you had at work. Do you stop? Do you pause and whisper, "Dear, my mind just wandered, and I started thinking about other things. Can we wait a few minutes?" How many are that honest with their sexuality?

More often, partners decide to follow through to protect the other's feelings. Whose feelings have been protected? Do you really believe your partner doesn't know you left the room? Maybe these things are never discussed, but in truth, the body knows when it's abandoned. It might be more loving to tell your partner you've left for a while. That can let you both come back honestly. It's not a personal affront. It's not malicious or insensitive. It's just honest, human, and true. Who could ask for more?

If your body signals to you that you aren't ready, then you aren't ready. There is really no logical reason to be dishonest in bed, except if you are concerned about weak egos and fragile self-concepts. In your new recovery programs, both you and your partner learn that you are much more than your image, and you both deserve the chance to be real. When you are saying no to the food obsession, you need to learn to say no to other things that aren't on your timetable or in your best interests as well.

If you avoid the difficult work of finding out what is right for you and standing up for yourself without putting others down, you might run the risk of returning to food obsession. You have to become your own champion and have the courage to show who you are. In this chapter, you will experience coming home to yourself. You will learn techniques to be more grounded and secure so you won't need the weight. When you can represent your own position clearly and from a strong center, you won't need to amass excess flesh to feel substantial. Without this grounding, you'll get too scared and return to excess food. Lost poundage will quickly reappear. Now is the time to say no to food and yes to your own life.

Tiffany learned to say yes to herself. She was a budding Hollywood starlet, making every casting call and audition. She was also anorexic and a periodic vomiter. From time to time she landed a walk-on part or a brief appearance on the soap operas. Her career was just getting off the ground, but her vomiting was growing more excessive. She had even been talked into a few producers' beds. Tiffany accepted many of the dehumanizing aspects of her chosen career and began to use herself as a commodity on the casting couch.

She starved herself painfully for weeks at a time and then resorted to weekend pig-outs. She also vomited after every sexual foray with men she didn't like. *As an actor, I use myself as my instrument,* she rationalized. *Everyone knows a great part of an actor's life is spent in seeking work rather than working. This is just one of the methods I use for job hunting. And it works.* Tiffany had effectively rationalized behavior that her soul could not tolerate. In *Hot & Heavy,* I advise you not to take your body anywhere your soul can't follow.

The more Tiffany jumped in and out of Hollywood beds, the more she vomited in rage at what she "had to do" to get work. When she asked for help with the vomiting, she found that to change her relationship with food she had to change her sexual behaviors. She had to learn how to say no. She also said no to the part of herself that told her she couldn't make it without violation and humiliation. She could no longer chide herself. Ultimately, for each person in recovery, the issue is the need to reevaluate life choices. It's not just the eating pattern that has to change. Tiffany's decision came on a soap opera set during lunch. Alan was the star of the show and the latest heartthrob to millions of women. Everyone on the set knew that he and his wife, Vanessa, had an understanding about his need to sleep around, both to further his career and so he wouldn't feel cramped or tied down. He was a womanizer, but no matter where he wandered, he'd never take anyone other than his wife seriously.

Tiffany saw Alan as the perfect vehicle for furthering her career. Everyone on the set, including writers, listened to what Alan wanted. He was the show's main attraction. She mapped out a plan that traded a closeness with Alan for a few more appearances on this particular soap. For two weeks, she slyly played hard to get, just enough to keep him very interested. She acted both coy and indifferent—he liked challenges. While in the midst of this seductive game, however, Tiffany began an abstinent food plan and a commitment to herself and her sponsor that she would not vomit. After only three days of abstaining from vomiting, Tiffany found herself becoming edgy, scared, and terribly angry. Her irritation came out at saleswomen who wouldn't answer her queries intelligently, or waitresses who didn't move quickly enough for her. In the midst of this irritable stage, Alan sat down at her table. "I've been noticing you," he said, "and I can tell you've been noticing me."

"Of course I've noticed you. You're the star of the show."

"Well, I can also star in a number of other performances."

"So I've heard."

"How'd you like to give me an audition? No strings attached. I really like seeing you around here."

This was just the proposition Tiffany had been working toward. It clearly offered promise of furthering her career. However, without either the excess food to bolster her bravado or the outlet of vomiting to relieve her self-disgust and rage, Tiffany's answer had to come out differently.

"No thanks, I want to play a starring role in my own life." The words flowed out of her from somewhere deep within. "Your wife has top billing in your play, and I want the same billing in my own life." With that first refusal, Tiffany set out on a new career path and a new feeling about herself. The elation she felt at taking the risk of saying no to Alan buoyed her up for days. Before this, the only highs she felt were the euphoric feelings of power she had after starving. Now she felt strong and confident and very excited about the riskiness of it all. He might be offended and want her off the set. She might never work again. Who knew? All Tiffany knew was that she had to say no to preserve her abstinence. She couldn't handle those quick trysts without bingeing and vomiting. Her behavior was determined by her abstinence. This is such a switch from the idea that you control food. Here a food plan determines a life plan.

Saying no to Alan did not hurt Tiffany's career. The writers and director saw her value to the show, and she was written in for two more months. They were impressed with the strength of character she brought to her part. Now that she was admitting her vomiting at OA and no longer hiding, Tiffany was able to freely show all of herself. She had no secrets and nothing to hide. Today she's a star, and she came by it honestly and abstinently.

Tiffany is one of thousands who have said no to some parts of their old lives in order to say yes to abstinence and recovery. This chapter will teach you how to say no and feel okay about it. You will learn to play a starring role in your own life with a healthier cast of supporting characters. Most of us are initially scared to be the star, let alone actually direct the play. Giving up the power to say no and the ability to direct your own life is what keeps you bingeing and self-destructing—because it's a lie. Every time we say yes when we need to say no, we are lying. The only way to live a lie is to eat. A good way to avoid sitting down to an excessive meal is learning to stand up for yourself.

You have spent a large part of this book taking stock of your situation and how you got here. You have looked at your personality and traced the stages you and your loved ones need to go through to achieve lasting recovery. Now it is time to practice new ways to handle old situations, which will help you feel comfortable and stay abstinent.

F-Os and C-Ps each swing back and forth on the pendulum between passivity and aggressiveness. Neither has achieved the moderate, middle path of assertiveness. Many people who aren't food obsessed can live their whole lives without ever changing such stagnant roles. They don't have to change. They never have to practice assertiveness. As F-Os and C-Ps, you can't afford the luxury of the unexamined life. Your previous behaviors have kept you obsessed. When you become more conscious in life, you will eat and live more consciously.

Fat Ladies Are Giant "Thank-You" Cards

You are busy overcompensating. You feel morally inferior and legally guilty. You are slavishly grateful for any crumbs of human kindness and actually encourage others to punish rather than reward you. Therefore, if anyone treats you well, you need to make it up to them by paying back a thousandfold. An aged and beloved OA member in Los Angeles often tells the story that whenever anyone offered her a ride to a meeting, she'd have to pay them back by sending over a present from Tiffany's. Everyone at meetings who hears that story laughs first but deeply understands feelings of indebtedness.

When you give up eating compulsively, you will find that much of this ingratiating behavior stops. You don't need to impress anyone because you aren't feeling guilty. You know you are doing the best you can about your illness, one day at a time. With nothing to hide and nowhere to run, you start feeling firm about what you can and can't do. In order to manage staying abstinent, you may have to slow down many of the tasks you previously performed so speedily and perfectly for others. Other achievements will recede as abstinence becomes your primary focus. This change is bound to have effects on all your near and distant relationships.

As a C-P, you have adjusted well to the F-O as a guilty, self-loathing person. You'll both have to change old behaviors. Together, one F-O and one C-P make up one whole, nurtured, responsible person. In recovery you each must reclaim the missing part of yourself and become more independent.

Who's on Center?

Remember, the body doesn't lie. It is no accident that F-Os have bodies that change shape almost as often as the weather. Your body is showing confusion at not knowing how to stand in the world. It undulates like a giant mushroom cloud pushing out to occupy more space and power and then rapidly shrinking

225

again. Because you have not learned how to represent yourself adequately to others, you feel the amassing or diminishing flesh will create the effects you seek. Unfortunately, the body rarely catches up with how you truly feel about yourself. Saying no gives the body a leading edge on reality.

We want to avoid extremes and try to stay centered on moderate food plans and moderate behaviors. Passivity and aggressiveness are intimately allied with food obsessions. In the following paragraphs, I'll show a tendency toward either extreme isn't healthy. The better choice is more moderate "center" behavior, or assertiveness.

PASSIVITY. The passive person is generally characterized as quiet and shy and usually tends to withdraw from situations with any risk or conflict. This person is the wallflower at parties or the resentful employee who never asks for a raise or the fat lady tugging at the folds of her muumuu or the child who hangs on to Daddy's leg, peering meekly around the trouser to see without being seen. We have all felt this way at one time or another. Passive people often prejudge themselves and others, saying, "You're okay; I'm not okay."

Polly Passive is often admired, sometimes pitied, rarely invited, usually tolerated, and never envied. Avoiding envy is the bottom line and the essential reason to remain passive. The following sentiments are the rallying cries of many passive F-Os:

"I don't want to make anyone else feel bad. I'll be uncomfortable instead."

"I'm already so physically large; I want to minimize any other effects I'm causing."

"I don't want anyone to feel uncomfortable around me."

Passivity can also be used as a way to subtly but powerfully control others. Polly Passive whines about how helpless she is so others will come in and do it for her. In that way, she never lives up to her own potential and is living in that dress rehearsal, waiting until "I get strong enough . . . rich enough . . . thin enough . . ." As long as she remains rigidly passive and someone else is the actor in her life, she hides in food. Her lament rings:

"I never seem to accomplish anything."

"I sure wish I could help, but I'd mess it up."

"What can you expect from a fat person."

"Don't ask anything of me. I'm starving myself."

Passive behavior can be healthy and nurturing occasion-ally. Sometimes, it may be a strategic advantage to keep quiet instead of raising the roof. Withdrawal is sometimes actually more active than jumping in with both feet. But when a passive mode becomes your automatic, robotized response, then it is self-destructive. You have limited options. You have to be passive when every instinct in your body is crying out for action. When you rigidly remain passive no matter what, you are going to have troubles when the body screams, "I wanna come out and dive into my life." Sometimes the only way you know to shut up the wailing inner self is with food.

If related to such a person, you may not like this passivity. You don't have to. In the past you became more active to counter the passivity. Now you must give up being the care-taker. Instead of rescuing, you will be making more demands on the F-O; you must state your needs. If you are trying to take care of yourself and the F-O at the same time, you will have too much conflict. Imagine if you want to satisfy the F-O, but by satisfying your loved one, you feel deprived. What if you both need comforting at exactly the same time? You could end up like two-year-olds battling over toys in a playpen. At this point, it's better to seek your separate solutions with your individual sponsors.

AGGRESSION. Andy Aggressive hits others before they have a chance to hit him. Much of his energy is spent covering all bases so no one can criticize him for anything or take advantage of him. His tombstone will read "Nobody got the best of him." His aggression stems from the same inadequate feelings as Polly Passive, but he found another way to cope with them. He strikes out with, "I'm okay; you're not." He will do all he can to make you and himself believe that. He has to gorge himself to keep his true fear hidden. He loudly disclaims any vulnerable feelings, often using direct attack, personal ridicule, or subtle sarcasm:

> "You'd better not try to take advantage of me."
>
> "I'll make you pay for that."
>
> "So you think you're hot stuff, eh?"
>
> "I like my belly. Doc told me to watch my weight, so I've got it right out there where I can watch it—ha, ha, ha."

Aggression protects. The best defense is a good offense. Just as Polly used passivity as a subtle form of control, Andy uses aggressiveness as another. If he looks tough and keeps you distant, either laughing or quivering, then he feels safe. How could anyone suspect that such a tough guy could be so vulnerable? You buy his facade and leave him alone. His aggressive posture is really too much to take on. Others buy the act and leave. But without excess food, the aggression breaks down and the scared little boy comes out.

Some aspects of aggressiveness work for survival. Aggression helps you overcome fear and succeed in a competitive environment. It helps you mobilize energy for difficult tasks. It warns you when threatened. Some aggressive instinct is necessary. Without it, you'd be victimized all the time. You don't want to completely discard this aspect of yourself.

Instead, you need to choose when and where to mobilize aggression. Make it work for you rather than against you.

ASSERTIVENESS. Ideally you will strive for a neutral position—neither passive nor aggressive but having access to a full range of behaviors at any time. The assertive person mobilizes either passive or aggressive behavior as needed. Life has its ebb and flow, and the assertive person has enough personal security to roll with the punches and adopt a style to fit the occasion.

The assertive response to conflict is "I'm okay and you're okay. If there is a problem between us, we can work it out." As an assertive person, you watch out for your best interests and make decisions accordingly. You might decide it is better not to defend some positions and to take a stand on others that some people would let go by. You become your own judge, little motivated by what others want or expect. Pliant and flexible, you become truly natural and alive.

Even though we will explore the language of assertiveness and present correct alternative responses to dicey situations, please be aware that so much of our communication happens nonverbally. I began treating alcoholic families right out of graduate school in 1972. In those days, there was as yet nothing written about such work, and my intern, Alan Berger, and I were running multiple family groups all day on Saturdays. We really weren't all that sure about what we were doing, but we gave these families our exquisite attention, and they responded.

One family had a mother who was alcoholic and seven children, two of whom were still at home. The youngest boy was about ten years old and got noticed by swiveling from side to side in a desk chair. This drove his father up the wall. He yelled at each group, "Stop that fidgeting!" The boy's fidgeting actually diverted the father from talking with his wife about her alcoholism. The father's behavior was usually loud, aggressive, and controlling, but rarely effective. His wife drank, and his kids ignored him or cowered in fear.

Over months of treatment, this aggressive gentleman learned to speak directly to his wife about his sadness and helpless feelings. His aggression had masked painful helplessness. He felt if he kept shouting, then at least he was doing something. As we encouraged him to stop fixing and let go, his wife started speaking up in family sessions. As she took more responsibility for her own recovery, he felt more comfortable focusing on himself rather than his wayward wife and son. The boy stopped fidgeting and sat up quietly in his seat.

I have seen this kind of diverting communication go on even with infants. A baby will be squealing during a family session, keeping Mom busy and diverted. When the couple starts talking honestly, the baby stops crying. Baby seems to pick up that the right topics are being addressed and finds that being quiet serves the family system better and lets the process unfold.

We know as much as these babies do, but we often choose not to notice. Your body will notice things and have instinctive corrective responses long before your head catches up. You can study assertiveness more extensively, but an abstinent body will be most helpful in indicating needed change.

For detailed descriptions of all assertive techniques, I recommend a book by psychologist Manuel J. Smith, Ph.D. Its title clearly highlights the lament of F-Os and their C-Ps, *When I Say No, I Feel Guilty.* He teaches assertive responses to guilt and criticism. Whether truly mentioned, merely implied, or subtly alluded to, we usually internalize guilt and criticism no matter what. We default to guilt and criticism. Few of us need much help in responding to praise. We usually weather that fairly well.

In recovery you will learn to weather criticism. Even if it isn't the other guy criticizing, your own judge sits on your shoulder and reads you the riot act. This internal judge is with you all the time and works overtime to tell you when you are wrong. When you believe this judge, you turn to food to punish yourself. Instead, you need to learn an assertive response. Sometimes you might have a family member around to abuse you. You each end up guilty. There is a better way out. Let's see how to say no to our judge (whether internal or external) and instead say yes to life. As a person in recovery, you learn new choices about where to focus your energies. You gain a new sense of priorities. Keeping abstinence first helps move the judge aside. The Shaker communities of the last century held as their motto "Strive to improve." Buddhists recommend "Begin at once and do your best." Twelve Step groups encourage "Progress, not perfection." Your motto can be "I may not be perfect, but at least I'm following my committed food plan. For today, this is as good as it gets."

In the following sections, we'll look at and practice some ways to apply assertive techniques to situations around food obsessions and confluence. Most of these techniques involve new behaviors, which feel awkward at first. Give yourself a chance to be a beginner and a student. Everyone needs practice. You are practicing developing more separation in relationships. When you can feel grounded and separated, you won't have to amass great flesh to feel secure or starve yourself to feel in control.

For all your interactions, the most important ingredient is your own active listening. Pay careful attention to what others are saying. Try to figure out the bottom line of what they really mean and what they really want. In many cases, it will help to actively mirror back to them what they are saying to you. Keep asking for clarification so they will become more and more specific in their criticisms. You want them to see themselves, and you want to get out of the way of their scathing criticisms. Good luck.

Agreeing

You can tackle criticisms by agreeing. First, you can try agreeing with the *truth* of the critic's statement or agreeing with the *probability* of the statement.

When you feel criticized, try to agree with the truthful *part* of the criticism. You do not have to buy the *entire* criticism. For example, when someone says, "You are really fat and ugly," you reply, "I am big, aren't I?" End of sentence; say no more. Just agree with the part you find to be true.

Sometimes it works to agree with the probability that what the other person is saying is correct. For example, you would use phrases such as "You *may* be right," "That's *possibly* true," "*Odds are,* you are correct," or "*Chances are,* that is so."

You can also use this technique in response to criticism such as "You always . . ." or "You never . . ." For example:

They Say	You Reply
"You're gonna die if you keep eating like that."	"You *may* be right."
"You never follow through with diets."	"*Sometimes* I don't."
"You probably weigh three hundred pounds."	"That *could* be true."
"You always embarrass me."	"*Sometimes* I have embarrassed you."

You have agreed. Don't disagree. Disagreeing only encourages argument. You have shown you don't wish to argue. That is assertive. You represent yourself without violating anyone else. There is no cause for guilt here and thus no cause for punishment. You will find this helpful when others are using scare tactics to get you to do things their way.

Sorting the Issues

To cover over your own self-loathing, you often avoided saying no and were thus continually manipulated and later angry. Your solution was food. Now you can find new ways to handle the con artist. People manipulate through phrases that start with "if." These statements involve other people's ideas of how *they* feel *you* should act.

"*If* you loved me, you'd bring me candy."

"*If* you were a good friend, you'd cook for me."

"*If* you cared, you'd stop my eating."

"*If* you valued your health, you'd diet."

In sorting the issues, separate the phrases. You may respond with the following:

"I do love you, *and* I don't want to bring candy."

"I am a good friend, *and* I won't cook for you."

"I do care, *and* I can't fix you."

"I do value my health, *and* dieting is not a good style for me."

Emphasize the "and." You show there is no relationship between the first and second statements. A loved one does not have to bring candy. You can value your health and develop your own plan without explaining.

It is important to use "and" rather than "but." When you say "but" you imply a relationship between A and B. When you say "and," you are clearly separating. Notice the difference.

"I really like you, but [hedging] I can't have dinner with you."

"I really do like you, and [definite] right now I'm not able to have dinner with you." (It also helps to say "right now" so later you have the option to change your mind.)

To maintain your own assertive position, you can remain interested in the opinions of others but not dominated by them. You invite engagement but not evaluation. It is a thin line. You can show that you are genuinely interested in hearing more from others as long as they keep criticisms to themselves.

Clarification

In "clarification" you ask questions so that others can refine their comments. Ask them to be specific and really itemize their particular objection or criticism. You want them to own their own criticisms. You keep asking questions so that they change their critical questions into actual statements of what they want. Then you can deliver statements back.

They Say	You Reply
"When are you going to lose some weight?"	"I am not really clear about why you think I haven't been trying to lose weight. Can you explain more fully what you mean?"

Do not ask this question to start an argument but rather with genuine concern. You want others to be clearer in owning their judgments of you. Let's follow this through.

They Say	You Reply
"Well, you keep talking about losing weight, but to me you look as fat as ever."	"So you want clarification of my poundage?"

They Say	You Reply
"No. It's just that I'm concerned for you, and it doesn't seem like you are doing anything about the problem."	"And what leads you to believe that I'm doing nothing?"

You want them to directly state how they feel. You'd like them to move from making "you" statements to making "I" statements. Then you can take it or leave it.

They Say	You Reply
"Well, I see you eat, and I see you staying fat."	[You assertively repeat their statement for the sake of clarification and then ask them to say what they want.] "So you believe I'm not doing anything. What could help you here?"

They Say	You Reply
"Well, I guess I'd like to know what you are doing to help yourself."	[They have said what they want. You can choose to give it to them or not. You might reply as follows.] "Well, I can assure you I am dealing with it and taking active measures, but I'd rather not share the specifics with you. I am availing myself of outside help and doing my best. I hope watching me doesn't cause you too much pain. It is a difficult and quite personal problem for me, but for today I actually am doing something about it."

You'll close with, "Thanks for sharing your concern."

You may have to say no to others' criticism and also to your own. You may have to give up trying so hard to please so many and instead take care of yourself.

Gracious or Selfish?

Although we believe keeping promises to others is *gracious,* we think keeping promises to ourselves is *selfish.* We can use our helpfulness to others as an excuse to hurt ourselves. Laments such as "I couldn't help myself" are borrowed from Top Forty music charts. They are a deadly tool F-Os use to break commitments to themselves. When you start seeing that your food obsession is an illness rather than a morality issue, you will be able to say no as a part of your prescription for recovery.

If not, you hold on to the option of using other people as excuses for slips in food commitments. For example, you continue to give to them, do for them, and worry about them so you can lament:

"They made me do it."

"It was Aunt Rebecca's favorite recipe. She'd be insulted."

"I had to get my daughter off to college, kids off to camp, husband set in his new job. . . ."

"The whole family was celebrating Thanksgiving. How could I refuse?"

"Do you really think I would insult the bride by not having a piece of wedding cake?"

Let's face it. There is only one person at the whole wedding who gives a damn one way or the other whether you eat the cake or not. That is *you.* The bride has plenty of other things to occupy her time. The groom isn't going to think you wish them forty years of bad luck. No one else cares. But you do.

It's your obsession talking you into eating. A committee holds a meeting in your head and starts talking you into "just one piece." Your committee is working overtime to talk you into it. You envision a giant spotlight shining down while everyone in the room waits in hushed anticipation to see which way you will go with the cake. All you need is for one well-meaning, sympathetic friend to say, "Go ahead. It's a special occasion, and it's only one piece."

You may complain, "Well geez, Ma, the devil made me do it." But in reality, it is your obsessive love affair with food that makes you do it. You only use others to talk you into what the sick side of you had already planned. You say, "Well, everyone else was having some. It's not fair. Why me?" (This is a classic example of your anger and denial.) Others at the wedding will eat one piece and forget it. You will have one piece, then a few stolen bites off a friend's plate, then a small fingerful of icing that Janet pushed away in disgust, declaring, "It's just too sweet for me." Later that night you wonder what happened to the rest of that big cake. Others are thinking of many other things besides the cake. You, instead, lie awake wondering whether you should have taken a piece home. The cake drama doesn't stop at bedtime. The next day finds you barreling down a supermarket aisle tearing open cellophane bags of malted milk balls trying to recapture yesterday's sweetness.

There is a way out of this scenario. You need to put just as much energy into a new response as you previously put into bingeing. You have to see abstinence as a reward rather than a deprivation. The reward will be that you are available to feel and live your own life. Let's see how Denise gave herself a gift by not having the cake at her sister's wedding. Her Aunt Ann was the most forceful pusher at the party. Denise gave herself the gift of abstinence while Aunt Ann was slicing.

Ann: Here, Denise, have a piece and wish your sister luck.

Denise: No thank you.

Ann: Come on, Denise, this is no time to be on a diet. [Notice Denise's refusal of the cake was not followed by "I'm on a diet." There's no need to say that. If we do, we set others up to try to talk us into breaking a diet. Never say diet. Notice how normal people don't make big shows of explaining the whats and whys of their eating. They simply say, "No thanks."]

Denise: No thanks. I'm not on a diet. I just don't care for any right now. [Notice how Denise repeats the "no" for herself as much as for Ann—it's reinforcing. She also says no *for now,* which implies she may have some later. Sometimes that can put off someone who is pushing. It didn't stop Aunt Ann.]

Ann: What's the matter, Denise? Are you resentful and jealous that your sister is getting married before you? [Here come the criticisms. These questions appear well-meaning, as if the inquisitor is really interested. In reality, it is a very cheap shot implying sibling rivalry and all that "psychobabble." None of us needs such instant analysis. If Aunt Ann is really interested in what Denise is feeling, she is not going to ask such an intimate question while slicing wedding cake. She really doesn't want an answer; she wants to let Denise know she's got her number. This type of interchange is a violation. A quick response is to pick up the

cake and stuff it in to keep your mouth shut.
If you grab the cake, you cop out on yourself.
That scenario creates the self-loathing that
keeps you eating even more. Your head says,
*These are loving, nurturing people with
my best interests at heart.* Your body feels
stab wounds all over your chest. If you feel
wounded, it's because you *have* been
wounded. Remember, the body doesn't lie.
Don't eat the cake; feel the pain.]

Denise: Actually, Ann, I don't think that's it. Thanks
anyway. [Denise answers the criticism by
simply saying she doesn't agree. She'll judge
her own behavior, thank you. She also does
not offer any further explanation or argument.]

Ann: [relentless] Well, if I were you, I'd take a
look at my real feelings about this wedding.
[Again, a criticism. She's implying "Auntie
knows best. You don't even know your 'real'
feelings. I have to interpret for you."]

Denise: Thanks for your concern, and no thanks
to the cake.

Case Closed

Denise offers no explanations and gives Ann the benefit of the
doubt. Maybe Ann's comments are out of concern, and she
doesn't notice how violating she is. Denise got out alive
without overexplaining herself and, most important, without
eating the cake. During this interchange, Denise secretly
cheered herself on: *No matter what, this woman won't make
me eat.* Although angry at Ann's veiled judgments, Denise
decided not to let them ruin the fun wedding by confronting
her aunt. She had to overcome a very strong power struggle

within, but refusing the cake left her exhilarated. Her strength and confidence lasted through the afternoon and well into the night. The cake didn't dominate her thoughts; self-respect did. She knew she was terrific. She felt so good that, later at the party, she walked up to a good-looking, unattached man and asked him to dance. She'd never done anything like that in her life. Incapacitated with shyness, her usual mode was to linger around buffet tables, bingeing as a way to ignore the shyness trauma.

She felt high and deserving because she refused the cake. Saying no to food made her more committed to saying yes to life. When not eating compulsively, there is much more impetus to go for it. Why not? We deserve it all. The good-looking man took her phone number. She spent that evening very pleased with herself for resisting the cake and Aunt Ann and dreamily contemplating a new relationship. Without shutting herself up with food, Denise found an outgoing, risky woman inside. What a surprise.

"Aren't You Getting Too Dependent?"

Annabelle, a diabetic, was referred to me by an internist. She knew that eating sugar was deadly for her but kept bingeing periodically. As an F-O, she couldn't control herself without help. When we met, she was highly deferential, extolling the virtues of Dr. Atwell. "He has been our family physician for years. He really knows his stuff. If he says I should get involved in this recovery program, I'm certainly ready." Unfortunately, at that point, Dr. Atwell knew very little about my newly instituted hospital program, the Obesity Recovery Service. He knew that he, like many physicians, had failed with Annabelle.

She had responded to doctor's orders in a fairly typical way. She giggled shyly and, with wide-eyed charm, promised the doctor that she really valued his advice and would follow his suggestions. She'd leave the office embarrassed about her apparent lack of willpower. As the nurse gave a few "tsks, tsks" while weighing her, Annabelle was humiliated by her own giggly behavior around powerful people. The situation was so demeaning that she heightened her self-loathing by "kissing up" to the professional. Her giggle and posing helped mask her rage at even having to visit the doctor's office.

Annabelle came to me with the same tell-me-what-to-do attitude. Her recovery was ultimately secured when she learned to tell professionals she didn't need them to tell her what to do. Her past behavior had shown she didn't follow doctors' orders anyway. She needed to find a way to say no out loud. Her chance came three months after her initial referral.

Annabelle had been abstinent from compulsive eating and refined carbohydrates for seventy-six days. She had a brief relapse one weekend but got back on her program. Best of all, her blood-sugar level and blood pressure had normalized. This woman had previously required daily insulin injections. At each of her weekly checkups, Dr. Atwell was more and more impressed with how well she was doing. Rather than passively waiting for him or the nurse to deliver a lecture, Annabelle took control of the visits. She talked animatedly about how well she was doing at Overeaters Anonymous. She got excited sharing with them how much fun the meetings were and how much support she was getting from her sponsor. She elaborated on how she managed to survive a family dinner party without bingeing and was looking forward to throwing away her injection syringes. This was a threat to Dr. Atwell.

At this juncture, Annabelle was changing the rules and the roles. *She* was telling the physician what *she* had planned in her recovery program. Understandably, Dr. Atwell became medically concerned, as he was responsible and, of course, had seen her relapse before. It was hard for him to believe this time would be different. He wanted more control of the situation.

Dr. Atwell: Well, Annabelle, it does seem like you are well on the road. We will want to keep monitoring you weekly just to make sure you have no problems. [Dr. Atwell was trying to continue the same old relationship. The physician will ultimately be in control, and Annabelle will passively reject his advice.]

Annabelle: Actually, Dr. Atwell, I don't think I should see you every week. It is better for me to only weigh in once a month. You see, I have a tendency to become obsessed with the scale, and it's best if I just stay abstinent in my eating rather than looking forward to weighing. [Annabelle made more explanation here than necessary, but this was because she was trying to educate the doctor about the needs of others like herself. This was definitely a role reversal and a threat to their relationship. Dr. Atwell was accustomed to passive, guilty patients. Annabelle was taking too much control of her own recovery. The doctor was concerned that she might relapse, and he was also somewhat disgruntled at her telling *him* how things will be.]

Dr. Atwell: You know, Annabelle, you do have a tendency to fall back on your commitments. I think we'd better continue a closer watch on you [staying with the past].

Annabelle: I understand your concern [active listening: letting him know she heard and
understood him], *and* I am finding that
daily contact with others in Overeaters
Anonymous is helping me stay abstinent
[sorting issues].

Dr. Atwell: Yes, but you do need a close watch so we
can detect any blood-sugar fluctuations.
[The doctor wanted to turn the discussion
to areas of his expertise so he could feel
more in control and move Annabelle to
her usual one-down position.]

Annabelle: I have been abstinent from sugars long
enough that my body is becoming a very
sensitive barometer. Since I talk daily
with someone else about my eating, I
think we would see a problem long
before it would show up on lab tests.
I'd rather head my eating off in advance
than dissect my blood after the fact.

This turn of events can be very disconcerting to medical
personnel. A patient who has been chronically obese and diabetic, having spent countless hours in physicians' waiting
rooms, is telling her doctor she would rather go to meetings
with laypeople and seek their help rather than his professional
services. Professionally concerned for the patient's health, the
doctor returns to what he knows best. He wants to be more
cautious and keep control of the situation. Unconsciously, the
doctor is personally threatened by this new development.
He is concerned that a group of nonprofessionals will accomplish what has stymied him for years.

It is the rare professional who can let the patient find his or her own personal and best recovery. The doctor must be secure that he has already done all he can and is willing to let others try. In this case, it was clear that Annabelle was definitely committed to taking over responsibility for her own health. This was a dramatic change from the doctor-patient relationship that had existed for the past twenty years.

Dr. Atwell did make one last attempt to turn her around. He saw that Annabelle's attendance at OA was definitely accomplishing what had stymied him in the past. He knew it was working. He congratulated her on her progress each time she came to his office. Despite all the indications that this was the way to go, he still doubted its validity. He was concerned that Annabelle said she had a lifelong chronic illness and would always need to rely on some type of help. (This dependency was not a problem for him if the help required was from a physician. He was concerned that Annabelle was accepting the idea that she'd need to rely on other suffering F-Os.)

He made one more attempt to warn Annabelle about the dangers of diminishing her visits: "Don't you think you've had enough of those meetings? Do you want to go to them for *the rest of your life?* It's just another dependency."

Annabelle smiled. "You *may* be right [sorting issues]. I try to take my recovery 'one day at a time.' For now, this seems to be what I need. I'd like to follow through with this just for today. I like the idea that 'if it works, don't fix it.'"

Dr. Atwell stared blankly. What could he say? He couldn't argue with results. In taking responsibility for her own recovery and going for help where she was an equal rather than subordinate, Annabelle started actively participating in her life. As she became more successful in her food plan, she felt more secure and assertive.

Dr. Atwell's concerns bring up a commonly voiced criticism of successful members of Overeaters Anonymous.

While they are still fat, no one criticizes their attendance at meetings, but after most of the weight is lost, others start doubting the necessity for attendance. "Don't you think you've been going to those meetings long enough? You've lost your weight. Don't you think you could cut down now? After all, you don't want to develop dependency." This thinking is puzzling. Wasn't the obsessive addiction to bingeing a dependency? Aren't many in our culture dependent on other drugs and obsessions?

What is wrong with transferring the dependency to something healthy and nurturing? It's not such a terrible thing to admit that "Yes, I am a person who likes supportive, loving people, and when I go to meetings, I feel nurtured and don't have to go home and binge." What is wrong with depending on love? Our little dog at home doesn't consider all this when he rolls over to have his belly scratched. Why are humans so afraid to get love? A person with a broken leg would be foolish to refuse a cast and crutches. Can't a sick and suffering F-O turn to others who can help heal and support? Why not? So you need a crutch. . . .

Critics who tell you not to get such help are trying to live by the American macho myth: "I can do it myself." Even if you could, why *should* you?

What's Your Fortune, Cookie?

As a confluent personality, you must also learn to stand up for your own feelings. You have spent so long developing a chameleon-like ability to walk in their shoes and adjust to their moods that it is hard for you to learn that how you feel is important. How you feel does not have to be explained, justified, or excused. It just is. Emotions are not right or wrong. They just are. Your hardest job is learning to take care of yourself, not others.

Roberta got a chance to test her new assertive skills when

she took her overeating daughter, Claire, out to lunch. Claire had come home on a pass from the treatment unit and asked her mom to take her to lunch. "I'm just dying for some Chinese food. Let's go to Foo Long's."

As soon as these words were out, Roberta began to panic. She saw Claire's eyes light up. She noted that burn smell one can sense when there's overtime devoted to thinking about a binge. Roberta knew she didn't want to take responsibility for Claire's food plan, that it was not her business how Claire ate, but she felt sick inside. It was the glow, that look. Family members can see that haze reappear when a binge is imminent. Claire looked like a convict, just released, ready to commit another crime. Roberta didn't want any part of it. She tried to respond by expressing her own feelings rather than telling Claire how to act or feel.

Roberta:	Honey, I don't feel comfortable going to that restaurant.
Claire:	Oh, wow, Mom. You're trying to control my food again. If you weren't so controlling, we'd go there.
Roberta:	It's not control. I just don't want to go there today. [Note the allusion to "not now."]
Claire:	Would you want to go if it was someone else rather than me?
Roberta:	[Self-disclosure must be the truth.] Well, yes.
Claire:	[attacking] See! It's just that you want to keep me from eating Chinese food.
Roberta:	I am not concerned with what you eat. That is your business.

Claire: [escalating] That's right. I'll eat what I
           want, when I want, and I don't have to take
           orders from you. If you'd stop controlling,
           we'd go there.

Roberta: I don't want to control, *and* I don't want
           to go to Foo Long's today [sticking to "I"
           messages and sorting issues]. I don't want
           to give you any orders.

Claire: Then why won't you go to Foo Long's with
           me?

Roberta: [She asked, so it's not butting in to answer.
           Roberta sticks with "I" messages about her
           own feelings.] Well, dear, since you asked,
           I will share with you how it is for me. It is
           hard for me to be with you when I sense
           this panicked, ravenous feeling about food.
           It makes me feel bad to watch you. I feel
           that when you are in the midst of that, it's
           better we be apart. I'd love to eat with you
           when you are in a calmer state about food.

Claire: Do I really seem ravenous? I thought I just
           wanted to return there for old time's sake.
           I didn't even know. [Her mother's honest
           statement of her own feelings helped
           Claire to really hear what was said. This
           let her open up to look at herself.]

Roberta: We've been there often during binge times,
           and it may just be my memories, but I'd
           rather not go there right *now*. [Notice
           Roberta states "just for today." This is how
           she feels about it today. It may not be for
           all time. She just has to express where she

is today.] I do feel a little anxiety from you. Like, it's really so important to make it that place. I'm just uncomfortable.

Claire: Now that you mention it, I think I'm uncomfortable too. I really noticed myself getting excited about Foo Long's. Come to think of it, I was really kind of obsessing about their sweet-and-sour pork. I felt like I had it coming to me.

Roberta: I guess that's what I picked up, that excitement.

Claire: I really don't want to eat anything that is calling to me that much. I can only eat it if I can take it or leave it. If I've got to have it, I can't.

Roberta: Well, sweetheart, your food is your business. I just had to tell you that I felt too much anxiety to go there today.

Claire: Thanks, Mom. Wanna go to the coffee shop where they make that nice salmon?

Roberta: Well, salmon may not be as sexy as sweet-and-sour pork, but you do seem calmer when you mention it. I'd feel okay going there with you.

Trading Roles for Realities

Sometimes one person is both an F-O and a C-P and attends both Overeaters Anonymous and Al-Anon. Sometimes couples occupy both slots and mix and match the roles. It is very easy to begin comparing, competing, and evaluating your partner's recovery instead of your own. You need to find a positive way to tell your mate to mind his or her own business. Racine and

Joe had to work this out after Racine planned to meet a friend at a salad bar restaurant.

Joe: [trying to be helpful] Racine, since I've been in the recovery program, I've been advised that it's not a good idea to go to salad bar restaurants. [Joe is trying to come across as assertive, but underneath, he is implying that "father knows best" and "you'd better listen to me."]

Racine: Oh? [She knows he wants her to change her behavior and do it his way, but she doesn't react. She waits. Her response is a form of clarification. She is asking him to provide more information to get to the point of what he really wants to say.]

Joe: Yes, dear. I don't think you should go to that salad bar.

Racine: I see. How does that affect you, Joe? [Racine is trying to get Joe to make an "I" statement and stop telling her what to do with her life.]

Joe: Well, I've been watching, and I really think you are packing in more food than you need. You don't notice yourself at salad bars.

Racine: And how does that affect you, Joe?

Joe: Well, it really doesn't affect me at all. I'm just telling you for your own good. Take it or leave it. [Joe is becoming defensive because he is being asked to own his own judgments and be more direct and assertive. He'd rather tell her what to do than state how he feels. He could have made an "I" statement, saying,

"I don't like it." But that might be too risky for him at this point.]

Racine: [letting him know that she is feeling secure with her own food plan] I hear your concerns, *and* I feel I am getting enough help with my food plan [sorting issues]. My sponsor and I feel the salad bar fits in well. [This is *end of report*. Racine has let Joe know that she will be a person who judges her own behavior, and she will not need to explain herself to anyone. Because she is also working actively with her sponsor in OA, she can feel secure that her food plan is organized, disciplined, and healthy and that she isn't kidding herself about her eating. Security about the food creates security in interpersonal relating.]

With Lynette, who'd been bingeing and purging through her early marriage and two full-term pregnancies, her husband's monitoring of her food plan almost came to blows. The stress on her body created by vomiting had caused loss of her menses. Sam, her husband, wanted more children and felt it was his right to monitor and push for her to eat more. Each time she developed food plans with sponsors, he ranted about how sick it looked for her to be measuring her food at home and eating what he considered so little. She tried to explain to him that if she didn't follow some rigid guidelines for a while, she would feel too guilty and scared about what she had eaten, and that her fears of weight gain would push her to vomit. She assured him that she also wanted more children but would have to move slowly. She also noted that she'd gotten pregnant in the past even while vomiting. Sam yelled at each meal about her small portions. He kicked chairs and shook the baby and ranted around the house. (Sometimes C-Ps become violent when they become frustrated at their loss of control.)

Lynette's responses to him were weak and withdrawn, making her seem extremely guilty. I tried to push her to stand up to him and tell him that her food plan was none of his business. In group sessions we all talked about how important it is to feel safe around food and how in early recovery that only happens if you follow some guidelines that you share with another OA member. This food plan could not be open to judgments from family members. In family sessions, I tried to play the "heavy" for her, trying to convince Sam of all the husbands I'd known who had failed at trying to control their wives' behavior around food. Lynette admitted to him that even with his close monitoring, she had returned to vomiting. None of this worked. He still believed he could control her. Sam wouldn't listen to me or his wife. He was adamant about his rights and truly felt abused by her, that she was denying him more children.

At one family dinner, Sam picked up her plate and hurled it across the room. She called me screaming hysterically. I instructed her to quietly tell him she would have to leave for a while to give him a chance to cool down. I asked her to tell him that she could not accommodate his attention to every drop going into her mouth and that she might have to take all her meals outside the home. I asked her to be strong, quiet, and direct. She said she couldn't pull it off. Feeling so guilty about her eating for so long, she wasn't able to mobilize a strong, quiet, confident response that told him she'd be in charge of her food and would only remain at home if he butted out. Instead, she cowered and lurked in a corner while he ranted.

Afterward, Sam felt so guilty about his behavior that he refused to come back to group or couples therapy, although he did stop yelling for a while. I gave Lynette an "amends assignment." You might be shocked here wondering why *she* should make amends when *he* exhibited the bad behavior. Well, it takes two. And we can only take care of our part in the equation, cleaning up our own side of the street.

Amends don't come until Steps Eight and Nine (in a Twelve Step program), as you have other work to do first. (Most newcomers feel so guilty that they want to apologize for breathing. It is quipped at AA that you can always tell newcomers at a meeting, because when you spill coffee on them, *they* apologize.) Although you might not be ready to begin working the Steps, sometimes life intrudes, and with guidance from others, you begin the deep psychological work.

Here is the assertive amends note that Lynette wrote to Sam:

> I am sorry I have encouraged you at times to monitor my food plans. I realize how confusing this must be for you and how it can generate such rage. When I am feeling good about what I am doing with food, I want to show off to you, telling you all about what is working and why and how good I feel. I realize this draws you in. Then, when it turns on me, I act guilty and withdrawn, and you are so sensitized to me that you pick up my slinking behavior, and it makes you very nervous. You think you'll feel better if you can control my food. I feed into this by not standing up to you. The whole thing escalates. I apologize for giving all these mixed messages, and I apologize for letting you think that you could so abuse and mistreat me with this violent behavior. It isn't good for me or the children. Therefore, I want you to know that I love you and care about your feelings, but I can't subject all of us to this rage. When it happens again, and I say *when*, because without

further counseling, it is bound to explode some more, I will remove myself and the children for a while. I will eat my meals in peace. That is the only way I can keep food down. I am sorry for my part in provoking this and mixing you up in my illness, but if you can seize the moment, this is also a great opportunity for you to uncover where that rage comes from. My behavior can't be the only provocation. I happen to be the convenient source for your anger right now. That's why I want to remove myself so that you might examine more about it for yourself. Again, I am sorry for all this, and I do love you.

Lynette was using an effective tool in writing her feelings so she could gain clarity.

Self-Disclosure

It is ideal to be able to express your own feelings and thoughts to another without hurting them or yourself. How you express your feelings depends on the nature of your relationship and how strongly you feel about yourself and your position.

It is important that you make "I" statements about yourself and your feelings rather than "you" statements about the other person. You are best at representing yourself and how you feel.

Example: "I am hurt by your criticism."

"I really wish I felt more liked by you."

"I'm afraid you don't like me."

"I'm afraid you might leave me."

"I feel bad about disappointing you."

"I am embarrassed by my fat."

"I feel a lot of pressure when you ask about my weight."

You must pay careful attention to the effect you create with the other person. Obviously, it is easier to be strong and state your case with someone who is not a near and dear loved one. Practice assertiveness first with distant people, even strangers, and then move to directness with those you love. You don't want to wound the other person, either in the ego or the heart. You want to leave the situation feeling good about your own actions and liking how you behaved. You want to be able to look back at the situation and say, "I really like how I handled that." When you feel good about how you behave with others, neither dominating nor being dominated, then you can relax and admire yourself. You won't have to punish yourself with food.

Rita had been anorexic, and her mom was grateful she was finally eating again. However, Mom wanted to move their relating away from food. They were always discussing food and diet. While earlier we saw Roberta, who didn't want to eat Chinese food with her daughter, this mom found all food forays difficult. She lamented, "Is this all there is?" She wanted more. Her sponsor helped her learn a more assertive response to the following typical phone call from Rita.

Rita: Hi, Mom, how about dinner next week?

Mom: Well, Rita, I'd love to see you, and I'd rather not go to dinner.

Rita: What do you mean? You have to eat, don't you?

Mom: Yes.

Rita: Well, why not with me? Don't you want me to eat?

Mom: It's up to you if you eat or not. Whatever you like. I'd just rather do something else.

Rita: I get it. You're trying to control my food again.

Mom: I miss having other experiences that don't center on eating or not eating. For me, it gets in the way. I'd rather do other things with you. Truthfully, I do tend to watch what you eat an awful lot. I get overly concerned when you pick at your food. I watch how you work your plate. I think it interferes with our relationship. I'd like to do something with you that has nothing to do with food. Let's see what else we have going for us.

Mom remained secure with her own "I" messages about what she would like. She did not respond to Rita's invitation to fight about control. She is saying she would like to see Rita, that she cares, and that she is owning her own tendency to want to control. She is also opening up to the idea that food is getting in the way, and she wants to be close to Rita instead. She's tired of hovering over her daughter's plate.

In this case, even though Mom did very well in being direct and stating her own wishes, Rita was really looking for a binge buddy. The best binge buddy is often a punitive parent. They join in and then punish. With that, you can have it both ways. However, this mom didn't want that role anymore, and Rita wasn't ready to stop the game.

Rita: [angrily] Well, I think it's just you trying to make me eat your way again. If you weren't such a control freak, you could stand to watch me eat whatever and however I want. You are letting your problem with my eating get in the way. [Actually this is improvement for Rita. In the past she never expressed rage. A benchmark book on anorexia is titled *The Best Little Girl in the World*. Rita was always a good girl while starving herself.]

Mom:	[agreeing with the odds] You may be right, and rather than test myself or you, I'd rather move our relationship to another arena. I'd like to go to the museum.
Rita:	Too bad, Mom. If you can't accept me as I am, eating as I do, then I want nothing more to do with you.
Mom:	You seem to be angry with me. I'm sorry you feel that way. Please do understand that I really would like to go to the museum or a street fair or a crafts show, or anything else you might like. Please let me know if you'd like to try something like that. [Mom continues with "I" messages despite the attack. She doesn't let her agenda be swayed by Rita's anger.]

Both of these women are changing their old roles with each other. For today, they are able to stand separately and express themselves. This interchange highlights a crucial issue in eating relationships. Maybe Rita and her mom have nothing in common other than their power struggles over food. When one person withdraws from that struggle, there may be nothing left. They deserve the chance to find out.

Beat Me, Baby

Many obese women beg their passive husbands to be stronger with them. Often, the husband is really not too interested in interacting anyway and, even if he has tried, can't seem to match his wife's intensity. This issue is explored in *Hot & Heavy*, where we see that since the women's movement, females got down off their pedestals and told their men they are very interested in sex. Then the males got the headaches. Because of the men's reactions, many women reach for their plates instead of their mates. They channel their sexuality into food obsessions. Men sometimes retreat into a passive acceptance of their situation. Sometimes the passivity comes out in sideline aggression rather than direct frontal attack. The following story shows what can happen when the husband does finally assert himself.

Elizabeth had been after Joel for years, demanding that he stand up to her. She complained that she felt spoiled and out of control and wanted him to set limits for her. This is part of the F-O's wish to stay child-like, yet in control. Joel was a former truck driver. He had dislocated a hip in an accident and was now permanently retired. He also suffered a hearing loss and counted on Elizabeth to be his ears. He rarely went anywhere without Elizabeth and never asked others to speak up. It was easier to have Elizabeth translate. In exchange for this, Joel was Elizabeth's servant. She weighed more than four hundred pounds and found it difficult to walk or breathe. Joel answered her every need. He picked up her dropped pencils, prepared her meals, buttoned her clothes, helped her out of low-slung chairs. They functioned well together, both as invalids. As their relationship became more and more dependent, neither left home much. He cooked; she ate.

Recovery was a definite threat to that self-enclosed system. However, Joel secretly feared for Elizabeth's health, suspecting an imminent heart attack. He was also, frankly, tired of picking up after her. Like many spouses of chronically ill and addicted people, he suffered too and felt both grief and anger at the same time. Confluents have compassion for the suffering of the addicted person but also feel helpless watching the slow and gradual deterioration. Joel felt enraged by an inability to help. He even admitted he would prefer Elizabeth end it all quickly rather than to watch the daily trauma of her slow suicide. He felt it was inappropriate for him to feel anger toward a sick person. He was frustrated because he had no emotional outlets. Elizabeth often asked him to express himself but actually feared he would. She knew he was angry. His behavior let her know. But he never said anything directly. There was too much to lose.

Joel had to confront his own denial system. He began saying no. He sat tight while she struggled to pick up a pencil. Stopping old, predictable behaviors is another way of saying no. Actions speak louder than words. Elizabeth had never had to suffer the consequences of her disorder. Joel was always there to rescue her. She occupied a PIP, or Privileged Invalid Position, in the family. Elizabeth actually felt she deserved special services from Joel because she had worked hard raising his two children from a previous marriage. Although she did deserve to be treated well, their arrangement was killing her.

After a few weeks, Joel became more assertive with Elizabeth and told her, lovingly, that he would not be her servant anymore. No one likes to be told no, and Elizabeth was no exception. She attacked Joel, accusing him of neglect. Joel had worked hard to suppress his anger for many years and found it hard to fight back. He found his strength in a family therapy session with the support of other family members. He finally summoned the courage to answer back. He stood up and with a quivering jaw and stern look shouted, "Dammit, woman, either respect me or leave me!"

The room echoed with silence. Elizabeth was

stunned and then beamed with respect. She cried, "I'll never say another mean thing to you again." She feared he would really leave her if things didn't change. She was scared. He had options. She marveled at the realization that he was a separate person. She also knew he meant what he said. He had support from others and didn't feel guilty. He learned that her recovery was *her* job. He had never been that strong with her before, and she loved it. For years she had whined at him to be stronger. Each time he was, it was meaningless because she had asked for it. This time it was totally his idea. Neither one of them has forgotten that night. It signaled the beginning of a new life—no going back and nowhere to hide.

As a way of pretending she didn't mind her Privileged Invalid Position, Elizabeth often made fun of herself and played the clown. This way she stayed in control; she made fun of herself before anyone else could. Whenever she huffed and puffed into a room, she quipped, "I'm such a tub o' lard. I hope I don't break this chair. Ha, ha, ha." She had so dehumanized herself that she never respected her own feelings. When Joel broke through his own fear of anger, she was forced to take herself more seriously. If he could demand respect, so could she.

Elizabeth learned to see herself as a suffering person trying to get well and started respecting herself. She began to share the pain of her obesity. But she had to get close with strangers first before she could come closer to Joel. She had to hear herself say, "I feel really bad about my weight, and I'm tired of making jokes about myself." Today, both she and Joel attend separate meetings where they can talk about their own separate feelings; then, when they come together, they're both more assertive.

A year and two hundred lost pounds later, I asked them, "What if someone said that recovery has made you and Joel distant from each other? You used to be together every minute. Now you go to separate meetings, and you argue more than you used to." Both were incredulous at the idea. Joel explained the new freedom he feels when he's not managed by Elizabeth's dependency. "She's got her problems; I've got mine."

Elizabeth smiled coquettishly. "Since we've developed our separate identities, our sex life is coming back, and that's great."

It's not as much fun to have sex with yourself as with a partner. Developing their separateness helped them come together in a much more exciting way.

When I met with them after the first year, we were seated in low, engulfing, overstuffed chairs in the hospital lounge. Elizabeth asked Joel to bring her two straight chairs to use as support to help her up. There were only folding chairs available. She looked around and then wondered aloud if they were strong enough to help her to stand. Looking at Joel, the chairs, and then me, she said, "Oh, the hell with it. I'll do it myself." A deep breath, a slight sigh, a push, and Elizabeth was out of the chair. Joel beamed his approval. He had worked himself out of a job.

Healthy Neutrality

With new assertiveness, you won't have to force your ideas on each other, and you'll learn to mind your own business. As you attend your own self-help groups, you will be too busy to monitor anyone else. Getting your own house in order is a full-time job. Each of you deserves the support and nurturance of others. And you deserve to feel good about the love you give someone else. It is surely difficult when you do your best and give your all and the one you love and care for is still miserable and hurting. It is very hard to give up the job of helping this person. However, that often proves to be the most loving thing you can do. By removing yourself from your loved one's struggle, you allow other help to come in. That doesn't make you inadequate; it just means the job was not yours to take on. Perhaps you are too close and love too much. It is difficult to see that letting go is helpful.

Again, we encounter the message "lose to win." You are working toward developing a new loving relationship with an equal partner, not tackling him or her as a project. If you wanted the job of battling illness, you should have become a doctor. It is good to separate the person from the disease. You may continue to love the person, but you do not have to enjoy the sickness.

Once you have mastered a healthy neutrality toward one another, you will undoubtedly encounter the usual struggles others have when food obsessions are not in the picture. In any relationship, despite whatever goodwill exists, conflicts occur. One wants to go to the show, and the other wants to stay home. One wants to wallpaper the living room, and the other thinks plaster is best. Both want to use the car on the same night. Each is in a bad mood on the same day.

Even knowing the proper responses as outlined in this chapter won't help if your tone and attitude still hark back to the past. That is why the Twelve Step groups are so important. Others can see your attitudes better than you can. They can give you feedback about how you are really coming across. They will interpret your nonverbal messages and help you hear what you're not saying. The meetings will be your practice field.

Even before you begin to use your groups for practice, it will be helpful to review the following guidelines. The suggested don'ts and dos can be followed by both F-Os and C-Ps. You will both have a tendency to relapse into past behaviors, either becoming food obsessed or watching someone who is. If recovery lasts a lifetime, there is bound to be periodic relapse, which you should not judge but wait through and then go on. Try to realize that when there is relapse, the persons suffering are hurting themselves; they are not trying to hurt you. They are not doing it *to you*. They are doing it *for them*. Take care of yourself and work your own side of the street.

DON'Ts and DOs

Don't: *Don't* preach and lecture.

Don't have a holier-than-thou attitude.

Don't use the if-you-loved-me appeal.

Don't make threats you won't carry out.

Don't scold about the past.

Don't hide food or avoid social engagements.

Don't argue when bingeing.

Don't make an issue over treatment.

Don't assume martyrlike self-pity.

Don't expect an immediate, 100 percent recovery.

Don't be jealous of the recovery.

Don't be a doormat to the mood swings.

Don't try to protect.

Don't push anyone but yourself.

Don't take anyone's behavior with food personally.

Don't take on guilt at having caused the other person's problems.

Don't talk about food but instead about feelings.

Don't try to be too logical. It doesn't help.

Don't head downward with loved ones.

Don't expect quick and forever recoveries.

Don't talk about anyone as a patient.

Do: *Do* forgive.

Do learn the facts about eating disorders.

Do develop an attitude to match those facts.

Do talk to someone who understands (counselor, sponsor).

Do take a personal inventory of yourself and your behavior.

Do go to a clinic, treatment center, O-A, or Al-Anon.

Do maintain a healthy atmosphere in the home.

Do encourage new interests but don't nag.

Do take a relapse lightly if there is one.

Do pass on your knowledge to others.

Do be honest with yourself.

Do mind your own business.

Do take care of yourself.

Do try to relax and take it easy.

Do play—show you want a way out.

Do acknowledge the seriousness and power of the illness.

Do know that your loved one is not trying to hurt you.

Do try to see the person underneath the symptoms.

Do see the symptoms as an expression of something.

Do admit your own anger and frustration.

Do talk with others similarly afflicted.

Do get help from others.

Do appreciate other joys in life, even if suffering with food obsessions.

Do focus on "progress, not perfection."

Do take life one day at a time.

Do know that love has nothing to do with it.

CHAPTER 8

Fear of Flying

"This is it! This is my life. Whatever it takes, I want to spend the rest of it thinking about something other than food." That's what I screamed at a mirror, holding up fists like Scarlett O'Hara in *Gone with the Wind* right before the intermission. She holds up the potatoes she's clutched from the soil of Tara and screams to the heavens, "As God is my witness, I'll never go hungry again!" She was swearing *to* eat. I was swearing to *stop* eating compulsively.

I was six months shy of my thirtieth birthday and wanted to have something else going on in my life besides the endless focus on fat or the repercussions of fat. Of course that's what you want too. Then why have you spent the past twenty, thirty, forty, or fifty years in the throes of the illness, denying what was happening to you while you sank lower into the suffering every day? Because you were afraid of flying. You didn't believe you deserved the good life.

Having treated food obsessions for three decades, I still strongly recommend that people attend Overeater's Anonymous. That is not necessarily because I believe in an addiction to sugar (or that we are like all other addicts). It's that we have no tools for living once we get free of our obsession and are out in the world living successful but scary lives. I want people to learn about the Twelve Step way of life and see others who are further along in learning new techniques for enjoying the good life.

The book *Alcoholics Anonymous* carefully cajoles newcomers by emphasizing that all of the tools and Steps are "suggested only." At meetings, members continue to recommend, "Take what you can use and leave the rest." There is only one statement in all the literature that is said more forcefully: "We absolutely *insist* on enjoying life." This concept is not open for interpretation or rejection. We *insist*. If we can't offer you a better way of life, a way to feel comfortable within your own skin, a way to accept the good life with gusto, then what's the good reason to give up obsession? Things should get better.

We must believe that people do things for good reason. You had good reason to stay suffering with your food obsession. One reason, of course, is because you didn't know an alternative. But now you've read this book. If you don't make any effort to follow the suggestions, you are choosing consciously to suffer rather than accepting the alternative. The alternative is life without pain and guilt.

Many of you are afraid to be truly happy, fearing you will become reckless and hedonistic. Many of you fear you'll be irresponsible and shallow if not suffering. "I suffer, therefore I am." Dragging around the excess suffering is a way to symbolically announce to the world that you care and are involved with its woes. So many popular public causes, whether banning bombs, helping the poor, eliminating hunger, or saving whales, find their ranks swelling with bingers who demonstrate how much they care for others as a way to not appear self-involved. If nothing else, this book is about learning to care for yourself *before* saving the world. Here we offer the same advice as the flight attendant giving you the air safety instructions. Put on your own oxygen mask first before you try to help anyone else. Understandably, your new commitment to self might not be welcomed quickly by others who have come to depend on you for certain services. They may turn out to be the C-Ps who need to keep you in the same old role.

As an alternative to bingeing, you may find yourself going for weekly massages, manicures, or lunches with friends—activities you previously judged as too self-indulgent when there was so much important work to be done. For now, the most important work is to do whatever it takes to keep yourself serene and secure so you won't need to binge. Abstinence from the compulsion has to become your number-one priority. Let yourself become a fanatic for your own cause.

There is a larger issue at hand here than just losing weight or getting a manicure. To truly gain a lifelong recovery, you will be renegotiating a basic commitment to yourself about your whole life. Are you ready and willing to become a person who actively responds to the good things in life? The suffering is always easy to find, and you know how to react to it. While the smooth, comfortable old shoe of pain fits, the good life brings problems.

The world will come at you as if you have always looked this way, as if you were always "normal." You'll feel angry at others' kindness toward you. You'll pout, "Where were you when I really needed you?" You may feel inadequate in simple polite social situations. If you were formerly a fat buffoon, you may not know how to sit quietly as an equal participant at a party. There will be jealousy and competition, two things you rarely encountered while still fat or self-loathing. You'll be surprised by this and question, "Who, me? They're jealous of me?" And then, of course, there's the sexuality issue—the come-ons, flirtations, sometimes even whistles. Sexuality is such a large issue that I wrote a whole book about it (*Hot & Heavy*).

If accepting the good life were not a crucial aspect of

recovery, we would not see so many people falling back into the throes of their illnesses. Why is there a 98 percent failure rate for people who have undertaken weight-loss programs? As the richest nation in the world, why are we also the fattest? Maybe we feel more stable when fat. Many extremely obese people who lost major weight functioned well when still up in the seven-hundred- to eight-hundred-pound range. When they approached normalcy, they plummeted into depression. Their bodies tightened up, but their psyches became wobbly.

If you could handle the good life, you certainly would not have picked up this book. If I'd found it easy to handle the good life, I'd never have amassed excess poundage and then become a therapist to try to figure out why. If you knew how to endure your blessings, you would not have gone back to food obsessions so many times. In this last chapter, you will take a look at the imminent possibilities for your new life. You will see fears of success and how they relate to separating from home. Having been reparented with more distant mentoring, you'll now have the security, encouragement, and self-worth to go for it.

Fear of Success

In a one-hundred-mile journey, ninety miles is halfway. It's also true that the last ten pounds is often the killer for those overeaters who can't stand success. Of all Americans who undergo weight-loss programs, after two years 98 percent gain all their weight back plus more. Even for those who have lost hundreds of pounds, the responsibilities of success weigh them down. If you've been one of these yo-yo dieters, you've witnessed this disappointment time and time again. The first few years, all the accolades and compliments seem to increase incentive and keep you committed. Eventually, however, applause for weight loss recedes and the world starts expecting more and different things from you. You used to be able to brag at parties showing your "before" pictures. For my first three years in recovery, each time I met a new person, I quickly pulled out those pictures to show who I used to be. I wanted to be compared to my former self rather than evaluated on what I brought to the table in the present. It was a variation on my lifelong theme of "look what she's overcome."

To be accepted in the present for exactly who you are today is much more terrifying. How do you live as an equal among equals, an average Joe instead of a freak? While all were impressed with your success, you were able to revel in the attention. What happens when you are just expected to suit up and show up to live the life put in front of you? Some of us continue in chaos, taking on even greater challenges to ensure being the center of attention.

Sometimes, that attention itself is aggravating. We seek it and then hate it. A dieter's body is public domain. Just the fact that the world comments about it makes it everyone else's province rather than your own. "Well, hi there, skinny," someone says. "You're really losing weight."

You smile meekly and thank her, but a part of you feels violated. You don't comment on *her* body. Her body seems to be her own business. You want the compliment; you like being noticed. At the same time, it's a slight attack. It opens you to the possibility later that she and others will readily comment if they see you gaining weight. You live in fear. What business is it of theirs?

You may have held the fat person's unrealistic sense of what the thin life is like. By imagining life will be perfect as soon as you lose weight, you face a number of disappointments when you lose weight and still have normal human problems. I thought my disappointments in love happened because I was fat. Then I lost weight and there were still people who weren't interested in me. What could I blame it on then? Was it me? The *real* me? The *thin* me? It's easier to be rejected for your fat than for yourself.

You may decide you'd rather regain the weight and keep food obsessions as your problem. At least you know how to deal with that. Returning to the starting gate in the weight-loss race is easier; you know how to run that one. In other words, you won't have to learn any new tools or techniques for how to be a thin, "normal" person. If not diets, what else will you have to talk about? Even patients who lose hundreds of pounds with bypass surgery find that after two years, many pounds creep back on. The surgeon balks, "It's not possible that you can gain so much weight." He or she doesn't understand that you have to gain the weight or else face the harsher reality that you don't know how to live with the success you've always wanted.

In my office hangs a picture poster showing a bright, newly hatched yellow chick staring into space asking, "What do I do now?" That's the dieter's dilemma. The answer is, "Stick with the winners."

If you spent all these years in suffering, it is going to be hard to adjust to accepting the good life each day. You will need to seek out and stay close to other successful people who will be happy for your success and not feel threatened. If you expand your circle of friends to include people who themselves are successful, they can teach you how to tolerate success and will also have no need to pull you back to old failures. You'll get the nudge to "go for it." Your success will only enhance and motivate them. They will have no need to see you fail but will instead motivate and encourage you.

Common Barriers to Success

Some meetings of Overeaters Anonymous are specifically designated as maintainer's meetings, where success is the order of business. Discussions at these meetings center around living through the stress of success and problems of abundance. Members need help to endure the good life. Let's take some time to look at some of the struggles with success voiced by effective maintainers. See whether any of these statements could be voiced by you.

EQUALITY. "I don't know how to deal with equality. I'm used to being with people I feel better than or less than. I don't know how to have an equal relationship. I walk on eggshells fearing you can't handle my strength. I don't want to talk much about my happiness in case you don't feel the same way."

LONELINESS. "I've done so well. Why do I feel so bad? Things are great, but I feel lonely. Many of my old friends don't want to be with me anymore."

FRIENDSHIPS. "Without you I'm nothing, but with you I lose my sense of identity. When I'm not complaining about problems, I have very little to talk about. If we don't go out to dinner, what can we actually do together?"

DEPENDENCY. "I have to destroy myself and be needy in order to survive in a relationship. When I am not needy, nobody wants me."

EMOTIONS. "I need to express my feelings, but I must be careful not to upset anyone. I have to balance on a tightrope —honest but not too honest."

DIFFERING OPINIONS. "If I don't see things as you do, I must be wrong. It's hard for me to believe I could be right. Does that make me wrong?"

CONFLICTS. "I have to learn to resolve differences without taking issues head-on and embarrassing anyone. I've got to make others feel better."

GUILT. "I feel responsible for everyone's feelings, and at the same time, I don't have a clue what to do about their pain."

MYTHS. "I was taught to strive for success, but it's a hollow victory. Even when I'm a winner, I feel like a loser."

MODELS. "I don't know who to emulate. It seems like no one has trod this ground before me. No one I know lives the way I'd like to live."

HEALTH. "It's not so bad to get sick. Then I don't threaten anyone. I can get some nurturance without risk. If not weight problems, a migraine will suffice."

SEXUALITY. "But men don't like women who come on too strong. If I like myself too much, no one will want me."

FEARS. "I want to try weird new things, but no one would even understand that I might like to. Where do I talk about this?"

Models for Success

Few F-Os have been given effective models for living with success. These models have to be someone who's traveled the road, a person who's farther along in recovery. You can't hear it from people who haven't been there. Let's face it. Every Tom, Dick, and Harry has some kind of helpful hint or words of wisdom about diet and exercise. That's not what you need. You need someone who has faced the depths of degradation over this obsession and been pulled out with the help of others similarly afflicted. You also need to hear from people who've been at it awhile and have been successful for a while. You won't benefit from overzealous ninety-day wonders who give strong rah-rah pitches but haven't put in the time and effort for long-term personality change.

Early on, your struggles will be with food plans, and that is why OA has specific sponsors to just serve as food sponsors. Later on, the problems of success and the struggle with abundance and joy will emerge. That's when you'll need guidance from someone who has been successful for quite some time and can share with you some of the Twelve Step principles of how to live a successful life without punishing yourself further with food.

It is senseless to talk to those "maintainers" until your own struggles come closer to theirs. Wait to discuss those struggles until you are actually *living* them. We are so accustomed to *talking about* ourselves that we often don't wait for our real life experience to catch up. You must avoid intellectualizing and philosophizing before you get there. It is of value for you to attend maintainer's meetings even in early recovery, as they present the hope of what's possible for you as well as alert you to what is in store. However, don't investigate these problems until you are actually in them. Remember how I explained to my early sponsor that I was afraid to get thin. She gently told me to "get thin and then we'll talk about it." Help in accepting the good life with gusto is the most important reason I recommend attending Twelve Step meetings forever. You may need more help when successful than you do in the early stages. One patient of mine went to only one meeting a week for her first three years in recovery. Later she found that life got so much "better," with dating issues, job promotions, and what we call "problems of abundance," that she needed to fit in more meetings for a while. She complained to me that though now thin, she wanted to sing along with Peggy Lee: "Is that all there is?"

Opposite the hatched-chick poster in my office is my grandmother's midwife diploma. She helped people be born physically; I help them become reborn psychologically and spiritually. In this new birth, you will be finding a way to tolerate success and avoid returning to past failure. You've already lived and died a thousand deaths. Your little chick will be born with wings and tools to stay aloft.

Growing Up

The fear of moving along to success and accepting the joy in store stems from an even deeper fear of growing up and leaving home. If you really stop being a suffering person and begin to take care of yourself, you are making a statement. You're saying that you will be responsible for your life and are giving up patterns you learned as a child. You are also giving up some ways you might be punishing your parents. Your bingeing and starving can illustrate their failures as parents. But that's explained thoroughly in *Fat & Furious*. For our purposes here, we'll look at how difficult it is to wriggle free. Often the confluent, whether it is your actual mother, a spouse you married who is like your mother, or a helpful friend who protects you like a mom, will have to find another job. As you become willing to do whatever it takes not to eat compulsively, you are abandoning old patterns and won't need rescuing.

It is no accident that we see an epidemic of food obsessions in an age when youngsters are given so many conflicting messages. Food obsessions are a way to remain a child and stay at home. Some people abuse hard drugs; F-Os choose a more acceptable drug. In growing up, the relationship most difficult to renegotiate will be between mothers and daughters.

"A Son Is a Son Till He Takes Him a Wife, A Daughter's a Daughter All of Her Life"

From Nancy Friday's *My Mother/My Self* and Colette Dowling's *The Cinderella Complex* to Susie Orbach's *Fat Is a Feminist Issue* (I and II) and my book *Fat & Furious*, we've outlined the struggle between mothers and daughters to separate and develop equality. Many daughters are living out a struggle their parents have not negotiated well. Dad urges his daughter to succeed and make him proud; Mom sends the message that if she doesn't pursue home and hearth, she is choosing against her and forsaking her values. Many women are choosing not to marry, and some are choosing to remain childless. This is often difficult for mothers to bear. As a daughter works to gain her mother's approval, Mom only feels defeated and rejected and thus never approves. It becomes a losing battle. Seeking that mother's approval sends many to compulsive eating to gain the needed comfort.

> When I began to grow in a different direction, when I left her house, became independent, then conceding my love and admiration of her would have meant an acceptance of beliefs and attitudes which I consider a threat to my existence.... During her life I fought her influence, and she fought in me the kind of women who had displaced her.
>
> —Anaïs Nin, *The Diary of Anaïs Nin*

In psychological diagnostic manuals, eating disorders are classified as diseases of childhood. Adolescent eating disorders signal the inability to leave home. The daughters are unable to detach from the nurturance-independence struggle and thus continue to cling emotionally to Mom, refusing to move out psychologically. This "living at home" exists even if the two reside three thousand miles apart and the daughter has married and had her own children. If you are living out a script programmed into you from childhood, you are still not operating from choice and are thus still at home.

When a daughter grows up feeling good about herself, she will probably attract her own mate, marry, and make her own home away from her mother. The current generation of maturing young women is experiencing conflict in this area. By staying fat, women keep mates at bay and don't compete. Susie Orbach had early explained in *Fat Is a Feminist Issue* that fat women were opting to stay out of the race to send in their thin sisters to compete instead.

Some women do manage to find partners, but their continued enmeshment with their mothers jeopardizes their relationships and keeps them food obsessed. Mandy's story is a good example. Mandy once told me, "I'm not going to any Twelve Step group. I've heard those people talk, and I can tell they want to break up my marriage." Her first marriage survived as long as she kept her 350 pounds. This was her second marriage. Her first husband was arrested for drunk driving three times, refused alcoholism treatment, and also refused to work. Mandy's mother, Colette, paid off their debts, financed a divorce, and also paid for the intestinal bypass operation that was to save Mandy's life and give her a new start.

Down to 150 pounds, Mandy remarried. Mandy and her mother spent most of every day together while her new husband, Ned, was consumed with work and getting ahead. As he worked, Mandy and her mother shopped. They also plotted to have a baby. Ned didn't want any more kids; he was supporting two from a previous marriage. Mandy and Colette wanted a child. They also felt it would bring Ned home more, and Mandy knew the pregnancy could explain her recently encroaching weight gain.

Despite Ned's protests, Mandy secretly removed her IUD, and a year later gave birth to Jeffrey. She also strayed back up to 350 pounds. Mandy and her mom became engrossed in caring for Jeffrey and talking about dieting. Jeffrey seemed to know his daddy didn't want him and grew into a hyperactive, raging little boy. Mandy kept eating. She and her mom remained very close. At this juncture I suggested OA, but Mandy adamantly refused, "for the marriage."

In reality, this marriage was a sham. Mandy was living out a scenario she and Mom had written, and it had nothing to do with Ned. Any guy could have filled the role. Ned knew this and so did little Jeffrey. The significant relationship in this household was between Mandy and her mother. They saw each other daily and shared all their intimacies. Both knew every piece of silverware in the other's drawers as well as every maneuver the other's partner played in bed. The guys were pawns in the women's game plan. Never could this mother-daughter team say this out loud. Instead, Mandy and Colette talked of male domination and female victimization in the home. Believing they were victims kept them close. Actually, the men had moved out emotionally long ago.

One winter Colette went on a cruise, leaving Mandy at home with her husband and son. Within a week, Mandy called me sobbing and immediately attended an OA meeting. She said she wanted out of her fat. Two weeks later, they came for family therapy as Jeffrey's acting out became more pronounced. With Mandy's mom out of town, Mandy and Ned faced each other. Little Jeffrey escalated his problem behavior to provide a diversion from impending intimacy.

Not for long. After the cruise ship docked and Mandy drove her mother home, she stopped going to OA and canceled the next therapy appointment. She feared, *They want to break up my marriage.* Actually, there was little in the marriage to break up. Ned worked and complained. Mandy ate and complained. Jeffrey kicked walls and complained. The relationship that had to break up was between mother and daughter. That excessive closeness was defeating the marriage and taking Mandy's life. Instead of negotiating this separation, Mandy and Colette worked out another solution. Colette paid for a second surgical procedure, this time stomach stapling.

I wrote the foregoing in 1985, where I remarked we would have to wait and see how things developed as Mandy lost weight again. Regretfully, I must report here that Mandy regained the weight as quickly as she lost it, she and Ned divorced, little Jeffrey finally grew up and left home, and Mom moved away to Florida. Even then, the mother-daughter tie was excessive as Mandy's life was filled with constant new projects and failed relationships and businesses. Her mom rescued her from every one of them. Two years ago, her mother died. This may be the moment for Mandy to grab hold of her own life. Some daughters have not managed to lose weight until their mothers pass on. However, sometimes the failure message is embedded so deeply that it even calls back from the grave.

Unlike Mandy, Lynn did take some lessons home from OA. She had always had an ideal relationship with her mother, especially after she had her first baby and gained the final 100 of her 360 pounds. She and her mother were never closer than when they shared child-rearing stories. Just after the birth, Lynn's younger sister, Natalie, quit smoking. Natalie had always been the acting-out child, in contrast to Lynn's good-girl image. When Natalie quit smoking, excess rage welled to the surface, and she began yelling and screaming at her mother every day. To soothe that painful situation, Lynn moved herself right in to be an even better good girl so Mommy wouldn't hurt.

Lynn and her infant visited every day. She would stop at the store to prepare for the visit. She appeared each morning with bags full of ice cream, pistachio nuts, popcorn, bagels, noodles, and, for the sake of being "healthy," cottage cheese. With these creations, Lynn set out as family mediator. Keeping Mom active in the kitchen kept her out of raging Natalie's path. Mom cooked; Lynn ate. Lynn knew just how to tell a joke and turn a phrase to keep her mother and sister from picking at each other. Whenever she got tired or couldn't think of anything to say, she ate. The system worked well until Lynn cut out the excess food. With a committed food plan, the daily visits became more difficult. Lynn didn't know how to listen to the complaints from Mom and her younger sister.

She also couldn't joke while others were angry. Abstinent, she got quiet. One day she had to ask her mom for something new.

Mom: So what's wrong with you? You sit around so quietly all the time.

Lynn: I'm just feeling sort of raw since I'm not eating like I used to.

Mom: [She is really missing the good times she used to have when her daughter ate. She feels helpless to make her feel better. She decides to use the family's favorite, time-honored remedy.] Well, I think you're really trying to do too much too fast. Why don't you eat just a little here and there, and you'll feel better. I read an article that said it's better to eat many small meals a day instead of waiting for three big meals. Here, have a taste of this cobbler I made, and you'll eat less at dinnertime.

Lynn: I really want to stick to my food plan, and I don't want to snack.

Mom: Don't you understand what I'm saying? It's not a snack. You have to get into new ways of thinking with many small meals. You shouldn't have to suffer so much. This OA is really making you bitchy.

Lynn: I'm sorry if I'm bitchy, and I can see you really want to help, but I want to follow the direction I'm getting from my sponsor in OA.

Mom: [feeling left out and threatened] So who is this sponsor and what does she know? Is she a doctor?

Lynn: No, Ma, it's another person who has been through this. and she is instructing me in what she did to lose over two hundred pounds.

Mom: Well, everyone is different, and I don't think you should be listening to any old nobody in OA. Why don't you read the article I mentioned and eat like I told you?

Discussing how Lynn should eat is a way to stay focused on food. Previously, mother and daughter shared recipes, cooked together, and ate while they talked. Now there's a void. The void can be filled with discussions of dieting, but Lynn doesn't want to discuss food at all. She really wants to minimize the importance of food in her life. When food is gone, will there be something else with Mom to take its place?

Lynn: Thanks for your concern, but I'm really trying to find one plan and stick to it. I know there are millions of good ideas out there, but if I just find one and stick to it, it won't matter which one it is. In the meantime, Mom, let's talk about something else. I'm getting so I really like to stay away from food talk as much as I can.

Mom: [long silence] So what should we talk about?

Lynn: [Also quiet, she realizes that it had previously been her responsibility to carry the major direction of family discussion.] I really don't know, Ma. Maybe I just have to be quiet for a while. I'll wait and see.

Mom: [fearful that Lynn will become like her other daughter who rages most of the time] I sure wish you'd eat something. I know you'd feel better. I just want you to feel better.

Lynn: [sensing her mother's need for reassurance] Thanks, Mom. I know you love me. I just need to be quiet and without food for now. I think I'll go home a little early today. I do love you and appreciate you. I could take a nice hug instead of the cobbler.

Since Lynn married, her mother had rarely ever touched her. Feeling so close to Lynn, she didn't want to smother her. Mom figured that when Lynn left home to get married, that was the signal to cut the cord. She set out to stop touching. Her head told her it was best, but her arms ached to hold her "little girl." She offered food as a way to get closer. With food, she was even inside her daughter's skin. To Mom, if Lynn wouldn't eat, that meant she didn't accept her. Instead of taking in the food, Lynn asked for a hug. She asked for warmth instead of sugar. Mom grabbed her and shook as she held her close. With tears of joy streaming down her face, Lynn wouldn't have taken a doughnut if her life depended on it. She was getting all her needs met in her mother's arms. It's hard to cry and chew at the same time.

The difficult work of separating, growing up, and leaving home has to be effected gently, but forcefully. If you don't take on this strategy, you will continue to react to your mother as well as feel inadequate yourself. I have treated so many young corporate women who put on the corporate suit with shoulder pads but also the imposter syndrome that went with it. They just never felt right in either the suit or their own skins.

Menacing Mentors

Some women who move out of the home and kitchen often re-create excessive dependency in the business world. They may seem to reject their mothers' ideas about success, but they still want a big daddy to take care of them. A profile of a typical binge vomiter would be a woman twenty-five to thirty-five years old, successful, attractive, with a career in a "man's world," who appears totally self-assured and confident but is carefully not so successful as to pose a threat. These women re-create separation struggles on the job. They only go halfway in celebrating their gifts. They will work very hard, but then leave it to their supervisors to take credit. They will secretly resent this, but feel safe that they don't have to stand behind their work. The job becomes the oppressor their mother once was. A secret life at home with food helps fill the "victim" with enough self-loathing to keep her from flying too high. She thus poses no threat.

Wanda was a successful management trainer for a large firm. Her clients valued her expertise and she was respected by others, but she hated herself. She was one hundred pounds overweight. Always in the back of her mind was "If I'm such a good people manager, why can't I manage myself?" She was sure everyone else thought the same thing. She was also certain that she achieved success because she had really fooled everyone. She feared they would soon find out she was a fraud and had nothing to offer.

Despite professional accolades, Wanda believed she was worthless. This attitude kept her fat. Fat is a symbol that something is wrong. It is a warning to others: "Lest you think I may have my act together, take heed first of this enormous bulk of a body, and you'll see I still suffer." It's a signal that we need comforting and don't know how to get it. Wanda did not want to let others see what a truly competent professional she was. She didn't want to believe it herself. As long as she stayed fat, she could postpone living up to her fullest potential. After she lost weight, she quipped, "My potential almost killed me."

Because her basic self-concept was one of inadequacy, Wanda spent many years doubting her professional skills. She needed constant validation before she could work.

Before giving training seminars, she attended those given by others, comparing herself to them. For many years, she maintained a working contact with a former professor, a powerful mentor who "had all the answers." She depended on him, a forceful personality who expressed his views with assurance. She found it easy to accept his opinions and reject her own if different. She needed constant reassurance to prove that she was okay. That relationship seemed to work extremely well. Dr. Gordon liked teaching insecure students who were always questioning and seeking his opinion.

The system worked very well until Wanda decided that she'd get thin no matter what. She joined OA and followed directions from a sponsor. As her weight loss progressed, she began to feel more confidence in herself and respect for her own views, many of which differed from her mentor's. She found his easy answers too superficial. She wanted more complex, careful considerations and found she had differing professional experience. Her voicing different opinions stressed their relationship.

When Dr. Gordon advised her, she rebelled by calling him bossy and arrogant. He was shocked. He was just continuing to assume responsibility for her as he had done in the past. She used to like it when he told her what to do and how to act. Wanda didn't need that anymore. Her recovery was progressing, and she no longer had fat to keep her down. She was willing to risk being fully who she was, standing up for her own opinions. She now needed equal colleagues, not a big daddy. Dr. Gordon felt left out and unnecessary. Actually, when Wanda no longer needed him, he saw her as arrogant and self-centered. Many heated arguments ensued. The insecure student who had once adoringly sought his guidance was now rebelling and moving out on her own.

Here were two gifted people who worked helping others. They needed their own help in renegotiating a changed relationship. Wanda practiced finding a way to lovingly assure her mentor that she valued him but had to grow up and leave him. She was encouraged to handle the situation in such a way that she would feel good about herself when she walked away. She was to strive for a feeling of well-being, assured that she had not hurt herself or anyone else. If she did not negotiate this well, she might return to bingeing, or she might have to continue the dishonest game of pretending she felt inadequate and needy. That was no longer true.

Wanda found that, as a recovering person, she had a responsibility to consider his feelings as well as her own. When she was the needy child, she didn't owe him anything, just homage. Now, because she was a more secure, self-confident adult, she had to consider how her behavior would affect him. She had to be aware of her own strengths and, though scared and shaky herself, she had to think about the other guy. Most of all, she waited until she felt truly loving toward him so she could show him appreciation while breaking away. She had learned that "love without honesty is sentimentality, but honesty without love is brutality." At all costs, she had to avoid being brutal. If she felt guilty, she'd punish herself later with food. She wrote the following letter:

Dear Dr. Gordon,

How unfortunate it must be that when you have been out-standingly terrific at teaching and training, you eventually work yourself out of a job. I sure have difficulty giving up feeling needy around you. I still value your pearls of wisdom and time-tested answers for complex problems.

Unfortunately for us, you taught me a great lesson. It has developed me into a valued professional. You taught me that, above all else, I should trust my own judgment. When I didn't have any confidence in myself, that was hard to believe. Surely my opinion didn't make sense. I needed you to fill in all the blanks. I was so afraid to risk taking a gamble on my own thoughts. Now, I want to trust my own judgment. I feel I've been brought out of my suffering into a whole new way of life. I look like a normal, healthy person, and as the world treats me that way, I feel more confident and secure.

I so appreciate the confidence you had in me at a time when I couldn't have it in myself. Just like they say in OA, "We'll love you until you can love yourself." I really couldn't have made it this long way if you hadn't had the confidence to trust me before I could trust myself.

Thank you for teaching me so much and instilling me with such confidence. It's like "Give a man a fish and he eats for a day; teach him to fish and he eats for a lifetime." You are the one who taught me fishing and now my duty is to teach others the same. The ocean sure seems big enough for us all. *Good catch!*

After receiving this letter, Dr. Gordon quietly and anonymously attended one of Wanda's training seminars. He clearly saw she'd learned from him and had also developed more on her own. He later sent the following card:

The apple doesn't fall far from the tree. Your view has merit, even if you did get it all by yourself.

Today, these two serve on the same faculty. They represent similar and opposing points of view on a variety of subjects. Most important, each respects the other. The value they have for each other is based on equality and reality. Neither has to play big daddy or darling little girl. Instead they each have something to gain and learn from the other. Difference is exciting, not a threat. Wanda is maintaining a large weight loss. So far, her body has weathered the changed relationship.

Flying Is Threatening

It didn't go quite the same way for Brenda. When she became successful, she outsold the office manager three months in a row. All the wasted hours she had abused in planning and negotiating binges were now, in recovery, put into late hours at work and ready availability for clients. Although excessive workaholism is often a transferred addiction for persons new in recovery, Brenda needed the diversion from food. To her office manager, Brenda's success was a threat. After four months of abstinence, self-confidence, responsible behavior, and a fifty-pound weight loss, she was fired. Her boss told her he didn't appreciate her attitude and felt she was a detriment to the workforce because her sales intimidated others. Clearly, she had a choice. She could minimize herself, perform under capacity, and not threaten anyone. However, that form of underselling would be a lie. Living dishonestly, she'd have to go back to overeating. Instead, she lost her job.

Her months of good sales had helped her put away some savings, which helped her get by until a new position came along. She found that, as long as she stayed abstinent, no matter what hallway she'd have to wait in, new doors would open. When you are living true to who you really are, you will attract exactly what you are supposed to get. What at first looks like a loss may ultimately be preparing you. It opens the window for something new to fly in. Brenda's new job was with a more prestigious firm with wealthier clientele and more expensive properties. She moved up because she stopped fearing success. The Chinese say, "Only a small fish swims in shallow water."

Take No Prisoners

This time you're not going back. There's nobody left at home. When you negotiate the stress of success and cut the ties to your old, failing way of life, you have to ride the horse in the direction it's going. When your C-Ps are also doing their work, everyone is on the new road, and there's no "there" to go back to.

You will find a way to take your old self—that sick, suffering fat kid—along for the ride. Every other time you took on controlling your food problem, you threw away your old self. How disrespectful. No wonder the failing self has to reappear to drag you back. Now you have a chance to live a whole new way of life within this very same lifetime. You've already been dying. Let's move on to flying.

This time, welcome your former self into your new life with love and respect. After all, that poor little kid helped you out of a lot of tough scrapes. That is the person whose best efforts walked you right up to the threshold of this new life. This person can't be all bad. He or she, too, deserves the chance to fly.

As you advance in the OA program, you will be encouraged to work with newcomers and help them gain serenity. You may in turn become a sponsor and help reparent a newcomer. I caution you, though, that helping others is the last Step in a Twelve Step program. It is only to be taken on after you have done the necessary work yourself. You can't get by with doing what OAers call the "two step," dancing between Steps One and Twelve. The First Step is an admission that you need help. You can't just jump to the Twelfth and start helping others. The intervening Steps help you learn how to become teachable and vulnerable and grateful. After all that, you'll have more to offer the newcomer. In essence, this action is a way for you to heal the wounds of your own childhood. Each time you offer understanding and support to the newcomer, it is a chance for you to give to your own suffering kid the things that were missed. In that way, you keep reparenting yourself and welcoming your former self into your new life. That suffering kid has to be laid to rest gently and with love so he or she won't rise up and rebel in fear of flying.

With a gentle, nudging welcome, your sick, suffering self won't devour you in recovery. Instead, you will have joined all your forces and let the kid come along for the ride. Jean-Paul Sartre said, "Freedom is what we do with what was done to us." You don't have to continue painful patterns set adrift in previous generations. As the Unity Church prays, so can you: "Let there be peace on earth, and let it begin with me." It can actually begin in your generation. You just want to keep your body slightly less than stuffed and your mind obsession free. That will keep your own channel open so you can resonate with your own true vibrations. You are the artist who, with careful guidance and help, can create a totally new life for you and others. Referring to the dance of life is an appropriate closing to this book. Think of your own life as a creative dance for which you are the choreographer and the diva.

The famous dancer Agnes DeMille was a protégé of Martha Graham. Though often confident and well praised as a genius in her own right, she had periods of self-doubt and despair about her dance. She wrote to Martha asking for some guidance, looking for a way out of her self-doubt. Here is Martha's response:

> There is a vitality, a life force, an energy, a quickening that is translated through you into action, and because there is only one of you in all time, this expression is unique. If you block it, it will never exist through any other medium and it will be lost. The world will not have it. You must keep that channel open. It is not your business to determine how good it is, nor how valuable, nor how it compares with other expressions. It is your business to keep it yours, clearly and directly, to keep the channel open.

You do not even have to believe in yourself or your work. You have to keep yourself open and aware to the urges that motivate you. . . .

Keep the channel open. . . .

No artist is pleased. . . .

There is no satisfaction whatever at any time. . . .

There is only a queer, divine dissatisfaction, a blessed unrest that keeps us marching and makes us more alive than the rest.

ABOUT THE AUTHOR

Dr. Judi Hollis has been counseling addicted families since 1967, when she helped open New York City's Phoenix House Programs. Since that time she went on to open the nation's first eating disorder unit and has been training counselors internationally as well as opening alcoholism and eating disorder units around the world.

She holds graduate degrees in rehabilitation counseling and counseling psychology from the University of Southern California (USC) and is a licensed Marriage, Family, and Child Counselor (MFCC). She has taught at USC, Goddard College, Chapman College, the University of California–Los Angeles (UCLA), the Omega Institute for Holistic Studies, and at many community groups and hospitals around the country.

Her best-seller, *Fat Is a Family Affair,* has served as a groundbreaking treatise in the treatment field. It was followed by *Fat & Furious* and then *Hot & Heavy* and many workbooks, videos, and audiocassettes. She currently maintains personal consulting practices on both coasts, dividing her time between New York City and Palm Springs, California, as well as providing worldwide phone consultations.

With her radio show, *Dr. Jude's Ladies Locker Room,* Dr. Hollis developed an international audience. She is now completing work on a book about resisting the spiritual path. She appears often on TV with Oprah, Sally, Maury, Leeza, and others, and her work has been featured in *Shape, Teen, Glamour, Self, Cosmopolitan,* and *Elle* magazines.

She can be reached at 1-800-8-ENOUGH or
www.judihollis.com.

Judi Hollis has devoted the last thirty years to educating recovering individuals and their families. Thousands have benefited from her residential and inpatient treatment programs and nationwide seminars. The following resource list is provided to assist you in your further exploration of the ideas presented in this book.

Also by Judi Hollis:

BOOKS

Fat & Furious (Ballantine)
Hot & Heavy (Health Communications, Inc.)
It's Not a Dress Rehearsal (HOL SEM Productions)
Let Them Eat Cake (HOL SEM Productions)

PAMPHLETS

Accepting Powerlessness (Hazelden)
Relapse for Eating Disorder Sufferers (Hazelden)
Resisting Recovery (Hazelden)
When AAs Go to OA (Hazelden)
Humility vs. Humiliation (Hazelden)
Transferring Obsessions (Hazelden)
I'm Not Ready Yet (Hazelden)

VIDEOS

Family Matters
    (Hazelden, Dick Young Productions, New York City)
Dark Secrets, Bright Victory
    (Hazelden, Dick Young Productions, New York City)
The Divine Dine™ (HOL SEM Productions)
Live to Eat—Eat to Live (HOL SEM Productions)
Starving for Perfection (HOL SEM Productions)

AUDIOCASSETTES

Hope for Compulsive Overeaters, vols. 1 and 2 (Hazelden)

Fat Is a Family Affair (Hazelden)

Codependent Compulsions (HOL SEM Productions)

Y2 OA? (HOL SEM Productions)

Let's Talk Radio (HOL SEM Productions)

Going Deep (HOL SEM Productions)

Fat & Furious (HOL SEM Productions)

From Fat & Furious to Hot & Heavy (HOL SEM Productions)

Bloom Where You're Planted (HOL SEM Productions)

Sunlight of the Spirit (HOL SEM Productions)

For ordering or more information about videos, audiocassettes, and seminars, please call 1-800-8-ENOUGH or go to www.judihollis.com on the World Wide Web.

About Hazelden Publishing

As part of the Hazelden Betty Ford Foundation, Hazelden Publishing offers both cutting-edge educational resources and inspirational books. Our print and digital works help guide individuals in treatment and recovery, and their loved ones. Professionals who work to prevent and treat addiction also turn to Hazelden Publishing for evidence-based curricula, digital content solutions, and videos for use in schools, treatment programs, correctional programs, and electronic health records systems. We also offer training for implementation of our curricula.

Through published and digital works, Hazelden Publishing extends the reach of healing and hope to individuals, families, and communities affected by addiction and related issues.

For more information about Hazelden publications,
please call **800-328-9000**
or visit us online at **hazelden.org/bookstore**.